Barn Burning, Barn Building

BRIGHT SKY PRESS
ALBANY, TEXAS

Barn Burning Barn Building

Tales *of a* Political Life, *from* LBJ *through* George W. Bush *and* Beyond

by **BEN BARNES** *with* Lisa Dickey

b̓

BRIGHT SKY PRESS

Box 416 Albany, Texas 76430

10   9   8   7   6   5   4   3   2   1

Library of Congress Cataloging-in-Publication Data

Barnes, Ben F., 1938 –
Barn burning barn building : lessons of Lone Star
politics that can improve our country's future by
Ben Barnes.
    p. cm.
Includes bibliographical references.
ISBN-13: 978-1-931721-71-4 (alk. paper)
ISBN-10: 1-931721-71-8 (alk. paper)
1. Barnes, Ben F., 1938-
2. Legislators—Texas—Biography.
3. Texas. Legislature. House of Representatives—
    Speakers—Biography.
4. Texas—Politics and government—1951 –
I. Title.

F391.4.B37 A3 2006
328.764'092—dc22

2006042546

Book design by Julie Savasky
Jacket design by DJ Stout and Julie Savasky,
Pentagram, Austin, Texas

Printed in China through Asia Pacific Offset

For my wife, Melanie
my children, *and*
my grandchildren

Table of Contents

Foreword

by Robert Strauss

I FIRST MET BEN BARNES BACK IN DECEMBER OF 1961, AT THE CATARINA Ranch down in South Texas. He was just 23 then, a lanky young man from a farming family who'd just finished his first year in the Texas House of Representatives. I'd never met Ben before and didn't know a thing about him, but that was soon to change.

We'd been invited to the ranch by my friend John Connally, who was planning his upcoming 1962 campaign for governor of Texas. Connally had worked on Lyndon Johnson's campaigns, but this was the first in which he'd be a candidate himself, so he called together a group of about 20 friends to meet with him and talk strategy. Connally and I had been good friends since our college days together at the University of Texas, so he asked me to come along as an extra set of eyes and ears.

With its spacious and comfortable house, the Catarina Ranch, which was owned by our mutual friend Dolph Briscoe, was the perfect place to meet. On the first day, the whole group gathered in the living room to talk about what Connally needed to do to win. Most of us didn't really know each other well, but nobody held back, and pretty soon we were having a spirited discussion. I noticed then that Ben, who must have been at least 10 years younger than anyone else in the room, made more sense than most of us. He just jumped right in, not at all intimidated by the more experienced men around him. And although he'd been in politics all of one year, he came off like an old hand.

By about 10 o'clock or so, the evening was over and everyone had gone to bed except Connally and me. We sat up in the living room and talked over what we'd seen and heard. "John," I told him, "I believe that big old dumb-looking redheaded boy made more sense than any of the rest of them." Connally just laughed, as he already knew Ben Barnes was a political prodigy. Now the rest of Texas was about to find out too.

During Governor Connally's first year in office, Ben took care of getting the votes needed to pass his legislation in the House. It was only Ben's second term, but he already knew better than anyone how to work the floor and count votes, and he used those skills to help advance Connally's vision for the state. Then, at the beginning of Ben's third term in 1965, he got himself elected Speaker of the Texas House — at 26 years old, the youngest man to do so since the Civil War era.

And Ben was only getting started. For two terms, he was one of the most effective House Speakers that Texas had ever seen. As a legislative leader, he showed a rare skill for keeping his eye on the bigger picture — he and Connally teamed up to push through all kinds of progressive legislation, including education reform, tax reform, and improvements in human services. The Barnes-Connally political alliance was one of the most productive and important in the state's history, and it's no exaggeration to say it pushed Texas into the modern era.

In 1968, the last year of Connally's governorship, Ben ran for lieutenant governor — an election in which he received more than 2 million votes, setting a record for most votes garnered by any candidate in Texas to that time. Then, during his two terms as lieutenant governor, he worked the Senate with as much skill as he had the House, bringing liberals and moderates together in a way that was — and still is — all too rare in Texas politics. Ben just seemed to have an instinct for bringing coalitions together and keeping the focus on what was important.

By this time, most people believed Ben was heading for a long and productive career in elective politics. But his career was soon stopped, and not by anything he did himself. The strongest Democrat in the strongest Democratic bloc in the South, Ben was in statewide office at a time when several other statewide Democratic officials got accused of wrongdoing. Seeking to damage him politically, Ben's opponents were quick to tar him with the same brush — even though Ben had nothing to do with the alleged misdeeds. Their leaks and rumor-mongering did enough damage to cost Ben the 1972 Democratic primary; he came in third place, and his political career seemed finished.

Yet in the years since, Ben Barnes has never really gotten out of politics. Though he didn't ever run for office again, he's continued to pour his energy, time, and resources into state and national Democratic party politics, making himself into one of the party's premier fundraisers and strategists. Ben's influence on Capitol Hill is such that former Senate Majority Leader Tom Daschle once called him the "51st Democratic senator." He still has the same political savvy and insight that thrust him to the top of Texas politics before he reached the age of 30. And what he has to tell us today is desperately important for the future of the party and of the American political system.

In *Barn Burning, Barn Building,* Ben gives us a first-hand look at a truly extraordinary political period. He takes us inside the workings of the great Democratic stronghold of the 1960s, and gives us personal insights into lions of history such as Lyndon Johnson, John Connally, and Barbara Jordan. But Ben does more than just tell great stories. He shows why the history of that era matters so much to today, and explains how we can use the knowledge of that era to help put our ailing political system back on track.

In Texas and across the country, we're facing some of the most difficult and thorny problems we've seen in decades. From education to infrastructure to health care and social services, we need to start making some tough choices. Ben Barnes has been here before; he's made those tough choices and helped improve people's lives. There's no one who has played a more important role. As Lyndon Johnson put it so memorably at a fundraiser for Ben back in 1970, "Show us the way, Ben! Where you lead us, we will follow!"

ROBERT STRAUSS
January 2006

Prologue

IT WAS A RAINY AFTERNOON IN LATE 1960 WHEN SAM RAYBURN, IN A SINGLE comment, told me the future of American politics. He couldn't have known it then, but he also foretold the future of my own political career. I didn't even realize it myself until I looked back years later, long after Rayburn was dead.

It was November of 1960, and I'd just been elected to the Texas House of Representatives. I was a baby-faced 22-year-old, and probably had no business even running, but I'd worked like a dog to win. I'd worn out a couple pairs of shoes walking from door to door, stumping for votes across the three counties that made up my West Texas district. And when I won the Democratic primary that May, the seat was mine — no Republican opponent had filed for the general election in November. It's hard to imagine now, but in Texas politics then, Republicans were so scarce, the joke was that they could hold a caucus in a phone booth.

Once I'd won the primary, I was considered a Representative-elect, and I started meeting the giants of Texas politics. I met Lyndon Johnson that summer as he campaigned across the state for the Kennedy-Johnson ticket, and got to know Texas Governor Price Daniel, several of our U.S. congressmen, and most of the members of the Texas legislature. But it was the encounter with Rayburn that really stuck with me.

We were with a crowd of other elected officials at a standard-issue political event — I believe it was a dedication ceremony for a new dam — and the rain was just spitting down. It was cold and miserable, and as soon as the festivities were done, I hurried back to my green Ford, pried open the door with half-frozen fingers, and jumped in. Just then, the passenger-side door opened, and Rayburn plopped himself down in the seat next to me. I'd never met him before, and he wasn't supposed to ride with me, but mine was the first car he'd seen and he was anxious to get out of the rain.

At that time, "Mister Sam" Rayburn was one of the most respected and beloved politicians in the country. He'd served as the Speaker of the U.S. House of Representatives for longer than anyone in history, and he'd done it with a grace and efficiency that won over even his political opponents. He flat knew how to get things done, and was so good at playing every side of the political game that the *New York Times* named him "Mr. Everything."

Rayburn also held another record: in 1911, he'd been elected the youngest Speaker of the modern Texas House at the tender age of 29. That much I knew. What I didn't know was that, just five short years after that rainy November afternoon, I'd beat Mister Sam's record, getting elected Speaker of the Texas House at age 26.

But that was a long way off yet. For the moment, I was just as excited as could be to have a Texas legend like Rayburn in my car — and truth be told, I was a little nervous, too. As we rode to the nearby restaurant that was hosting the reception, I decided to try making some small talk. "Well, Mr. Speaker," I asked him, "what kind of president do you think John Kennedy will make?"

"Son," he answered, "I'll tell you what. I like Kennedy. He's got a lot of bright people around him, and I wish some of them would have run for office too. But that's not what's important." Rayburn leaned over, gripped my knee with a gnarled hand, and squeezed hard. "What's important," he went on, "is that Richard Nixon got his ass beat."

I didn't know quite what to say to that, but fortunately I didn't have to think about it for long, as Rayburn went right on talking. "Nixon's gonna try to come back," he said. "And I want you to promise me one thing. I want you to promise me you'll do everything you can to keep him from coming back. Because if he ever gets elected, that man could destroy the presidency."

━━━━━━━━━━

NOW, I DIDN'T KNOW WHAT EXACTLY RAYBURN MEANT BY THAT COMMENT, but over the years I never forgot it. When Nixon lost his race for California governor in 1962 and told reporters "you won't have Nixon to kick around anymore," I assumed, like a lot of other people did, that his political career was over. But it wasn't, of course, and a little more than a decade later, Nixon would indeed come close to destroying the presidency.

What's less well known is that he also wreaked all sorts of havoc on the Texas Democratic party during that time, and helped bring down my own political career as well. In the process, he helped hasten the decline of the Democratic party in the South and launched the kind of partisanship and smear tactics that have now become so prevalent in American politics.

Telling that whole story was a big reason I wanted to write this book, but it was far from the only reason. I was lucky enough to enter Democratic politics at the beginning of the party's heyday: throughout most of the sixties, Democrats dominated the national scene, holding the White House, both houses of Congress, and the majority of governorships and state legislatures. Texas politicians, led by President Johnson, were at the center of that dominance — and I was fortunate enough to be right in the middle of Texas politics. It was an amazing time to be a witness to, and a part of, history.

Today, of course, the parties' roles are reversed. Republicans — and specifically, Texas Republicans — are every bit as dominant nationally as the Democrats were in the sixties. Where once the names Johnson, Rayburn, and Connally were synonymous with political power, the 21st century brought us Bush, Rove and DeLay. Two of the Democrats' most pressing questions after the painful 2004 election losses were: "How did we get to this point?" and "Where do we go from here?" To find answers to these questions, you've got to start by looking back to the period when Democrats were strong. That's what I intend to do in this book.

As Sam Rayburn used to say, "Any jackass can kick down a barn, but it takes a good carpenter to build one." These days, there's a lot more barn burning in politics than barn building, and that's a trend I'd like to see reversed. *Barn Burning, Barn Building* is my story, but it's also the story of a great era of Texas politics. And beyond Texas, it's a story whose principles and lessons ring true for every state in the union. I love my state and my country fiercely, and I hope that by looking back at our past, we can start to craft a better future. The people of Texas — and of America — deserve nothing less.

BEN BARNES
Austin, Texas
January 2006

Chapter One

From Peanuts to Electrolux

I WAS EIGHT YEARS OLD THE DAY I BECAME A DEMOCRAT. IT WASN'T BECAUSE my Daddy was a Democrat, or because I admired — or even knew about — anybody who was in office at that time. It was because a couple of men drove up to our house in a pickup truck and gave my parents some news they'd been hoping to hear.

My family owned a peanut farm in Comanche County, in central Texas. We cultivated about 40 acres, growing peanuts and corn and raising hogs and chickens. We didn't have much, though I didn't know it — I had two pairs of jeans and my mother made sure one was always clean for me to wear, so I figured we were doing all right. From the time I could walk, I did chores on the farm, planting and hoeing peanuts, picking cotton, slopping the hogs, and milking our two cows. Like any farm, ours took a lot of work to keep it running.

Now, I know it seems like every Texas politician of a certain era — Lyndon Johnson, Sam Rayburn and John Connally among them — has his own story about growing up on a farm without two nickels to rub together. You're probably thinking that these childhood details sound like the worst kind of Texas cliché, and that you really ought to have picked up another book to read. But my point is, we got up at dawn and finished work after dark, and because we had no electricity — no refrigerator, no electric appliances, no electric lights — we had to heat water over a flame, use kerosene lamps for light in the evenings, and cure or can our food to keep it from spoiling.

That's why, when those men pulled up to our house that day in 1946, the news they brought was so welcome. They told my father that the government was going to bring electricity to our little farm.

President Franklin D. Roosevelt had created a program called the Rural Electrification Administration by executive order in 1935, with the sole purpose of bringing electricity to farms and rural areas like ours. Before the REA, just 10 percent of American farms had electricity — even though 90 percent of city households already had it. And the numbers were even worse in Texas, where less than three percent of farms had electricity in 1935. Farmers wanted it, of course, but power companies wanted them to pay the costs of stringing power lines over so many miles to bring it, and no one could afford that.

Some members of Congress had fought against the REA, saying it promoted socialism. The utility companies fought it, too, arguing that the government ought not to get involved with private business. But President Roosevelt had a grander vision than that. He saw a need, he understood that the government could help fill that need, and he took the steps to make it happen. The REA brought electricity not just to our farm, but over the next 40 years, to nearly every farm in the country.

That was my first experience with government, and it made a big impression. From then on, I thought of government as something that helped make people's lives better. I was too young to know what the New Deal was, or to know about the many other progressive programs — the Tennessee Valley Authority, Social Security Act, Civilian Conservation Corps, and others — that Roosevelt's administration was putting into place. But I knew the government could make a difference for good, like it did for us, and I never stopped believing that it could, and should, continue to do just that. It's a bedrock Democratic principle and the reason why, even sixty years and a full-scale national political swing later, I'm still a Democrat.

Of course, in mid-20th-century Texas, calling yourself a Democrat was like declaring you had a pulse. If you were alive, you were a Democrat, and that's how it had always been; from the time political parties arrived on the Texas scene in the mid-19th century, there really was only one party to speak of. Most of the settlers who'd made Texas their home had made their way from the Southern states, and they shared the same kind of conservative, states'-rights philosophy that Southern Democrats did. These are the people who formed the core of the party.

Save for a few scattered Republican victories, Democrats more or less had their way in Texas for the hundred years between 1850 and 1950. But in the absence of a strong opposition party, the Democrats themselves split into two factions, the conservative / moderates and the progressives. That split would continue well into the time when I served in Texas politics, first as a member of the House, then as Speaker, then as lieutenant governor. The story of my political career is in many ways the story of trying to hold these two sides together, to keep the party strong. Ultimately, though, that rift was one of several factors that led to the Democrats' decline in the '70s. And it's only through understanding that history that we can start to make the Democratic party strong again.

But I'm getting ahead of myself. Let me back up and start where any good story starts: at the beginning.

═══════════

THE LEON RIVER SNAKES QUIETLY THROUGH THE PLAINS OF COMANCHE County, past waving prairie grass and the oak trees that line its banks. In this part of Texas, where bands of Comanche Indians once roamed, the hills roll gently and the pace of life is slow. From the air, the land is a patchwork of farms — carefully tended squares where peanuts and melons grow, and where pecan and peach trees bear their fruit.

The Barnes family has lived in Comanche County for generations — long enough for the land to feel like a part of who we are. My grandfather, Benjamin Franklin Barnes, was the first postmaster for the town of Comyn, the nearest town to where I grew up. Located about 100 miles southwest of Fort Worth, Comyn had been built around a depot for the Texas Central Railroad. With a population of 27 in 1939, it had all the basics of a tiny Texas outpost — a cotton gin, a few stores, a lumberyard — but not much more. It also was home to an oil pipeline built by the Humble Pipeline Company, which employed my father, B.F. Barnes, for many years.

My dad worked at a pump station along the pipeline, spending eight-hour shifts making sure there was enough pressure to get the oil from the distant oilfields to the refineries. There were rotating shifts — morning, afternoon, and graveyard — and when my dad would finish up his eight hours, he'd more often than not come back to the farm and get right to work again. He'd hoe and pick cotton and thrash pecans, and so I grew up just assuming that everybody in the world worked a 14-hour day.

He'd come by his work ethic naturally, as one of 16 children who'd grown up on a farm. He and his six brothers all had to drop out of school at early ages — in my dad's case, in the eighth grade — to help their father make the payments on the property. My mother, Ina B. Carrigan, was raised on a farm too, about 15 miles from where my father grew up. She made it further in school than he did, graduating from high school in a little town called Proctor.

I was the first in my family to be born in a hospital, on Easter Sunday in 1938. At five o'clock in the morning, my father loaded my mother in the car and drove her 18 miles down the road to the nearest hospital, in Gorman. As it turned out, she spent most of the day there before I finally made my appearance that evening. My parents' excitement at having their firstborn was tempered by sadness when she also gave birth that day to a stillborn boy who would have been my twin brother.

In keeping with family tradition, my parents named me a variation of "Benjamin Franklin" — Benny Frank Barnes. The name suited me fine until I decided to run for office at age 21, at which point I figured "Benny" was a little too young-sounding for a candidate who needed every ounce of maturity he could muster. I changed it then to Ben Frank Barnes.

My younger brother, Rick, was born 21 months after me, and the two of us worked the fields and ran around together. We learned to swim in the Syrup Hole, a deep pool in nearby Cow Creek, and played every kind of sport. With no television or even radio in the house, we spent just about all our time outside, either doing farm chores of playing games. On the weekends, we might get to go into DeLeon or Dublin and see a Western for 10 cents — and if we were really lucky, we might then get treated to a cherry Coke or an ice-cream cone. In Texas in the summertime, nothing tasted better than a cool drink pulled by the soda jerk down at the drugstore.

Rick and I were young boys during the World War II years, and we'd go around the neighborhood collecting scrap iron for the war effort. We didn't really know what it was for, or what the war was about, but when President Roosevelt gave his "fireside chats," our parents would ride us down to my grandfather's house so we could crowd around the big radio in Pawpaw Barnes' living room.

Working on the oil pipeline was considered a national defense job, so my dad was exempt from military service. But all six of his brothers served, as did two of my mother's brothers. Some of my earliest memories are of seeing my uncles in uniform when they came home on leave. One Christmas Eve, my Uncle Ray showed up at our door, covered with snow after walking a mile to our house from the highway. We welcomed him in like he'd been to the end of the earth and back, which for all I knew, he had.

My only other war-related memory is of my father coming into the house excitedly one afternoon. He'd left the car idling outside, and even as young as I was, I was worried about him using up our ration of gasoline. He said something about an "atom bomb," and I of course had no idea what that meant. But he also told us the Japanese were going to surrender, and by the look on his face, he was a lot happier about the war ending than he was worried about that new kind of bomb.

————————

THE TEXAS OF MY BOYHOOD WAS A PLACE OF DUST, SWEAT, AND HEAT. MORE than half the population lived in rural areas, though the number of city dwellers was growing fast. The number of farms was falling steadily, from half a million in 1930 to about 385,000 in 1945. Yet nearly a third of the Texas work-force toiled in agriculture, compared to less than three percent who worked in oil and gas. Growing up in Comanche County, everyone I knew was tied to the land in one way or another.

Politics wasn't a big topic of conversation at our house, but even so, I apparently developed a taste for campaigning early. I found an old whistle in the house, and I'd go out in the back yard and blow it as loud and long as pos-sible, until all the neighborhood kids came running. I held an election and got myself named president of the gang, and I'd send everybody off on various chores and errands — most often things my father had asked me to do myself, like cleaning out the garage. This urge to run things was pronounced enough that, years later when I was elected Speaker of the Texas House, my old Sunday School teacher told reporters, "I had trouble with him. He was always wanting to organize the class and teach it himself." I suppose the world might have just spun right off its axis during my boyhood, if I hadn't been there to make sure it stayed on track.

Rick and I played baseball and football, and even though I was nearly two years older, we developed a real rivalry. Once, when I was pitching in a Pony League game, I found myself facing him at the plate. Now, usually Rick was catching when I was pitching, but this season we'd ended up on opposite teams. The bases were loaded, and sure enough, he hit one of my best pitches over the fence. I could have handled it gracefully, like a proud older brother, but I was mad enough to spit. I was convinced he couldn't have hit me unless he knew all my pitches from catching me, and so I refused to speak to him in the car on the way home.

I might not have acted out so much if I'd known what would happen in a game not long after that. This time, Rick and I were on the same team, and he'd roped a hit into the outfield. He always was fast, and he rounded first, then second, before the outfielder could even get to the ball. But suddenly, halfway between second and third base, he went tumbling. At first, we figured he must have tripped. But then, he couldn't get up.

My parents took him to the doctor, who gave them terrible news. Rick had polio, and he might never walk again.

Rick's illness knocked me over. He was always a better athlete than me, even though I never would have admitted it out loud at the time. I was 15 and he was 13 when he got sick, and I couldn't sort out how something so awful could happen to someone like him. In the end, he was able to walk again, but only after a year of treatment, surgery, and then two more years of healing. My mother spent hours at his hospital bedside, and my father and I were often alone at the farm. It was a rude introduction for a 15-year-old to how unfair life can sometimes be.

With Rick laid up, I had to work harder than ever on the farm. But though I mostly liked farm life, there was one part I couldn't abide. Out in the fields, hoeing peanuts, picking bolls, and thrashing pecans, I got the worst sunburns you could imagine. With my red hair and fair complexion, I didn't stand a chance — every summer, I'd blister and peel, blister and peel. Sunscreen hadn't been invented yet, and even wide-brim hats weren't enough to keep me from turning red as a lobster whenever the sun shone, which during a Texas summer was just about all the time. When someone eventually came up with the idea of those big umbrellas you could prop up above your tractor seat, I thought I'd died and gone to heaven.

Looking back, maybe it was lucky I got sunburned so bad. If I hadn't, I might well have stayed on the farm and never gotten into politics. But I wanted to get away from the sun, the grit, and the peanut straw that always found its way down my collar, and so I decided I ought to get an education.

My mother encouraged me every day in this pursuit. She wasn't an overly expressive person, but she did take time to praise me as having some smarts and some promise, and I was ready to believe her despite the evidence to the contrary. She'd say, "You gotta get out of this peanut country, Ben. You don't want to work on a farm your whole life. You ought to get yourself a college education and do something with yourself." That, combined with my often-blistered skin, instilled a little ambition in me.

I worked hard in school — a little schoolhouse in nearby Comyn, where I studied with about a dozen other pupils. By the time I graduated in 1956, they'd consolidated all the schools in that part of Comanche County, and we had a hundred students in our senior class. That's probably the largest graduating class DeLeon High School ever had — and certainly the whitest. At that time, in the mid-fifties, there were very few Mexican Americans, and I don't believe there was a single African American family in the county.

All of that seemed perfectly normal to me, partly because I'd never really been anywhere else. In high school, the farthest I'd been from home was Fort Worth, 100 miles up the road. I'd gone there for a stock show and come right back, and that trip gave me the extent of my knowledge about the "outside world." Yet Fort Worth did seem far away at the time, as the interstate highways hadn't been built yet, so it took a good two and a half hours to get there.

Comanche was a dry county when I was growing up, and there weren't many places people could go to socialize. Like every other town in Texas, the biggest social event of the week was the Friday night high school football game. I played for the DeLeon High School Bearcats, and I swear that at some games we played, there were more people in the stands than there were residents of the entire county. I don't know where all those people came from, but they surely never missed a game.

Football games offered a lot more than just an opportunity to come see a bunch of teenage boys run around in helmets. They were the hub of community life. People would come to see and be seen, to talk about crops, trade horses, admire new pickup trucks, swap gossip. Those games were the gravity that pulled everybody in the community together — and in many parts of Texas, they still are. Texas is the most football-crazy state in the country, and 50 years after I ran around on those fields myself, there's no sign of that abating.

Like any high school student, I liked some teachers better than others, and a few made a lasting impression on me. Al Langford, the head coach for the DeLeon football team, taught me about teamwork and how to use whatever talent you've got — even if it's less than the other guy's — to succeed. But it was a lesson from my English teacher, Lucille Duke, that really stuck with me.

She had assigned the class to do a book report on *The Egyptian*, a then-popular novel by a Finnish writer named Mika Waltari. I'd finished the book early, and went up to Miss Duke in class and said, "I'm ready to do my report."

"Well, Benny," she said. "If you finished that so quickly, then you've got time to read another book. I want you to get yourself a copy of *Les Miserables*, by Victor Hugo."

I didn't think it was quite fair to get extra work just because I'd finished my assignment so quickly, but once I started reading *Les Miserables*, I didn't mind. That book had a greater impact on me than anything else I've ever read. The story of the rogue Jean Valjean during the French Revolution, the book touches on the grandest themes of the human condition: suffering, poverty, heroism, and redemption. It lit a spark in my 16-year-old soul, and I became aware for the first time that we can either choose to seize the time we have or waste it. I literally thought to myself, "This is your day. Do not waste an hour." And as corny as it may sound, I've tried to live that way ever since. I must have had some success at it, because years later, Texas Governor Ann Richards described me publicly as "an oscillating fan" — someone who never seemed to stop moving.

The only person who had more of an influence on me than my teachers and coaches was my father. He was a quiet sort, not one to draw attention to himself, but his actions spoke louder than anything he could say, anyway. Once, when a neighbor family's house burned down, my father insisted on taking some money he'd saved to make a payment on our farm to help them out. He gave them about $500 or so — a huge sum at the time — despite the fact that his banker was ready to kill him for it.

One August afternoon, he also taught me a powerful lesson about accepting other people — a rare enough lesson in those days of segregation and overt racism.

Comanche County had been more or less hostile territory for blacks ever since 1886, when a black man had been accused of murdering a white woman in the area. That summer, a white vigilante mob had gone after the few black residents of the county, driving them out violently with weapons and threats. And even though 60 years had passed by the time I was growing up there, I'm embarrassed to say that when I was growing up, there was still a big sign at the county line that read, "Nigger, don't let the sun set on you here."

I almost never saw any African Americans in DeLeon, Comyn, or any other of the towns in the county, but the one notable exception was the time my father and I went to have lunch at the Bearcat Grill during DeLeon's annual Peach and Melon festival. During festival time, people come from all over Texas, and that year a traveling carnival had set up nearby.

While my dad and I sat at the grill eating our lunch, a black man, probably in town working the carnival, came in and asked for a hamburger and French fries. The woman behind the counter refused to serve him and told him to leave. He didn't make a fuss or anything, just turned and walked slowly toward the door.

He hadn't even made it out before my father was at the counter, ordering a hamburger, fries, and a Coke. Fortunately, the food came out of the kitchen quickly, and my father grabbed it and headed for the door. He found the man and invited him to sit in our pickup truck, out of the sun, to have his meal. It was a blistering August day, and the man gratefully took him up on his offer.

We sat there with him as he ate his food, and when he was done, he thanked us and went off along his way. My father revved up the truck, turned to me, and said, "Let me tell you something, Ben. Anybody, no matter the color of their skin, is as good as you and me. You always treat people as your equal. Don't ever let me hear of you doing otherwise." I don't know how, in a culture of such deep-rooted intolerance, my father turned out to be that open-minded, but I've always been grateful that was the case. Later, when I voted against segregation bills in the legislature, the men who supported the bills would ask me, "Ben, you come from Comanche County — what are you doing voting against segregation?" The answer lay in the lunch of hamburger and fries my father bought at the Bearcat Grill that day.

━━━━━━━━

TEXANS LIKE TO THINK THAT OUR STATE IS SOMEHOW DIFFERENT FROM THE other 49. There's a mystique that people buy into, a "Don't Mess With Texas" attitude that perpetuates its own stereotype while irritating the hell out of people in states like Oklahoma.

But even looking at it objectively — or as objectively as a Texan like me can, anyway — Texas is unique. No other state has its combination of sheer physical size (second only to Alaska), large population (second only to California), and abundant oil resources (second to no one). Texas was even an independent country in the 19th century. And no other state, save perhaps California, can boast the same kind of national political influence that Texas had in the 20th century.

The discovery of significant quantities of oil beneath our dusty plains in 1894, and the influx of money that produced, vaulted the state into a position of national power. The first gushers led to a rush of exploration, and deeper, vaster — and richer — oil fields were discovered throughout the next few decades. Even modest taxes on oil production yielded huge windfalls for the state, and soon, growing numbers of wealthy oilmen began exerting their influence on local, state, and national politics. Dallas and Houston became major urban centers, and the culture of wildcatters and roughnecks became part of Texas lore. And it wasn't just the oil money that enriched Texas; it was the fact that we controlled such a vital resource for the national economy.

Though my father worked for the Humble Pipeline Company, I never did work in the oil business. Instead, I took a job extracting a somewhat less glamorous resource from the land — a mineral called molybdenum, used for strengthening steel in products like car parts, airplane parts, and construction equipment.

The summer I was 19, I followed one of my uncles out to Climax, Colorado, to work at the molybdenum mine there. It was a beautiful spot, as the town of Climax clung to the side of the Rocky Mountains, two miles above sea level. My uncle worked in the machine shop, but I worked deep down in the mine itself, fighting claustrophobia every time the elevator went down that shaft. There wasn't much to like about the job. The work was tiring. The older miners talked nonstop, like they were afraid they'd cease to exist the minute they couldn't hear their own voices. And molybdenum ore dust got into your eyes, nose, mouth, and any place else not covered up.

The pay was decent, and it rose depending on how many unpleasant things you were willing to subject yourself to. Base pay for working in the mine was $3.50 an hour. If you were willing to wear wading boots and get wet, you got another 75 cents an hour. And if you were willing to handle dynamite, you'd get another 75 cents. On top of that, Saturdays paid time-and-a-half, and Sundays paid double.

There was money to be made, but after just two weeks I was crazy to get out of there. I went to a union meeting, and one of the union men asked me how I liked working in the mine. "I don't like it one bit," I told him.

He eyed me for a minute, then asked me an unexpected question. "You play baseball?" I told him I did, and that I was a pitcher.

"Are you worth a damn?" he asked. I told him I'd pitched in high school.

That was apparently good enough for him. "The Leadville mine workers have a baseball team," he told me. "If you make the team, you can get out of the mine, play ball and work as a fire inspector, just riding around in a jeep and looking out for fires. You'll still get five bucks an hour."

I'll tell you what, I never threw the ball so hard as the day of the tryout for the Leadville team. I hadn't picked up a baseball in a year, since my last high school game, but throwing at 10,000 feet gave my fastball a little zip, and I made the team as a relief pitcher. The day I got out of that mine was the happiest day of my life.

By the time I worked that summer in Colorado, I'd already finished two semesters of college, the first at Texas Christian University in Fort Worth, and the second at a small college called Tarleton. I'd liked TCU well enough, but Tarleton was closer to my home town of DeLeon, and therefore closer to my high school sweetheart, Martha Morgan. Martha was just 17 and in the middle of her senior year at DeLeon High School, but we'd decided to go ahead and get married that spring. We'd dated for the past two or three years, and I don't think I — or anyone else in town, for that matter — ever doubted we'd end up married.

I'd gotten accepted to the University of Texas, and when Martha finished school, we packed up and moved to Austin. I was 20 and ambitious, and could hardly wait to get there. This truly felt like the beginning of my adult life — and politics was still the furthest thing from my mind. I'd never paid any attention to either state or local politics, and had never even shaken the hand of a politician. If you'd asked me who the mayor of DeLeon was, I'm not sure I could have named him.

In fact, the thing I was really focused on, in addition to my studies, was how to make a little money. I took more than a full load and went to classes year round, aiming to get my degree in just two more years, but even with the extra work, I still spent hours trying to earn a living. I took several different jobs, but the one that probably did me the most good was selling Electrolux vacuum cleaners door-to-door.

You couldn't invent a better training program for a political career than door-to-door sales. You've got to learn how to make your pitch succinctly, win a person's trust quickly, and persevere when you get doors slammed in your face, which is often — in fact, the company I worked for warned us we'd have to knock on an average of 30 doors to get one opportunity to demonstrate the vacuum. You develop a thick hide pretty quickly in that kind of work, and that definitely came in handy during my political career.

The key to making a sale was convincing the woman of the house to let me do a demonstration in the bedroom. I'd put a clean bag in the Electrolux, vacuum the mattress, and then dump the contents right out on the bed. You wouldn't believe how much dirt an ordinary mattress can hold. These women, many of whom prided themselves on keeping a clean house, would look at that pile of dirt on the bed and just about faint. Then I'd suck it back up with the Electrolux, and they were ready to sign up right there.

I sold a lot of vacuum cleaners that way, and the detail of my experience as a door-to-door salesman made for good newspaper copy when I started to rise in Texas politics. When I became Speaker, one "anonymous friend" told a reporter, "I'll tell you one thing, it's a good thing he quit selling vacuum cleaners because if he hadn't, every house in the city of Austin would probably have at least a couple of them by now."

It wasn't the vacuum cleaners that got me into politics, though. That came courtesy of another job, working at the Texas Department of Health in downtown Austin.

I'd started out working one of the more tedious part-time jobs there, filing birth and death certificates by hand. Today, of course, everything is computerized and automated, but back then we had to file records by taking the screws out of the giant books that held each county's records, putting the records in the right place, and then putting the screws back in when we were done. It was time-consuming work, and there was a whole team of part-timers like me doing it.

I worked hard and, within six months, got myself named supervisor of the part-time employees. One of my new responsibilities was to manage the money coming in from the little concessions stand selling snacks in the lobby of the building. Whatever profit we made on concessions went into the employees' "flower fund," which was used to pay for flowers when people died, or the little holiday parties the department would throw. I was supposed to co-sign any checks being written on the flower fund account, and that's when the trouble started.

An assistant to the Health Department commissioner used to bring me the checks to sign. One afternoon, he brought me a couple of checks made out to the Tower Liquor store and the Tower Club, a private club in town.

"What are these for?" I asked him. I didn't know of anything the department had planned that would require payments to either place.

"None of your business," he said, not smiling. "If you like your job, sign 'em."

"Well, I don't think I ought to sign 'em if I don't know what they're for," I said, at which point he told me I could think about it for a bit, but if I didn't sign them by the next day, I'd be sorry. He made his point further by bumping his car into mine in the employee parking lot that afternoon, leaving a dent. It felt like I was suddenly in a bad gangster movie.

I don't know what that guy expected me to do, but what I did do was go right away to Bert Hall, a former legislator who was then working at the Health Department. I told Bert about the checks for liquor and clubs, and told him I'd discovered by looking back through the checkbook that there were more than just the two the commissioner's assistant had tried to get me to sign. Hall took it seriously enough to send me up to the Capitol building to talk to a couple of people there.

If you've never been to the Capitol building in Austin, it's hard to convey just how majestic it seems — especially to an impressionable young man who grew up in a dusty outpost like DeLeon. Made of deep red granite and taller than the Capitol building in Washington, D.C., the Texas Capitol is a sleek, imposing dome that towers over the whole of Austin. I'd been there as a tourist, but this was something different: now I was going up and having meetings with my representative, Ben Sudderth, and two Appropriations Committee members, Truett Latimer and Bill Heatly. I'd feel a little thrill when I walked down those "corridors of power," and for the first time, it felt like I was really doing something important.

When Rep. Heatly heard my story, he said, "Well, son, it sounds like those people are stealing. But we need to have the proof. Can you bring me that checkbook?" I told him I could, and late that night, I let myself into the Health Department building and slipped the checkbook out of a desk drawer. I carried it up to the Capitol the next day, and that was all the evidence he needed.

Soon enough, District Attorney Robert Smith got involved, and three

Health Department employees — including the man who'd threatened me — found themselves facing the wrath of the state. They'd been caught red-handed, and when they were offered the option of either repaying the money and leaving Texas or facing charges, they knew there was only one real choice. Two of them slunk out of the state with their tails between their legs, though the third, a secretary, was allowed to stay.

The story was big news for a few days, and I got invited up to the Capitol to be officially thanked for my part in uncovering the scheme. For the first time in my life, it felt like I'd done something that really made a difference — and it was a feeling I was anxious to have again.

In a fluke of timing, Rep. Sudderth was planning to retire, opening up the seat from my district. And so, with the great accumulated wisdom of my 21 years, I made a snap decision to run for his seat in the 1960 election. By that time I expected to have my bachelor's degree in hand and be in law school at the University of Texas. I figured that, even if I won somehow, I could continue and get my law degree while serving.

Before making my decision final, I decided to go back home and test the political waters. I convinced a friend of mine from TCU, Brian Ingram, to drive me down to DeLeon so I could visit with a few people in my district. I asked about dozen different people — businessmen, community leaders, and local party officials — what they thought about my idea. They all told me the same thing: "Go on back to law school, Ben. That's the craziest idea I ever heard." They had a point. After all, no one knew me, I had no money or experience and I was just 21 years old. As Brian and I drove back to Austin, he said, "Well, I'm glad that's over with. You weren't really serious, were you?"

But I was. I took in everybody's opinion, then ignored them all and decided to run. Looking back, I can't believe I just jumped right in and did it, but at the time it felt like the most natural thing in the world. They say a politician needs both luck and timing to succeed, but I think, at least in my case, it helps if you have some ignorance thrown in. Not too much — just enough so that you don't know what you can't do.

Chapter Two

Up with the Baptists, To Bed with the Drunks

Once I'd decided to run, it was time to pay a visit to the man I was trying to replace: retiring Rep. Ben Sudderth. I didn't know him well, though we'd met a couple of times during the Health Department scandal. Judging from the look on his face, he was certainly surprised when I walked into his office one morning in January of 1960 and announced, "Mr. Sudderth, I'm going to run for your seat."

He looked at me a moment, then leaned over his desk and said, "Young man, I have to tell you, I don't think you have a prayer of winning." Sudderth had already declared for another candidate in the Democratic primary, a man named Ike Hickman, and he went on to tell me he just didn't think there was any way I could compete with him.

On the face of it, Sudderth was right. Ike Hickman had every possible advantage over me, and then some. He was from Brownwood, which was the largest city in the voting district. Compared to my home town of DeLeon, which had about 800 voters, Brownwood had 8,000 voters — most of whom could be expected to go for their hometown candidate. I, on the other hand, didn't know a soul in Brownwood.

Hickman ran a feed mill in town, but he also was locally famous as the host of his own daily radio show. Every morning, farmers tuned in to hear his farm news program, which was broadcast across all three counties in the district. He was also active in local politics, serving on the Brownwood city council.

As if that wasn't enough, Hickman had not only served in World War II, he was a bona fide decorated war hero and had spent time in a German prison camp. Quite simply, he was about the most perfect candidate you could have found. And because he was running at the end of the Eisenhower administration, he even had the perfect name, which he took advantage of by handing out "I Like Ike" buttons at campaign events.

I soon found out that pretty much everyone who knew anything about politics shared Sudderth's opinion about my chances. Even my own father offered less than a ringing vote of confidence when a co-worker at Humble Oil asked him what he planned to do about the fact that I was running. "Nothing," my father answered. "He's 21 years old."

In the beginning, the only thing people seemed willing to offer me was advice. After I handed out little cards with "Ben F. Barnes" on them at one early event, a former sheriff told me to get rid of that middle initial. "The first time I ran," he told me, "I used my middle initial, 'T.' I lost. The next time, I took it out — and I won!" I took his advice, and never used the "F" again. Another man, Cap Shelton, told me I ought to buy a hat, to make myself look older. I did that, too — bought a cheap little cowboy-style hat at a department store — and it worked. I wore that hat everywhere during the campaign.

All the advice was helpful, but in those earliest days, there were only two people who believed in me enough to put their time and resources into my campaign: C. H. "Ham" Locke and Howard Sparks.

Ham Locke was a rural mail carrier and a member of the DeLeon Chamber of Commerce, and he and I had been friends for a couple of years. When I told him I was planning to run, his first question was, "Do you have any money?" As he later recounted to the *Fort Worth Star-Telegram,* my response was, "No, but I've got a friend who is willing to print me some cards and I know where I can borrow a little money. I think I can win it on shoe leather."

Ham was the first to really believe in my campaign, and he took it upon himself to organize my first fundraiser, a breakfast in DeLeon that raised about three or four hundred dollars. Even back then, that wasn't big money, but it was just about the biggest chunk I'd get. Other donations began trickling in — a railroad union man gave me $50, the local REA electric co-op gave me $100 and some stamps, and a man who ran a dry-goods store in DeLeon gave me another $100. In the entire campaign, I reported a total of about $2,000. That just sounds impossible in these days of high-tech, consultant-heavy campaigns, but at that time all I really needed was enough money to fill my car with gas, and to get a sandwich or two when I wasn't getting fed at a pie supper or luncheon. Campaigns at that time were won with sweat and shoe leather, not attack ads and focus groups.

The second person who bought into my campaign was Howard Sparks.

Howard was a businessman in Brownwood, but he wasn't exactly a poster boy for the Chamber of Commerce. In fact, the Chamber pretty much shunned him as a renegade, because Howard rather famously liked to drink, and Brownwood had been a dry town until just the year before. Even though Prohibition had been repealed 27 years earlier, it's fair to say that in Texas, the battle between proponents and opponents of alcohol continued to rage as fiercely as ever. Even after Brownwood voted in 1959 to allow sales of beer and wine, you still couldn't purchase whiskey or any other kind of liquor. In fact, it would be another ten contentious years before the Texas legislature finally passed a "liquor by the drink" law allowing people to buy a single liquor-based drink in Texas restaurants.

At any rate, Howard and the "establishment" didn't mix very well, and I suspect he signed on to help me partly because Ike Hickman was the "establishment" candidate. But I didn't really care why he was doing it, as I just needed all the help I could get.

Howard ran a printing company, and he printed up a batch of business cards for me to use. Because he didn't have a lot of money to spare either, he made them out of cheap stock — those cards were so thin, you could barely pull them apart. They had a little picture of me in my hat and the words "Ben Barnes, State Representative: Honest, Qualified and Sincere." In addition, Howard wrote my campaign literature, producing bulletins and brochures that were as well-written as any I'd have in my career.

Once Ham Locke and Howard Sparks had gotten on board, I then set about convincing another group of young men to help me out. Groner Pitts, Stuart Coleman, and Putter Jarvis had signed on to work with Hickman's campaign, but soon after we met, I managed to talk them into switching sides. Those three advised me and campaigned for me, and they helped me try to plot a way I could win.

With this small group in place, I suddenly had a real campaign. But at one of the first events where Ike Hickman and I both appeared, I very nearly dropped out of the race right then. It was at a joint rally sponsored by the Veterans of Foreign Wars and the Farm Bureau at the Brownwood Community Center. Hickman and I were both scheduled to speak, and we drew straws to see who would go first. He won and took the podium, and for the next 15 minutes, I saw my fledgling political career going straight down the toilet.

He talked about fighting the Nazis in Europe. He talked about being taken prisoner and spending time in the German prison camp. He talked about how much he loved this country, and how he'd nearly died for it, and how the Nazis had tortured him but hadn't broken his spirit. And he talked about wanting to come back and serve his country one more time, for the people of Brownwood and of Texas. The crowd was going absolutely crazy.

When he finished, I thought, "Well, that's it. I'm going to get up and announce that I'm resigning this campaign and going back to law school." I stepped up to the podium — suddenly feeling like a big old overgrown red-headed boy, wearing the only suit I owned — and got ready to say my piece. But what came out of my mouth was not what I expected.

As I stood there, I started thinking about what I had been doing in World War II. "I was only three years old when Pearl Harbor got bombed," I told the crowd. "So there wasn't too much I could do during the war. But my brother and I, we had a little red wagon. And we'd take that red wagon every Saturday and try to fill it up with scrap iron, and our dad would put it in the back of the car to take to a scrap iron dealer for the war effort. And that was the way I tried to serve."

Now, there's not much comparison between what a young boy like me could do and what Ike Hickman did during the war. But as I talked, I saw some of the women in the audience nodding their heads about that red wagon. So I went on.

"When I heard Ike Hickman speak just now, I thought I might as well just pack it in," I said. "But I want to serve you and I believe I can serve well. So I'm in this race, and I'm asking for your vote." I probably didn't swing a whole lot of voters my way that day, but I did at least manage to stay in the race.

———

WHEN I STARTED MY CAMPAIGN, THERE WERE ONLY TWO REASONS THAT voters outside of DeLeon would ever have heard of me. Sports fans might have seen my name in the paper because I'd played basketball and football at DeLeon High School. And many of the farmers in Comanche County knew me because I'd worked one summer measuring peanut allotments in the district. Now, between those two, you might think that being a football player would bring greater political advantages, especially considering how popular high school football is in Texas. But it was that tedious, dirty peanut allotment work I'd done a few years earlier that got my campaign rolling, in two ways.

Because peanuts were a subsidized crop, each farmer was only allowed to plant a designated amount — and the government occasionally hired people like me to go make sure farmers weren't planting more than their share. Using a wheel at the end of a stick, I'd walk around the edges of the peanut plots, measuring how many acres each farm was cultivating. Just about everybody pushed their limit a little bit, to see what they could get away with. I knew that, but I also knew that there were plenty of peanuts — maybe up next to a fence or a tree line, or lying in a shady spot — that would ultimately die from lack of sun or water, and I felt those ought to be subtracted from the final amount.

Whenever there was a question, I always erred on the side of the farmer, and they knew and appreciated that. There probably weren't too many six-foot-three, red-headed, sunburn-faced peanut allotment surveyors wandering around West Texas, so even if they didn't know my name, those farmers remembered me when they saw coverage of my campaign.

The other big benefit to the peanut allotment job was getting giant soil conservation maps. These were made up of aerial photographs, blown up so big that they showed every road, farm, and house in each county. It might take 20 or so of these maps to cover all the land in one county, so I had a couple dozen of them, showing every single house in the three counties of my voting district. Using the maps, I began visiting every house, one by one, and marking each off with a red pencil.

For three months, I woke up with the Baptists and went to bed with the drunks, spending 18-hour days trying to shake every hand in the district. I'd show up at the dairy barns at 4 a.m. to catch the farmers milking their cows. I'd call on businesses during the day and visit homes during the late afternoon and evening. Then I'd go to the bowling alleys and the truck stops, which were the only establishments open until midnight.

In his later interview with the *Fort Worth Star-Telegram,* Ham Locke described a day in my campaign: "[Ben] went to a pie supper over at Stag Creek one night and had an appointment later that night in Brownwood. He finished up after midnight. I ran into a café owner over at Goldthwaite the next day and he said, 'When I opened up this morning at 5, there was Barnes standing out in the dark holding his hand out and asking for my vote.' Found out that Ben had opened up all the cafes, service stations, and stores that way and was gone by 9 a.m. to campaign someplace else."

Pie suppers were the heart of the campaign, and I must have gone to about a hundred of them leading up to primary day. I'd started off at such a disadvantage, with Ike Hickman being a local celebrity and me being a 21-year-old nobody, that I had to meet as many people as quickly as I could. At a pie supper, I could shake hands with a few dozen people, and stuff myself with pie in the meantime. At one such supper, though, I got a little bit of a scare when a gentleman who was a pillar of the community suddenly got up to speak.

We were in tiny Proctor, Texas, the town where my mother had graduated from high school, and while everybody was milling about, a man I recognized as a judge from Gatesville rose and tapped his glass.

Now, I didn't know this judge from Adam. I couldn't imagine what in the world he was going to say about me, unless it was that I had spilled some blueberry pie down my white shirt. I stood there frozen for a minute, and he started speaking.

"I've got something to say," said the judge. "I want to tell you a story." And he launched into a story from a few decades back, about a time when a gang of white vigilantes was getting ready to lynch a black man. The mob was fired up, yelling and pushing for the lynching to start, when suddenly two men passed nearby with a team of horses.

"Jesse Barnes was driving that team," said the judge. "And his father, Benjamin Franklin Barnes, was riding with him. Jesse held that team up while his father aimed his shotgun at the crowd. 'You let that man go,' he said. 'Or I'll make sure you do.' And he held that shotgun on the crowd until they let the man get away."

Jesse Barnes was my grandfather and Benjamin Franklin Barnes my great-grandfather. I had never in my life heard that story, and I stood there rooted to my spot. The judge went on. "I'm going to vote for Ben Barnes," he said, "because we need men who come from that kind of bloodline helping to run Texas."

In those days, that kind of simple moment could literally prove a campaign's turning point. Bit by bit, people began to learn who I was, and I started to earn the trust of the voters. And as the primary drew closer, I pushed myself harder. I didn't have enough time to drive home to my parents' place every night, or any money for hotels, so I just slept in my car. I'd shower and shave at truck stops, in exchange for filling my car with their gas — which I also could barely afford. It was just about as shoestring an operation as you can imagine, but it was the only way I had a prayer of winning. I spent months covering every square inch of those counties, and by the time primary day rolled around, every single house on those tattered soil conservation maps had a red "X" marked through it.

Ike Hickman hadn't taken my campaign very seriously at the beginning, but as time wore on he'd realized I was gaining ground on him. Whatever good news I received, he tried to counter by appealing to Brownwood's most conservative elements. When the REA co-ops announced they were supporting me, Hickman talked up the fact that he was for the utility companies, knowing that Texas Power and Light was a big political force in Brownwood. When the railroad's Brotherhood of Local Engineers endorsed my campaign, Hickman made a big stink over the fact that Labor was backing me. I was so green I didn't really even know what that meant — I just wanted those railroad guys to vote for me.

At the end of primary day, on May 7, 1960, a lot of people — including probably Ike Hickman — were in for a surprise. I'd beaten Hickman by almost a 2-to-1 margin, with 8,023 votes to his 4,293. And with no Republican opponent facing me in the November general election, I had effectively won the seat. I'd just turned 22 a few weeks earlier, and now I was headed for the Texas legislature.

———

IN 1960, TEXAS DEMOCRATS WERE NEARING THE PEAK OF THEIR POLITICAL power. For most of the 20th century, Texans had been among the power elite in Washington — but that year we held claim to the two most influential legislators in the U.S. Congress: Speaker of the House Sam Rayburn and Senate Majority Leader Lyndon Johnson. That spring, there was also a chance that Johnson might even win the Democratic nomination for President.

Texas Democrats had first gained national prominence in the early years of the century, when Houstonian Edward House was President Woodrow Wilson's closest adviser. House was an eccentric political mastermind who liked to stay behind the scenes, even turning down a cabinet position when Wilson offered to let him choose whichever one he wanted. (If he had accepted, he'd have been one of four Texans serving on Wilson's cabinet.) House was so close to Wilson that the press referred to him as "Assistant President House" or Wilson's "Silent Partner."

President Wilson's two terms were followed by 12 years of Republican domination in Washington, an era of fiscal mismanagement that finally led to the stock market crash and start of the Depression during Herbert Hoover's presidency. Americans suffered plenty during those years of poverty and uncertainty, and by the time Hoover's term came to an end in 1932, voters were understandably ready for a change. This was the moment Democrats had been waiting for — and once again, Texas Democrats were right in the middle of it.

In 1932, Franklin Roosevelt won the presidency with a Texan, John Nance "Cactus Jack" Garner, as his running mate. Garner was an old-school politician who loved to drink whiskey and play poker, and he was happy to do it with colleagues on either side of the aisle. When he was House Minority Leader in the late '20s, he and Republican House Speaker Nicholas Longworth liked to invite their fellow legislators to a back room in the Capitol for what they called the "Board of Education" — an evening of stiff bourbon and bipartisan shop talk. Garner's protégé, Sam Rayburn, would later carry on the tradition when he became Speaker of the House in 1940.

Garner once famously declared that the office of the vice presidency wasn't "worth a bucket of warm spit," but he proved his own adage wrong by becoming the most powerful vice president to that point in history. A stocky, white-haired lawyer with ruddy cheeks and a sharp tongue, Garner did much of the work of pushing through Roosevelt's New Deal legislation. His combination of charm and political wiles carried his efforts, but it couldn't have hurt that fellow Texans chaired eight of the major House committees at the time — more evidence of the state's outsize influence in Washington.

Another Texan who played a big part in the New Deal was Jesse Jones. A high-school dropout who went on to earn a fortune as a financier and builder, the dapper, silver-haired Jones was appointed by President Roosevelt to run the Reconstruction Finance Corporation. Set up by Roosevelt to lend money to the country's faltering economic pillars — railroads, banks, insurance companies, and the like — the RFC was a major factor in pulling the U.S. out of the Depression. As the man at the reins, Jesse Jones earned the reputation of being "the second most powerful man in Washington."

The New Deal and World War II got the U.S. economy running again, and during those years yet another Texan rose to the ranks of Washington's power elite. In 1932, Sam Rayburn had helped maneuver Cactus Jack Garner onto the Democratic ticket with FDR, and over the next decade Rayburn became one of the most powerful and influential supporters of the New Deal. In fact, as the co-author of the Rural Electrification Administration Act, Rayburn helped bring the REA to life — and electricity to my family's little farm in Comanche County.

Short, bald, and built like a fireplug, Rayburn wasn't necessarily the kind of man you'd picture as being a master of the political game — but there has never been his equal in the House, before or since. He began his political career in 1906, getting himself elected to the Texas House at age 24. By the time he was 29, he'd already won the Speaker's chair. Rayburn said he loved being Texas Speaker more than any other job, but he held it for only one term before setting his sights on the U.S. House.

Starting with his election in 1912, Rayburn served a record 48 consecutive years in the House. Between 1940 and his death in 1961, he served as Speaker for every congressional session that Democrats were in the majority — which was every session but two. Rayburn's longevity broke records, but it was his political aptitude that really set him apart. He knew how to pull strings in every which direction to get exactly what he wanted, and he managed to make it look easy to boot. Sam Rayburn absolutely owned the House — and when Lyndon Johnson moved up into the Senate leadership in the early '50s, the state of Texas suddenly had an unprecedented grip on power in the halls of Congress.

Now, with all this influence in Washington, and the dearth of Republican opponents back home, you'd think the Texas Democratic party was just about invincible during this time. But absolute power is a dangerous thing. In the absence of a strong opposition, the party began turning against itself, with two factions clashing along battle lines that had existed for decades but grew sharper by the day. The clash would finally break out into the open in 1952, paving the way for the Republican party to at last get a precious toehold in Texas.

The rift in the Texas Democratic party had gotten its start in early 20th century, during the days when the Prohibition movement heated up. Liquor has always been a divisive topic in Texas, with vocal anti-liquor forces on one hand calling for restrictions or bans on alcohol sales, and the pro-liquor side on the other hand, wishing everybody would just simmer down and have a drink. Like most "morality" issues, this one cut deep, and the Democratic party found itself split, with the "progressive" or "liberal" Democrats for Prohibition and the "conservative" Democrats against it.

That kind of labeling is simplistic — it's too easy to call someone "liberal" or "conservative" because of one or two things they believe, when their politics are usually more complicated than that. But over the years, Democrats in Texas began aligning themselves under these labels, with a clear divide growing between those who were more business-oriented and those who were more focused on various other constituencies. The two sides developed their own power structures within the party and, over time, began to fight almost as much as if they were in opposite parties.

In the '40s and '50s, the conservative Democrats began outstripping the liberals. For one thing, the culture of Texas is generally conservative, so the liberals already had a harder row to hoe. For another, more and more money started flowing into the state from oil, gas, aviation, and other industry, and as the state's coffers filled, the business-oriented conservative Democrats saw their power grow. Our most powerful politicians during this time — Sam Rayburn, Lyndon Johnson, and Governor Allan Shivers — all had strong conservative ties. And in fact, it was Governor Shivers who made the move that gave that first glimmer of hope to Texas Republicans.

Shivers was a tall, dashing World War II veteran who had become governor in a very unfortunate way. He was serving as lieutenant governor in 1949 when then-Governor Beauford Jester had a heart attack and died while riding on a train to Houston. Shivers and Jester were good friends, and Jester's death affected him deeply. But that didn't stop Shivers from jumping into the governorship like he'd been born to it.

Shivers was a man of opinions, and the subject that got him truly worked up in 1952 was the "Tidelands issue." Because Texas had been its own independent nation before it joined the union, the state still claimed mineral rights to all land up to three miles off its shorelines along the Gulf of Mexico — a claim that was worth a lot of money, since oil had recently been discovered offshore. That year, the U.S. Congress was scheduled to consider a bill that would codify the state's claim into law. The Republican presidential candidate, Dwight Eisenhower, told Shivers he'd support the bill. The Democratic candidate, Adlai Stevenson, said he'd veto it, turning the Tidelands over to the federal government.

That was all Shivers needed to know. He started the "Democrats for Eisenhower" and also pushed through a bill that would allow Democrats to cross-file, putting their names on both Democrat and Republican primary ballots. His actions led thousands of conservative Democrats — dubbed "Shivercrats" — to vote for Eisenhower. And despite the fact that Rayburn and Johnson supported Stevenson, Eisenhower became the first Republican to carry the state since Herbert Hoover had edged the Catholic, pro-liquor Democrat Al Smith in 1928.

With the advent of the Shivercrats, the rift between the liberal and conservative Democrats widened. And when Shivers helped Eisenhower carry Texas again in 1956, it looked like the rift might just become permanent within the party. If the Democrats couldn't even unite behind a presidential candidate, after all, what chance did they have of holding things together at the state level?

But then, in 1960, a presidential candidate emerged who might, it seemed, be able to reunite the fractious elements of the Texas Democratic party: Lyndon Johnson.

————

I FIRST MET LYNDON JOHNSON IN THE SUMMER OF 1960, AT A POLITICAL meeting in Austin about his presidential campaign in Texas. With my primary victory, it was clear I was heading for the Texas House that fall — but still, they must have invited everybody and their dog if I got invited to that meeting. Just inside the door, they gave me a name tag that said "Representative-elect Barnes," which I pinned proudly on my suit lapel.

Johnson came to speak at that meeting, and the thing that struck me first was how huge he was, and how big his hands were. I'm six foot three, but shaking Johnson's hand, it felt like I was looking at a colossus. He really did seem to fill up the room, and when he trained those hangdog eyes on me and grabbed my shoulder, I knew I was in the presence of a political master. It would be a couple more years before Johnson really registered who I was, but I was drawn to him right away, for both his charisma and his political pragmatism, which I aimed to emulate.

The story of Johnson's rise has been documented by dozens of writers. His boyhood in the poverty of the Texas Hill Country, his early career as a schoolteacher, and his election to the U.S. House in 1937 have become the stuff of history. And his razor-thin margin of victory in the 1948 Senate primary, which he won by just 87 votes, has been burnished into legend.

Johnson's beginnings in the Senate weren't exactly auspicious, but within five years he'd climbed his way up to become Minority Leader, and by 1955, a mere seven years after he was first elected, he became Senate Majority Leader. It was a meteoric rise — and Lyndon Johnson was not done yet.

Johnson ran hard for the presidential nomination in 1960, but he lost it to the younger, less experienced John F. Kennedy. The two men couldn't have been more different. Kennedy was a Northeastern liberal who'd been born into a life of privilege, and whose sense of entitlement led him to run for the presidency at a younger age, and with less experience, than most anyone else would have dreamed of. Johnson, on the other hand, had scrapped his way up the ladder, getting to the top rung of the Senate through sheer political savvy and will. It was no secret that Johnson didn't much care for the Kennedy clan, and during his campaign he wasn't above taking a few shots at the tanned, handsome junior senator from Massachusetts.

That's why, when Kennedy asked Johnson to become his Vice Presidential running mate, it created such consternation in Texas. The very idea of it was so divisive, in fact, that some have argued that the downfall of the Texas Democratic party can be traced to that moment.

As the Shivercrats had shown, being a Democrat didn't necessarily mean you'd vote for the Democratic presidential candidate. A great many conservative and middle-of-the-road Democrats in Texas weren't inclined to support Kennedy, not only because he was more liberal than they liked, but because they didn't believe he had a chance of winning. The idea that Johnson — who was older, more powerful, and more experienced — would hitch his wagon to Kennedy's presidential bid was almost too much for some of Johnson's allies to take.

A note written in Lady Bird Johnson's hand captures the depth of outrage Johnson's decision to join the ticket caused. Displayed in the LBJ Library, it's her jottings on a phone call she took for her husband in 1960:

> Ed Weisl says no. Would have to kill himself — violates every principle he holds near and dear — [Kennedy] merely using [Johnson] to control South.

South would consider him traitor and so would he. This fellow can't be elected — if thought Lyndon would dream of doing this would never have done what he did. It is unthinkable — sellout. Would have to campaign openly for Nixon. Kennedy only using him and would destroy him.

Across Texas, non-liberal Democrats howled at Johnson's decision. And while liberals rejoiced that one of their own had won the nomination, the addition of Johnson to the ticket set the state party reeling.

And it wasn't just Democrats who berated Johnson for his decision — some conservatives on the Republican side took their shots too. Barry Goldwater, who would run against Johnson for the presidency in 1964, wrote him a scathing letter the day after he accepted the VP slot:

> It is the morning after, so to speak, and as I sit here in my study I still have a numb feeling of despair over your actions of yesterday in accepting the candidacy for vice president. It is difficult to imagine a person like you running in a second spot to a weaker man, but it is even more incredible to try to understand how you are going to try to embrace the socialist platform of your party. I think many people, Lyndon, share my disappointment.
>
> You were intended for great things, but I don't think you are going to achieve them now.
>
> It is not easy to write this letter for I have always had respect for you.
>
> Sincerely, Barry

Goldwater's letter is telling, as it points to a kind of bond between moderates and conservatives, regardless of their party affiliation. During those times, partisanship wasn't nearly as fierce and unyielding as it is today — oftentimes, a couple of moderates who happened to be in different parties were more likely to work together than, say, a liberal and a conservative who were in the same party. And that's one of the reasons it became increasingly difficult to hold together the fractious elements of the state's Democratic party.

Holding the party together, and keeping it strong, should have been one of the main goals for Texas Democrats during these years. But at that time, with such a weak Republican presence in Texas, it just didn't seem like there was much of anything to worry about. In hindsight, though, the Democrats' eventual loss of Texas started with this small chipping-away at party unity in the late '50s and early '60s.

Once Johnson had agreed to the Vice Presidential slot, the race was on. People don't remember this now, but right through October of 1960, it looked as if Nixon was going to beat Kennedy. It also looked like Nixon would take Texas, despite Kennedy's choice of Johnson for VP. Things were touch and go during the last few weeks of the campaign, but as October ended, at last it appeared that the Kennedy-Johnson ticket was pulling ahead.

I spent election night down at the Driskill Hotel in Austin, where most of the Texas Legislature was gathered, and where Lyndon Johnson himself awaited the results. The Driskill is a real Austin landmark, a sprawling Victorian luxury hotel built in the late 1800's by cattle baron Jesse Driskill. With a dramatic limestone exterior, marble floors, and stained-glass chandeliers, it's the true "grande dame" of all Austin's buildings. It's also a popular place for politicians to "see and be seen" — not to mention the place where Lyndon Johnson had his first date with Lady Bird Taylor, back in 1934.

When I walked into the Driskill's ballroom that night, the excitement was thick in the air. I had no race of my own to worry about — no Republican had filed to run against me — but the presidential race ran close all evening. It was a thrill to be right there in the middle of it all, surrounded by the most powerful political figures in Texas. Looking around the room, I recognized many people who at that point I knew only by sight, but would come to know much better in the years to come — men like Frank Erwin, Jake Pickle, John Connally, and Governor Price Daniel.

That night was a big thrill for a political newcomer like me, but the next day things got even better, when we got the news that Kennedy and Johnson had won. Despite the party squabbling their pairing had provoked, Kennedy had made a shrewd choice in picking Johnson. There's no doubt that Kennedy wouldn't have carried Texas without him, and his margin of victory was slim enough that all it would have taken was Kennedy losses in Texas and Illinois to send Nixon to the White House.

It was a clear November morning in Texas, and the state's Democratic party was set to begin its extraordinary run of power throughout the next decade. Lyndon Johnson was the vice president-elect, Democrats had huge majorities in both houses of the Texas legislature, and Sam Rayburn was still Speaker of the House. And I couldn't wait to be sworn in and join, in my own small way, the great tradition of the Texas Democratic party.

Chapter Three

John Connally's Four Percenters

BEING 22 YEARS OLD AND A NEWCOMER TO THE LEGISLATURE, I FIGURED I'D probably take a few knocks in the beginning. Some were harder than others, but the funniest one came early on, when committee assignments were being handed out in January of 1961, just before the opening of the legislative session.

The story starts back in the summer of 1960, before I'd even officially been elected. I had jumped right into internal Capitol politicking by getting involved in the Speaker's race, a battle between the moderate Wade Spilman — a World War II hero who'd survived the Bataan Death March — and liberal Jimmy Turman, a schoolteacher. I put my chips on Spilman, and spent the summer trying to roust up votes for him among my soon-to-be fellow House members. Who knows what those veteran lawmakers must have thought when they saw me hurrying down the hallway, sticking my hand out and grinning ear to ear. I'm surprised now they didn't just turn around and run the other way, but just about everybody gave me some time, listening politely as I made my fledgling attempt at swaying a vote. I might not have known exactly what I was doing, but right from the beginning I was having fun doing it.

The Speaker's race turned bitter quickly, with Governor Price Daniel siding with Turman over the divisive question of whether or not to impose a new sales tax in Texas. On one side, Daniel and Turman were dead set against the sales tax, no matter the consequence. On the other side, Spilman didn't want a sales tax either — but as a conservative he preferred that over a corporate tax or state income tax as a way to raise much-needed funds for Texas. This was a classic battle between liberal and conservative Democrats, and the two sides went at each other hard all summer and fall.

Turman ultimately beat Spilman by just three votes out of 150, so my first gamble on playing politics didn't pay off. But even though my candidate lost, I'd managed to meet a lot of my fellow legislators while stumping for Spilman, and had my first taste of behind-the-scenes politicking. I felt like I was on the way to finding my footing in the House — but unfortunately, it soon became obvious that I still had a few things to learn.

As the Legislative session was gearing up, Turman asked me what committees I'd like to serve on. Turman was a former schoolteacher and a decent fellow, and even though we were on opposite sides in the Speaker's race, I respected him — and I was pleased to see that he respected me enough to ask for my committee preferences. I told him, "Mr. Turman, I don't really deserve any committee appointments, seeing as I campaigned and voted for Wade Spilman."

Turman considered my answer for a moment, then said, "All right. Are there any committees you don't want to serve on?"

"Well, yes," I told him, "there's one committee I'd really prefer not to serve on, and that's the Liquor Regulation committee. I come from a mostly dry district with about 27 Baptist churches, and I'd really rather not be in the middle of that particular issue."

"That's fine, then," Turman said, and that was the end of it. Or so I thought. Because of course, when they called out the lists of committee members in the Capitol a few days later, "Ben Barnes" was at the top of the list for Liquor Regulation. That was my introduction to the concept of payback. I can't say I thought it was too funny then, but when I think of what my face must have looked like when my name was called, it's pretty funny now.

The Texas Legislature, especially at that time, was about as colorful a group of people as you could gather under one roof. As legendary Texas political writer Molly Ivins once observed, the Legislature was "the finest free entertainment in Texas. Better than the zoo. Better than the circus." By state law, the Legislature convened in odd-numbered years, and then for no more than 140 days, unless special sessions were called during the summers. Most legislators had other jobs, at least partly since the base pay for serving in the House was just $4,800 a year.

My fellow representatives included bald-faced racists, Bible-thumping moralists, far-left liberals, and more than a few drunks. They also included some very savvy political minds and a host of genuinely hard-working, decent men (and three women — Myra Banfield, Virginia Duff and Maud Isaacks). But it didn't matter to me who they were or what they stood for; that first year I made it my goal to visit every single one of the other 149 members of the House.

It wasn't too hard to find everyone, because all the House members did their legislative work right there in the chamber. In 1960, Representatives didn't have offices in the Capitol building, so they'd work at their desks on the House floor, with their secretaries sitting right there next to them. There was a typing pool that everybody shared, and you could pick up your mail in the back of the House chamber — or, occasionally, someone would bring it to your chair. And if you needed to make or receive a phone call, you'd have to get up and walk to the bank of about 25 phones just outside the chamber. It's a wonder anyone got much of anything done.

That first session, I'd stop by my fellow legislators' desks just to stick out my hand and say hello. I told each of them that I was young and inexperienced, and that if they saw me doing anything wrong, they ought to let me know. I said that if I could help them with any legislative programs they were working on, they ought to call me up. I asked them for advice and tried to make friends with them.

By walking the chamber floor like that, I was able to make all sorts of friends in the House — on both ends of the political spectrum. I suppose I was doing it partly because I really did want to get to know my fellow legislators, but part of me knew my career would go farther if I had allies across the board in the House. I was already aligning myself with the moderate-to-conservative wing of the party — in fact, the *Houston Chronicle* dubbed me the "freshman Barry Goldwater" of West Texas in response to my conservative position on the appropriations bill that year — but it made no sense to me to choose sides to the exclusion of the other points of view.

I learned some valuable political lessons that year, including an unexpected one from the acknowledged master of the game. It started one afternoon when I received a phone call on the floor of the House.

"Barnes," said the man charged with receiving phone calls for Representatives, "The Speaker's on the phone. He wants to talk to you."

Well, that seemed strange. Speaker Turman had just been up at the podium a second ago — where in the world was he calling from? And why couldn't he just wait until he got back to tell me whatever it was in person? At that time, before cell phones made everyone demand instant connection every second of the day, it was certainly unusual for someone to go out of his way to call when he'd be seeing you in person shortly.

I went back to the phone bank and picked up my designated receiver to hear a familiar voice. "Barnes," said Sam Rayburn, "I need your help with something." I'll admit to feeling pretty special when I realized it was that Speaker who was looking for me.

A bill that was near and dear to Speaker Rayburn's heart had just failed on its first reading in the Texas House, and he asked me if I'd work the floor and request a reconsideration. The bill was a good one — it called for runoffs in special congressional elections, rather than a winner-take-all format. And it had gotten defeated not because my fellow legislators didn't like it, but because of the ongoing Spilman-Turman feud.

I couldn't have been more flattered that Rayburn called me personally to ask a favor, and so I got to work. And when the bill got called back up, and then passed, I felt proud but didn't expect a ticker-tape parade. I was just glad I could help out Speaker Rayburn, and happy that I was having at least a little bit of success so early in my legislative career.

But Rayburn had more than a simple thank-you in mind for the work I'd done. He went into his legendary card files, with the names of thousands of constituents, and sent a letter to everyone in my district, telling them what I'd done and singing my praises. I guarantee you what, that made a hell of a difference in terms of how my constituents saw me. Rayburn was the consummate politician on so many levels — he knew how to win over voters, but also how to win other politicians. I learned a lot from his generous demonstration of thanks, and from then on vowed to be as thorough with others as he'd been with me.

—————

LYNDON JOHNSON'S ELECTION AS VICE PRESIDENT WAS A PROUD MOMENT for Texas Democrats, but it also led to a significant crack in the state party's wall of dominance. It happened in a roundabout way, when a political move that had earlier seemed like a triumph suddenly looked like a big mistake.

Prior to Johnson's 1960 campaign for President, the Texas legislature had passed a law allowing him to run for the presidency and his Senate seat at the same time. That way, if he didn't make it to the Oval Office, he could still keep his seat — and his status as Majority Leader. This seemed like a great idea at the time, as it would allow Johnson to remain in a position of power in Washington regardless of how he and Kennedy fared in the presidential race.

So it was that on election night in November of 1960, the Kennedy-Johnson ticket won — and Lyndon Johnson also easily won reelection to the Senate, over an upstart Republican opponent named John Tower. But because Johnson was now the vice president-elect, he'd have to resign his Senate seat. The man who was chosen to fill it temporarily, until the special election scheduled for May of 1961, was Bill Blakley.

Blakley was a millionaire businessman and conservative Democrat, but he wasn't exactly a stirring candidate, especially in contrast to Lyndon Johnson. This was the second time he'd been appointed to fill a vacant Senate seat — the first time was in 1957, after sitting Senator Price Daniel had been elected governor the previous November. In the special election that followed, however, Blakley had decided not to run, and liberal Democrat Ralph Yarborough had won election to the Senate. Now, in 1961, Blakley was once again temporarily ensconced in the Senate — and this time, he decided to go ahead and run in the special election scheduled for that May.

The problem was, the special election quickly turned into a free-for-all. By Texas law, it was an open race, with all declared candidates running against each other, regardless of party. A whopping 71 Democrats filed for the race, and one lone Republican: John Tower. The top two vote-getters would face each other in a runoff, and the winner would take the seat.

With the Democratic vote split 71 ways, John Tower got the most votes — and therefore the momentum — in the preliminary election. If the Democrats had been able to pull themselves together and run just a few candidates, rather than almost six dozen, Tower might have placed third or lower and never even made it to the runoff. But now, he was scheduled to face the second-place finisher, Bill Blakley, in the May 27 election — and here the Texas Democrats made another critical mistake.

Blakley's staunch conservatism made him unpopular among liberal Democrats, and his vocal opposition to President Kennedy's "New Frontier" legislation irritated them even more. They just flat didn't like him, and didn't like what he stood for, and when it came time for the May election, they weren't inclined to vote for him — no matter that his Republican opponent, John Tower, was even more conservative than he was. This was the essential mistake the Texas Democratic Party made during these years: Every so often, they'd start to devour each other in fits of spite, allowing the Republicans to gain vital footholds in the state.

Liberal Democrats refused to vote for Blakley — and frankly, the moderate and conservative Democrats weren't too crazy about him either. In fact, many of those Democrats voted for Tower because they believed he'd be a one-term Senator, and easier to defeat in 1966 than Blakley would be. So it was that the young and energetic John Tower beat Blakley in the runoff by just over 10,000 votes. With that, he became the first Republican to be elected senator from a Confederate state since Reconstruction.

Tower was only one man, and this was only one election, but you can't overstate what his victory meant to Republicans in Texas. Up to that point, the history of the Texas Republican party was a long tale of futility and woe; you could count on one hand the number of political victories they had enjoyed. A Republican had won the governorship in 1868 — but the Democrats had responded by altering the state constitution to weaken the governor's office. In 1928, Republican presidential candidate Herbert Hoover had carried Texas — but only because he was a Prohibitionist running against a wet candidate. And the Shivercrats had pushed Republican Dwight Eisenhower over the top in Texas in two elections — but the Democrats had still enjoyed a lock on the legislature and statewide seats. Yet now, with Tower's victory, the Republicans had pried open the door and sent one of their own to the U.S. Senate for the first time since the Civil War.

The liberals had turned their backs on their party. And the conservative Democrats now found themselves in a dangerous position. With one of Texas's two senators a Republican and the other, Ralph Yarborough, a liberal Democrat, there was a real risk that conservatives in Texas would start turning their attentions — and money — to the Republican party. Psychologically, this was the turning point for Texas Republicans, the moment they began to grasp what was possible, rather than wallowing in what had always been inevitable.

John Tower was an unlikely field general for this revolution. Standing about five foot six in shoes, a plain-looking man with pomaded dark brown hair, he'd spent the last decade teaching history and political science at Midwestern University in Wichita Falls, Texas. He was just 35 when he was elected, making him the youngest man in the U.S. Senate. He didn't have the kind of bearing you'd expect for a successful Senate candidate — especially in a place like Texas, which typically takes a shine to larger-than-life, rough-hewn characters.

Tower seemed smart and savvy enough, but because of the way he'd been elected, he didn't appear to have much of a mandate. But over time, he'd make his mark in the Senate, and in Texas, as a vanguard of the right-wing Republican movement. And the real shame of it all was that he, like many Texas Republicans at the time, was a former Democrat who'd switched parties.

On the other side of the political spectrum was Tower's fellow senator, Ralph Yarborough. "Smilin' Ralph," as he was called, was a pure, unreconstructed liberal known far and wide as "The People's Senator." His rallying cry was "Put the jam on the lower shelf where the little man can reach it" — and his legislative career was one long exercise in trying to make that happen. Yarborough was a big-hearted, hard-working legislator who made a genuine effort to serve the people who elected him.

Unfortunately, Yarborough also had a few faults. He was, as even his friends admit, apt to take political affronts personally, and he tended a little bit toward the paranoid. After losing to conservative Democrat Allan Shivers in the acrimonious 1952 and 1954 gubernatorial primaries, and then losing to conservative Democrat Price Daniel in the 1956 primary, he made himself into the prime antagonist of the moderate-conservative wing of the party. He won his U.S. Senate seat in a 1957 special election, and for the next 20 years, he used his position to fight as hard against his fellow Democrats as he did for his constituents.

You couldn't help but admire many of the stands Yarborough took. He was one of only five senators from Southern states who voted for the 1957 Civil Rights Act, and his tireless efforts on behalf of minorities and the less fortunate were truly commendable. But the chip he carried on his shoulder about conservative Democrats ended up weighing down not just him, but the whole party. Yarborough was rather famously involved in a long-running feud with Lyndon Johnson that often took on the tone of a schoolyard slap-fight. Neither man was above offering a petty little poke here and there if he thought it might get under the other's skin. Sadly, some have also suggested that their feud — and Democratic squabbling in general — helped lead to the greatest tragedy in 20th-century Texas history, the assassination of John F. Kennedy in Dallas.

But as much as Yarborough disliked Johnson, there was another moderate-conservative Democrat that made his blood boil just as hot: John Bowden Connally, Jr.

I FIRST MET JOHN CONNALLY IN FORT WORTH IN THE SUMMER OF 1961. He'd been appointed Secretary of the Navy by President Kennedy, and had come down from Washington to make a speech at the Texas Manufacturers Association state convention. I was impressed by him right away, but not quite in the way you'd imagine.

Connally was blessed with a square jaw, a full head of hair, and rugged good looks. He was partial to Stetson hats and cowboy boots, and he exuded the kind of masculine confidence and charisma that most people associate with Hollywood stars. When he got up in front of the crowd and prepared to speak, people were already on the edges of their folding chairs.

He looked great for a moment, but then he started reading from a written text, and all his star-power quality just drained right away. Not only did he keep his head down, hardly ever looking up, but the speech he gave was just lousy. Whoever wrote that speech ought to have been put out to pasture — it put half the audience to sleep.

But even though his speech was terrible, it was already clear that Connally had all the raw materials to make a great political candidate. He'd been Lyndon Johnson's top congressional aide in the '40s, had worked on LBJ's first Senate campaign in 1948, and had been his campaign manager in the 1960 presidential race. He'd also worked for Texas oilman Sid Richardson for eight years, which meant he was equally at home in the worlds of big politics and big business. It was obvious that Connally was the kind of Texas insider I needed to get to know.

After Connally finished speaking, I made my way up to the podium and introduced myself. "Mr. Secretary," I told him, "I'm Ben Barnes. If you've got some time while you're here in town, I'd like to meet with you." Connally graciously invited me to come up to his suite at the Worth Hotel that evening to have a little chat.

We didn't talk long that night, but that marked the beginning of the most important and productive political alliance of my career. Over the next decade, Connally and I would work together on a shared agenda, trying to make Texas strong again in education, technology, and industry. We'd work to keep the Democratic party together, and when Lyndon Johnson became President, we'd work to help further his goals as well, both in Texas and nationwide.

But that night, at the Worth Hotel, my goals were less lofty. After Connally had met with me for a few minutes, he left me in the living room of his suite with a couple of his Naval aides, so he could go get some sleep. One of the aides had a pair of dice, and we got to rolling craps on the coffee table. We must have stayed up half the night playing low-stakes craps, and by the time we were done, I'd already made up my mind to take another kind of gamble: I decided to encourage John Connally to run for governor in 1962, and to join his campaign if he did.

Connally had been rumored to be considering a run, but he hadn't made up his mind yet. There was a lot of talk about whether Johnson wanted him to run, with some suggesting LBJ was putting him up to it and others saying he was dead set against it. The two men were as close as six is to seven, so there was no question that if Connally did decide to run, Johnson would support him. And Connally was, if anything, a man who followed no one's whims but his own, so he would be the one to make the ultimate decision whether or not to run.

I wanted Connally to run partly because he'd make a good governor, and partly because I didn't much like the current governor, Price Daniel. Daniel was in his third term in 1961, and he was gearing up to run for a fourth. I'd only been the legislature six months or so, but already we'd gone at each other a couple of times.

For one thing, Governor Daniel and I had come down on opposite sides of the sales tax issue. He was adamantly opposed to one, even though he offered no clear alternative for how Texas could bring in enough cash to meet the needs of the budget without it. After three contentious special sessions that summer, a sales tax passed — and I'd voted for it all the way. An angry Governor Daniel refused to sign it, but it became law without his signature.

Governor Daniel also wasn't too happy when I voted against a package of banking bills he was pushing. The package included an escheat bill that would have allowed the state to take over certain property that belonged to banks, and although it wasn't a terrible bill, I had my reasons for opposing it. When I was running for office that previous spring, the bankers who had financed my car had asked me if I'd vote against that bill. At first I joked with them, "Well, I can't promise you that, but I'll promise you this — I really appreciate y'all financing my car!" But after some thought (and after the car was paid off), I told them I'd vote against the escheat bill if I was elected.

I'd made a promise to those bankers, and as I told Governor Daniel, "I'm not going to break my word." So Governor Daniel retaliated by vetoing a bill that would have provided a new hospital district for Comanche County. It was a mean-spirited slap, one that did far more damage to the citizens of my home county than it ever did to me. At that point, I lost respect for the governor, and knew I couldn't work for his reelection.

But at that point, it was far from clear whether John Connally was the man to displace him, even if he did decide to run. A poll taken in the summer of 1961 showed that a whopping four percent of Texans supported a run by Connally. To be honest, most Texans didn't even know who he was, though the political establishment certainly did. Connally was the quintessential insider — not exactly a position of power for starting a statewide campaign.

At one point, early in the campaign, I tried to get my fellow representatives to sign their names to an invitation for a Connally reception. Not a single one of the other 149 members would agree to sign on. Nobody wanted to irritate Governor Daniel, and everybody had heard about the "four percent" poll. Several of the other members asked me, "Barnes, are you crazy? That guy doesn't have a chance." In the end, I only managed to get one other person to sign on for that reception — state senator Don Kennard, who was from Connally's home town of Fort Worth. Connally spent the summer mulling whether he should even run or not. In the end, bolstered by a die-hard group of supporters who dubbed themselves the "four-percenters," he decided to go for it.

In December of 1961, Connally sent me a telegram at my home in DeLeon. He was inviting me to a small gathering at the Catarina Ranch in South Texas, a massive, 165,000-acre spread owned by Dolph Briscoe, a wealthy rancher who'd served in the Texas House during the '40s. The meeting was to discuss Connally's campaign strategies for the '62 race.

This kind of meeting, usually replete with bottles of whiskey and steak dinners, was a staple of Texas politics — and in fact, it still is. You could hold them at a restaurant or at someone's house in Austin, but more often than not they took place in more rural settings, where a group of 8 or 10 people could get away, do some hunting, and enjoy the fresh air. A ranch was the perfect setting.

The truth was, nobody in Texas politics ever turned down an invitation to a ranch anyway. If a rancher asked you to come spend a weekend quail hunting, you didn't ever say "no" — the most you'd do is say, "I can't come this weekend, how about next?" It was almost like a White House invitation. Ranches are the most iconic symbol of Texas, and especially at that time, the families who owned and ran them played an enormous role in the social, cultural, and political life of the state. Even just hearing the names of Texas's most famous ranches — Lambshead, Four Sixes, Kings Ranch — is enough to bring back all kinds of memories and evoke a feeling of real, down-home Lone Star state history.

Some hunting seasons, I must have gone to 20 ranches — you'd just go to one after the other, from ranch to ranch. If you weren't a hunter, you'd become one quickly, as I found out one morning.

I had spent the night at a ranch with a few other legislators, and we'd been told to be ready before dawn, when a driver would come to take us each out to a deer blind deep in the woods. Well, I was about half asleep when the driver came, but I bundled myself into the car and tried to look forward to the next few hours, when I'd be sitting on an elevated platform built to give you a good view of a deer before he saw you. The driver dropped me off, and I scrambled up the plank leading to the blind, rifle in hand and dropping my jacket at the edge when I got to the top.

Once I got up there, it was so dark and still, I started falling right to sleep. I'd just about drifted off when suddenly a buzzing sound started up in the still-ness. I couldn't see a damn thing, but I knew what that sound was. It was a rattlesnake — and it was right there on that little platform with me!

I jumped to the very edge of that blind and started hanging off, as far as I could get from the snake without toppling off and falling the 20 feet or so down. As it got lighter, I could see him sitting there coiled up, his tail just a blur of buzzing. I'd crawled right over him when I put my jacket down and got on the platform! And I'll guarantee you — if that snake had bitten me, I'd have died right there, because that driver wasn't coming back until 1 p.m. or so, and it was about three decades too early to have a cell phone.

Fortunately, I had my deer rifle with me, though I knew there were only three cartridges in it. The rest of the bullets, wouldn't you know, were in my jacket pocket, not a foot from that snake. So I'd have three chances to shoot it while hanging halfway off that platform. And if I missed, it would just be me and one mad-as-hell snake for the next few hours.

I lifted that rifle to my shoulder and pulled the trigger. And I can't remember how many of those three cartridges I had to use, but fortunately, at least one found its mark. I kicked that dead snake right off the blind and sat there, shook up, until the driver came back. Even if a deer had wandered by, I think I'd done enough shooting for one day.

Most stays on ranches were a lot more pleasant than that one, of course, and when I got the telegram from John Connally to come to Briscoe's ranch, I was just as excited as could be to have been invited to such an important meeting. I drove my Ford Falcon down to the ranch, and when I arrived I found myself in the company of some of Texas's most powerful men — some of whom I was meeting for the first time.

Robert Strauss was there, a Dallas attorney who'd later become Treasurer, then Chairman, of the Democratic National Committee before being appointed the U.S. Trade Representative under President Carter and the U.S. Ambassador to Russia under President George H. W. Bush. Frank Erwin was there too, a political insider who would later become the head of the University of Texas Board of Regents. Eugene Locke of Dallas, a wealthy and influential attorney who would later run for governor, was there, as was San Antonio lawyer John Peace and former congressman Lloyd Bentsen, who would later become a U.S. Senator and vice presidential candidate.

Even in South Texas, there was a December chill in the air, so we were steered first to the bar for a scotch, and then to a living room with a giant, roaring fireplace. Eugene Locke was down on his hands and knees in the middle of the floor, studying a couple of big maps. Connally had just named Locke his campaign manager, and Locke had a new idea about how he thought the campaign ought to be run.

"We're gonna divide the state into 'shopping areas,' Ben," Locke told me. "It makes more sense than campaigning county-by-county." He asked me to get down there with him and help divide the state up, and so the two of us spent the next hour or so arguing over where people in each county went to shop.

Well, I thought the whole "shopping areas" idea was pretty stupid, but I just kept my mouth shut. Who was I to cross someone like Eugene Locke, after all? But later, when a small group was talking strategy in the living room after dinner, I couldn't contain myself.

Connally, with his flair for the dramatic, was calling on everyone in turn, asking their opinions about how he'd do in the race. Pretty much to a man, everyone told him he was destined to win, and that his opponents weren't likely to run nearly as strong as he would. Nobody in the room believed that Governor Daniel would run again. And everybody buttered up Connally with why Texas needed the likes of him in the governor's office.

I suddenly realized that, despite my relative youth and the greater experience of these men, I actually knew more than they did about how things were likely to play out. In fact, I believed they were dead wrong on most of what they were saying. But how do you say that to a room full of your political elders and mentors?

Here's how I did it: "With all due respect, Mr. Secretary," I began, "some of the things being said here tonight are about the dumbest things I've ever heard."

If there'd been any shuffling or chit-chat among the men gathered, there was none now. I went on.

"For one thing," I said, "Price Daniel is going to run again. I'll guarantee it."

"Ben," Connally said, "He's not running. I've got his word on it."

"Well, I can't help what he told you," I responded. "I don't have any doubt that he's gonna run. That's one thing.

"The second thing is, this 'shopping areas' idea is the wrong way to go," I went on. "We ought to run this campaign county-by-county, just like it's always been done. It's less complicated, and it keeps things in order so we can spend time on things we need to focus on.

"You've got a lot to overcome if you're going to win this thing," I said. "You don't have any name identification across the state. And you don't have any regional coordinators to help make sure you get some. You lack a solid money base. And you need a first-rate manager to get you up to speed." I ticked each point off on my fingers.

"There's just over five months until the primary, and you haven't got any of the elements in place that would lead you to victory. If you want to run, and win, you're going to have to get all these things together soon. Otherwise, you're sure to lose." I then went on to detail Connally's strengths, and how he could win the campaign, and when I finished, the room was silent. After a moment, Connally called on someone else.

Later, when everyone else had left the room but Connally and Bob Strauss, the two men discussed what all had been said. "John," Strauss told Connally, "I believe that big old dumb-looking redheaded boy made more sense than any of the rest of them." Connally laughed, and agreed. And a couple of weeks later, when he announced his candidacy for the governorship, he would have a plan for putting into action many of the suggestions I'd made that day at the ranch.

At the same time Strauss and Connally were talking, I was out in the bunkhouse drinking whiskey with Frank Erwin. They'd run out of beds for everybody, so Frank and I had gotten stuck out there, where the rooms felt about 30 degrees colder than the main house. Not that Erwin was feeling it — he'd been enjoying a bottle of Cutty Sark, and when he offered me some, too, I took the first sips I'd had in my life of straight-up liquor. Pretty soon, I wasn't feeling the cold either.

Frank Erwin was on his way to earning the reputation as "the most powerful backstage politician in Texas," as a UPI reporter would later put it. A partner in an influential Austin law firm, he was very close to both Lyndon Johnson and John Connally, and he was honing the art of using those relationships to help him get what he wanted. Frank could be aggressive and stubborn, but he also liked to play the role of mentor, and he often took students and young politicians under his wing. He wasn't a political mentor to me, though he often gave advice, both solicited and unsolicited. But he was a personal mentor, teaching me the kinds of things a country boy from DeLeon needed to know to succeed in the more sophisticated environment of the state capital.

When I met Frank, I'd never owned an overcoat. So he took me down to the Reynolds Penland men's store on Congress Avenue in Austin and helped me buy one. I'd never been to New York before, and Frank took me up there too. He bought me tickets to see my first-ever Broadway show — *Camelot*. He just tried to give me a little bit of tutoring in the kinds of things a well-rounded politician and educated man ought to know.

In return, Frank learned some things about the legislative process from me. He'd had no involvement in politics until John Connally ran for governor in 1962, and I already had a couple years in the House under my belt. Frank had served in the Navy before becoming a lawyer — he didn't have any special training that would give him a leg up in legislative politics. So it was that each of us gave the other something he lacked. From that first weekend out at Briscoe's ranch, our friendship grew.

———

JOHN CONNALLY WAS AN AMBITIOUS MAN, AND HE LOVED TO TAKE ON A challenge and win. He also happened to have at least his fair share of ego. These were a few of the reasons he ultimately decided to run for governor, but Julian Read, who worked on Connally's campaign, offers the best insight into why Connally ran — and why he ultimately proved to be such a transforming power in Texas government.

"Connally had gotten a good education," Read says. "He was a brilliant man in his own right. He had the background in Texas, the oil business and the cattle business. But in Washington, he got his eyes opened as to what was happening in terms of what states were doing to prepare for the future. He saw firsthand where all the grants were going, or technology study and development. He saw where the world was moving, and Texas was not in that forefront. He saw that investment followed education. He really got the baptism."

When Connally first asked Read to sign on to his campaign, he told Read, "We have to transform this state. We have to make the transition from an agricultural and minerals state." And as Read puts it, "Most people don't understand what a transformation that was, because we had a pretty easy world then. We were one of the few states that had so much income from oil, our universities were free. We were so blessed — no state income tax, a very low sales tax. It was a nice, comfortable world. So for Connally to have the vision to see, 'Hey — we've got to get ready for the future,' that was really a pretty revolutionary vision at that time."

This was Connally's vision for Texas — but to have a chance to make it happen, he'd have to win first. Despite his early "four percent" showing, Connally quickly gained ground in the primary race, thanks to a charisma and speaking style that was fortunately far better than what I'd seen in Fort Worth. Not only did he look like a governor from Central Casting (or as writer Mickey Herskowitz later called him, "The Marlboro Man in a tux"), but he had a grasp of the issues and a straightforward way of talking about them that drew in more and more supporters.

Still, Connally had competition from all sides in the primary. He was running against the incumbent, Governor Price Daniel, whose popularity had admittedly slid somewhat since the multiple special sessions and sales tax issue of 1961. But he was also running against the popular liberal Don Yarborough, as well as several other viable candidates. When primary day rolled around in May of 1962, Connally finished first — but he didn't win a majority, so he and second-place finisher Don Yarborough (whose greatest political asset was the fact that he happened to have the same last name as Sen. Ralph Yarborough) would now face each other in a runoff.

Connally was feeling pretty smug about his showing in the primary, and he campaigned like he expected to win. On the morning of the runoff, during a meeting at his office in Fort Worth, he got to speculating about his chances. I wasn't there, but Connally had called and put me on the "squawk box" so we all could hear each other.

"Let's go around the room," Connally said, "and everybody say how much you think I'll win by. I'm going to guess a couple hundred thousand votes."

A few other people offered their numbers, most predicting a similarly healthy margin for Connally. But I'd been out on the road ever since the primary, talking to ordinary folks and hearing something different. The sides who'd been splintered by multiple candidates in the Democratic primary were aiming to come together to defeat Connally, who still hadn't overcome the perception that he was just a tool of Vice President Johnson — "LBJ: Lyndon's Boy John," as his opponents taunted him. And when it was clear that no one else shared my concerns, I knew I needed to say something to get their attention.

"Well," I said, "I think it's as close as hell. I think you're gonna win, but not by more than about 25,000 votes."

That set Connally right off. "What in the goddamn hell are you talking about, Ben?" he barked at me, his voice a tinny roar in the phone. "That is the stupidest thing I've ever heard! Where did you get those numbers?"

"I'm gonna tell you what, Mr. Secretary," I said, my voice rising too. "You don't have a lock on this thing. There are people working all-out to beat you, and you shouldn't take anything for granted."

"You stupid son of a bitch," Connally spat. "You're crazy!"

"Well, fine, then," I snapped back. "You can go to hell!" And I slammed the phone down. I probably shouldn't have yelled at him, but besides the fact that I was working on just a few hours of sleep, I was as angry as I can ever remember being at him — before or since.

Fortunately, I'd earned Connally's respect over the past five months by working my tail off for his campaign. Even back then, Connally and I had a very good relationship, in the sense that he never treated me as anything but a political equal, despite our age difference. We fought like cats and dogs at times, but he always showed respect and even a certain amount of deference to me, because I'd already proven myself as a political strategist and ally.

That's one of the reasons why, later that night, Connally called me back — he wanted to apologize for having insulted me. But the other reason he called was that the early results were showing that I was right. When all the runoff votes were counted, Connally had won — by just over 25,000 votes.

I could try to claim some amazing political insight that let me predict the number almost exactly, but, to be honest, it was just an educated guess. Even so, I didn't go around admitting that to everyone else — it was all right with me if they thought I was some kind of great political genius for predicting almost exactly the right number.

CONNALLY HAD WON THE PRIMARY, BUT NOW HE HAD TO GO UP AGAINST Republican Jack Cox in the November election. Historically, Republican candidates for governor had averaged only about 12 percent of the vote over the prior two decades, but in the beginning at least, we needed to take Cox — who was a former Democrat and a very attractive candidate — seriously. Connally ran hard, traveling all over the state, and I continued to work on his campaign. But in the meantime, I was working on yet another race: Byron Tunnell's campaign for Speaker of the Texas House. My gamble with Connally had paid off, and now I was putting my chips on an established conservative for Speaker.

The previous Speaker, Jimmy Turman, had endured a very tough legislature in 1961, what with the multiple special sessions and the contentious battles over the tax bill. So Turman decided he'd had enough of the House, and filed instead to run for lieutenant governor in 1962. That left the Speaker's race wide open, and I quickly got behind Byron Tunnell, a white-tie-wearing East Texas conservative. Tunnell was about as plainspoken and candid a man as there was in the House, and I liked what I'd gotten to know of him. I became his campaign manager and started working to pull together the legislators on both sides of the spectrum to win him the 1963 Speakership, and hopefully to reunite what had become a deeply divided House.

Both my bets paid off. John Connally defeated Jack Cox to win the governorship in November of 1962, and Byron Tunnell won the Speakership two months later, in January of 1963. Because I'd bet early on them and worked my butt off for both, my political stock went up among Capitol insiders, too. And I'd won reelection, which wasn't too difficult because no opponent had filed against me in either the primary or the general election.

So it was that, by the beginning of my second term, I'd already earned a fair amount of political power. To reward me for my work on his campaign, Speaker Tunnell appointed me Chairman of the Rules Committee, a position that would allow me to deal with all personnel issues in the House, including assigning members' offices and parking spots. Tunnell was big on delegating, and he was happy to hand over whatever tasks I wanted, which would free him up to work harder on the issues. And I was ready to take whatever anyone would give me, and then some. By now, I was living and breathing politics, working 18-hour days, playing every angle I knew how to play, and having a lot of fun doing it. It wasn't so wonderful for my family, though, which now consisted of two young children, Amy and Greg, in addition to my wife, Martha. If I have any regret from those exhilarating early years in politics, it's that I was so focused on my work, I didn't pay my family the kind of attention they deserved.

I worked closely with Tunnell, but also with Governor Connally, who had never served in elective office before. He was a true executive personality, decisive and self-confident, but he needed some help understanding how to navigate the sometimes-murky waters of the Legislature. Connally trusted me, and he knew I was political to the core. We'd gotten to know each other well during the campaign, but during the 58th Legislature in 1963, we really began working together as a team.

Even so, I was sensitive to any perception that I was somehow Connally's "boy." In fact, I was sensitive to any perception of being a "boy" at all. I was so aware of being younger than everyone else that I tried hard to look mature — no smiling or laughing — in photographs. If you look at clippings from my early political career, you'd think my mouth had been sewn shut.

I tried to have a balance with Connally, working closely with him while maintaining my independence, just like during his campaign. I didn't make a point of going up against him, but I also didn't hesitate to let him know when I disagreed with him or with something he'd done. One such time came when he pulled a political trick on me early in the 1963 legislative session.

Connally wanted a bill introduced in the House to abolish the Texas Aeronautics Commission, which was the agency that built airports in rural areas of the state. He'd often ask legislators to sign their names to bills for him, and he wanted me to sponsor this one — but on this particular day he couldn't get hold of me, because I was off somewhere with Byron Tunnell making a speech. So he just had an aide sign my name to it.

Now, I wouldn't have minded that so much — after all, Connally and I were in agreement on many of the things he wanted for Texas. But after I found out he'd signed my name to it, I also found out that he'd told a member of the Aeronautics Commission that he didn't know why in the world I'd introduced such a bill, because he certainly wasn't for it.

I was so mad at Connally for that, I stormed into his office and said, "If you ever pull a trick like that again, I'll never introduce another bill for you."

"Oh, now, calm down, Ben," he said, "You're just upset." But I wouldn't calm down. I kept jawing at Connally until he finally said, "Come on, you need something to eat. Let's go down to the Headliner's Club and get some lunch." I may or may not have needed lunch, but Connally knew that, as a young legislator, I'd be more than happy to be seen out in public with the governor. So we went on over to the club, and I simmered down.

It's fair to say that the 1963 House session went about as smoothly as any session in memory. John Connally, Byron Tunnell and I worked well together, and there was very little of the contentiousness that had marked Jimmy Turman's term as Speaker two years earlier. I liked Tunnell and wanted to see him get reelected Speaker for the 1965 session, so I began working on it early, in the summer of 1963. What transpired as I went around drumming up votes for Tunnell would change my career — and, arguably, the face of Texas politics.

The way you got someone elected Speaker of the House in Texas was through a quaint arrangement called the "pledge" system. As campaign chairman, I'd go visit with a representative and ask him or her to support Tunnell. If they were willing to do it, they'd sign a little typed piece of paper "pledging" themselves to do just that. I'd hold on to those little pieces of paper until the vote was held, in the beginning of the legislative session. As long as people honored their pledges, the actual vote was little more than a technicality, as the candidates knew the outcome already.

One afternoon I was sitting in the office of Bob Bullock, who was a lobbyist at the time for the Texas Automobile Dealers Association. Bullock had served two terms in the House, and was about as tied in as a person could be to the Austin political establishment. He'd go on to become legendary in Texas, serving as secretary of state, comptroller and lieutenant governor before he and House Speaker Pete Laney helped to engineer George W. Bush's legislative success in the governor's office from 1995-99.

Bullock could be meaner than a snake but he was a brilliant political strategist, and as we sat and talked that day, he had an idea.

I was telling him that, after Tunnell served another term as Speaker, I might like to run for Speaker for the legislative session that would start in three years' time. At that point, Speakers generally served no more than two terms, so I presumably wouldn't have to go up against Tunnell himself, which would never have done.

It wasn't really much more than idle chatter, but Bullock peered across at me with his ice-blue eyes and said, "Well, Barnes, here's what you ought to do." He got up and walked across the room to a typewriter in the corner, and began clicking on the keys. When he finished, he tore the paper out and handed it to me. It read, "In the event that Byron Tunnell does not seek another term as Speaker, I pledge my vote to Ben Barnes as Speaker." I looked at it a moment, and Bullock said, "I've got a car downstairs at the curb. Why don't you go see Representative Armstrong right now and get his signature for both you and Tunnell?"

Bullock's idea was pure political genius. I'd get the pledges for Tunnell and, at the same time, collect the "second pledges" for myself. It was such a simple idea — but nobody had ever done it before. I went to Rep. Armstrong's office right then, and, sure enough, he signed the second pledge without question. Over the coming months, with Tunnell's knowledge, I got dozens of other legislators to do the same. For the moment, I didn't think those second pledges would do much more than just keep my name in the till for the future. But in another year's time, to everyone's surprise, they'd do a lot more than that.

Chapter Four

November 22, 1963 and Everything After

ONE AFTERNOON IN THE LATE SUMMER OF 1963, AFTER THE LEGISLATIVE session had ended, John Connally called me at my home in DeLeon. "Ben," he said, "I've got a job for you. I want you and Cliff Carter to be my official representatives for President Kennedy's trip to Texas in November."

Now, I'd spent a fair amount of my three years in the House trying to show that I wasn't overly awed by powerful people. I'd made a point of trying to act as mature as possible and demonstrate that I belonged in the "corridors of power" as much as anyone else in Austin. But when I put down the phone after Connally's call, I was just as excited as a little kid. I couldn't believe that, at age 25, I'd been invited with longtime Johnson aide Cliff Carter to help plan the official visit to Texas of the president of the United States.

Connally was rewarding me for my hard work on his campaign and in the legislature during his first year as governor, but there was another reason he'd called on me. Kennedy was coming to Texas for two things: to boost his poll numbers for the 1964 election, and to raise money. The truth is, Kennedy wasn't very popular in Texas at that time — in fact, there was a real fear he'd lose the state in 1964 — and not too many Texans were keen on giving him money. But I had raised a lot of money for Connally's '62 campaign, and Connally knew I'd be willing to work hard to raise money for Kennedy.

Connally was ambivalent about the trip. President Kennedy had been hinting for more than a year that he'd like to come to Texas, and Connally had, for the most part, simply ignored him. But finally, on June 10, 1963, President Kennedy made a quick stopover in El Paso while traveling, so he could confront Connally personally. Vice President Johnson came to the meeting, too, as well as a friend of mine, Larry Temple, who at that time was an aide to Connally.

"Kennedy had said he wanted to come down here to raise money," Temple recalls. "And that was the purpose of the trip. And Governor Connally discouraged the trip and the money-raising. He kept saying, 'No, it's not timely to do it, you need to build up your strength in Texas and your popularity before you do anything.'" But during that June 10 meeting, says Temple, "Governor Connally got a really big push from the President... So several weeks later, after multiple requests from President Kennedy's emissaries, including Vice President Johnson, the governor reluctantly said, 'Well, if you're gonna come, don't let it look like you're coming just to raid the state for money. At least act like you're interested in the state. Set up something to go around and meet people.' So that's how the trip got done."

If it weren't for the tragic events of November 22, 1963, the details of planning President Kennedy's trip would be forgotten political minutiae. But in light of the President's assassination in Dallas that day, it's worth looking closely at why things were planned the way they were — and how the rift in the Texas Democratic party might have played a part. As someone who was involved in the trip's planning, I can tell you the rift had quite a lot to do with it. But not in the way most people think.

A lot of people believed that Kennedy wanted to come to Texas to help patch up the ongoing feud between Lyndon Johnson and Senator Ralph Yarborough. But that simply wasn't the case. As Connally himself wrote in his memoirs, that feud "had nothing to do whatsoever with the trip, except that in a tiresome fashion it complicated the arrangements. Only later, after the tragic ending, would the feud assume larger and distorted proportions." After all, if President Kennedy had wanted to fix things between Johnson and Yarborough, he hardly needed to come all the way to Texas — the two men worked in Washington, D.C., just a mile or so down Pennsylvania Avenue from each other.

The way the rift did factor in, however, was in deciding what Kennedy's schedule would be during the two days of his visit. Not surprisingly, Ralph Yarborough had very different ideas than Connally and Johnson for what the President should do. And one of the things he pushed hard — over our objections — was having a big motorcade through Dallas.

I was at a planning meeting with Kennedy's people in Dallas' Petroleum Club one evening when Yarborough made his big push. We'd had a couple of meetings at the club, which was a stately, old, dark-wood, steak-and-red-wine haunt with an exclusive membership list. The room was dimly lit and stuffy with cigar smoke, and Connally's campaign manager Eugene Locke, Cliff Carter and I were going through the details of the trip with the Kennedy advance men. Even a two-day trip has a thousand details, and we were wrangling over this and that: Where would the president stay in Fort Worth? What time would he speak in Houston? Would his Dallas luncheon be held at the Trade Mart, or at the Women's Building at the state fairground?

We were a couple hours into the meeting when the maitre d' brought a telephone to our table. It was Ralph Yarborough on the line.

Yarborough didn't much like the fact that he'd been left out of the planning process, but Connally was determined to keep events under his own reins as much as possible. And because Yarborough wasn't raising any significant money for Kennedy, Connally didn't feel bad about trying to shut Yarborough out — not that he would have anyway, as Connally surely wasn't the type to shrink from a political power play.

On the phone, Yarborough began haranguing for Kennedy to have a motorcade in Dallas. The plan so far called for Kennedy to visit San Antonio, Houston, Fort Worth and Dallas, then end up with a big reception and gala in Austin on the night of November 22nd. But Yarborough, the "People's Senator," felt that the trip was too heavy on visits with "fat cats," and didn't provide enough of a chance for ordinary Texans to see the President.

Carter and I both argued heatedly against the motorcade, knowing that Connally would object to it. Connally wanted to build events around givers, so we could get Kennedy the maximum amount of cash and political momentum in the shortest time. He also felt that a motorcade would be too tiring for the President — it was such a whirlwind trip already, and Kennedy would need all the energy he could muster to win over the high-rollers who were reluctantly coming to Austin for the gala that night.

But Yarborough would hear none of this. He was dead set on having that motorcade, and after Kennedy's advance men responded with guarded interest, he called Bobby Kennedy and harangued him too, trying to convince him to intervene and get it on the schedule. For a while, the two sides were in deadlock. But Yarborough finally prevailed, and Connally reluctantly agreed to add the motorcade in Dallas.

At the time, of course, it just seemed like we were engaged in typical politicking. Yarborough flat didn't like Connally, and whether he truly wanted that motorcade or not, he would have fought like hell to get it just to make his point. But when I think back to those planning meetings at the Petroleum

Club, I wish to God we'd have found a way to talk him out of it. It makes me sick to think of it, even more than 40 years later.

———

A WEEK OR SO BEFORE THE KENNEDY TRIP, I HAD A CONVERSATION WITH Governor Connally's wife, Nellie. Nellie was — and still is — a charming lady, and just about the most perfect political wife Connally could ever have found. The two of them met in the '40s at the University of Texas at Austin, where Connally was president of the student body and Nellie was voted the campus Sweetheart. She had a wonderful ability to put anyone at ease, and she always looked you right in the eye, with a kind of frank sincerity that drew both men and women to her.

I told Nellie that we'd added a motorcade for the President in Dallas, and that the Kennedys wouldn't have very much time in Austin, only about 45 minutes, to check into the Driskill Hotel and get ready for the receptions and gala that night. Nellie's first reaction was one of concern for Jackie Kennedy.

"Well, this is the worst thing in the world to do to the First Lady!" she exclaimed. "She needs her time to prepare. She'll need to have her dress pressed, and to rest a little after such a long day." I don't know why, out of all the conversations I had about the Kennedy trip, that one stuck in my head all these years. Maybe it's because Nellie Connally, almost alone among those involved, seemed worried about the President and Mrs. Kennedy personally as opposed to how everything would go politically.

Cliff Carter and I had talked about the possibility that something could go wrong on the trip — especially in Dallas, which was the most conservative city in Texas. There was a right-wing contingent there, mostly supporters of the ultraconservative congressman Bruce Alger, that hated everything Kennedy stood for. The Alger mob had already been involved in a few ugly incidents — most notably one afternoon just before the 1960 election, when they'd surrounded Lyndon and Lady Bird Johnson at the Adolphus Hotel, jostling and spitting on them. And just a few weeks before the Kennedys were to arrive in Texas, a female protestor had swatted U.N. Ambassador Adlai Stevenson in the head with a placard after he gave a speech at the Dallas Memorial Auditorium Theater.

We were also concerned about possible racist backlash against the President. In September, segregationists had set off a bomb in a Birmingham, Alabama church, killing four African-American girls and adding a chilling new dimension to the battle for civil rights. In the nearly three years of his presidency, Kennedy had fought for several civil rights initiatives, and there were plenty of Texans who, to put it mildly, didn't much care for his point of view on the matter. So we were definitely aware that something could happen in Dallas — but still, neither of us ever dreamed that the President might be in mortal danger.

President and Mrs. Kennedy arrived in San Antonio on Thursday, November 21, for the start of their visit. Governor Connally, Vice President Johnson, Senator Yarborough and many others were there — in fact, there was even a public spat when Yarborough insulted LBJ by refusing to ride in a car with him — but I was in Austin, pulling together the final details for the big gala the following night.

The Austin gala was to be the grand finale of the presidential trip. President Kennedy had originally wanted to have a fund-raiser in every city he visited, but we'd managed to convince him to whittle it down to a single big dinner, where we hoped to raise $300,000 — a considerable sum at the time. I was one of seven men on the host committee for the dinner, and as the event drew near, I was running around trying to make sure everything was in place. At $100 a ticket, with many of the donors reluctantly being goaded into coming, we wanted to have a nice event — so we had the caterer prepare three hundred 16-ounce steaks and stock up on several different kinds of wine.

Meanwhile, the Kennedys were thrilling crowds of Texans at every stop. In Fort Worth, when a cheering throng clamored to see Jackie Kennedy, the President good-naturedly told them, "Mrs. Kennedy is organizing herself. It takes longer, but of course she looks better than we do after she does it." Everything was going smoothly — the crowds were happy, the press coverage was plentiful, and even the weather was good. But everybody knew that Dallas would be a tougher sell, especially after seeing the *Dallas Morning News* on the day of the visit.

The paper that morning ran a couple of provocative stories even before the President arrived. "Storm of Political Controversy Swirls Around Kennedy on Visit," read the top story on page one. And just below it: "Yarborough Snubs LBJ," describing the car incident from the day before. Even worse, an anti-Kennedy ad inside the paper sponsored by the "American Fact Finding Committee" was set off like a funeral notice, with a thick black border. In the ad's text, the right-wingers essentially accused Kennedy of being a tool of the American Communists.

So that was the greeting the Kennedys received in Dallas on the morning of November the 22nd. The motorcade would set off around noon, to be followed by a luncheon at the Dallas Trade Mart. Afterward, the President and first lady would make their way to Austin for the events that night.

In Austin, I spent the morning working on details of the gala, then headed down to a political watering hole called the Forty Acres Club to have lunch with Texas Democratic Executive Committee Chairman Frank Erwin and Deputy Director of the Peace Corps Bill Moyers, who was acting as an aide to Johnson. The three of us had just ordered when the bartender called out to our table, "Mr. Barnes? You have a telephone call." I excused myself, walked to the bar and took the receiver.

I couldn't tell you now who was on the other end of the line, but I'll never forget what he said. The President had been shot, possibly fatally. And John Connally had been shot and seriously wounded.

For a moment, it felt like my blood just froze. I couldn't believe what I was hearing. Could the President really be dead? Shot down, right here in the state of Texas, on the trip we'd planned so carefully? And would John Connally, who'd become not just a political ally of mine, but a good friend as well, survive? It was almost too much to take in, but there was no time to ponder. When I came back to the table, Moyers wasn't there — he'd gone to another part of the restaurant to take a call, and he was right then hearing the same news. I told Erwin what had happened, and then immediately dialed Homer Garrison, the man who commanded the state police and Texas Rangers as head of the Texas Department of Public Safety.

"Colonel Garrison," I told him, "I'm at the Forty Acres Club with Bill Moyers, and he's got to get to Dallas." Moyers was one of LBJ's closest aides, and though he'd skipped Dallas to come help with the Austin gala, it was obvious that Johnson was going to need him now.

"Come on down to the airport," Garrison told me. "We'll get him on a plane."

Moyers and I ran to my car, and I drove to the Austin airport at about 90 miles an hour. By the time we got to the Browning Flight Service there, a small Cessna was ready on the tarmac, and Moyers jumped out and climbed into the plane. It was about a 50-minute flight to Dallas' Love Field, and when Moyers arrived, LBJ was inside Air Force One. Moyers boarded the plane in time to see LBJ take the oath of office to become the new president of the United States. In the famous photo of Johnson taking the oath, with a shaken Jackie Kennedy standing at his side in her bloodstained suit, you can just see the bespectacled Moyers there in the right-hand corner.

President Kennedy was dead, John Connally was possibly dying, and the entire Texas political establishment was reeling from the shock of it all. No one knew quite what to do, so Byron Tunnell and I decided to invite people for a prayer service at the Capitol. We had a little mimeograph machine in the secretaries' pool, and I printed up a few programs, folding them over like church bulletins. They didn't look very good, but I felt like we needed something — some kind of official event — that would help people deal with what had happened. We invited the donors who'd come to Austin for the President's gala to come sit in the House gallery seats for the prayer service. It was a very emotional evening, a moving tribute to the fallen President.

Years later, I came across a copy of the official program for the gala that never took place. I'd never looked at it again after the assassination, but when I read it through this time, it gave me chills. Printed on the inside front cover was a welcome letter written by John Connally, parts of which are almost painful to read now:

> ...On this twenty-second day of November, 1963, the welcoming committee (consisting of all the citizens of Texas) greets the two leaders of our nation, in whose offices and persons run the bloodstream of liberty and freedom, fought for, died for, preserved, strengthened, honored by all men of all the states.
>
> We're mighty glad to have you with us, John Fitzgerald Kennedy and Lyndon Baines Johnson.
>
> We welcome the two Ladies of our Land, the wife of the President, and the wife of the Vice President. On her first trip to Texas, Mrs. John Kennedy has revealed to all of us her charm and the loveliness that has made her a welcome ambassador in other lands beyond the seas as well as the pride of her countrymen — a First Lady in every sense of the word...
>
> This is a day long to be remembered in Texas.
>
> John B. Connally,
> Governor of Texas

It was, indeed, a day long to be remembered — not just in Texas, but throughout the entire world.

━━━━━━━━━━

JOHN CONNALLY SPENT NEARLY THREE WEEKS IN THE HOSPITAL RECUPERATING from the bullet wounds that almost took his life. He'd had a sizeable hole blown into his chest cavity, and only Nellie's protective instinct, in pushing him down and inadvertently covering the sucking chest wound with his own arm, had saved him from suffocating or bleeding to death. When he was released from the hospital, he was a changed man, more reflective and even fatalistic, though that might not have been apparent to most. And he was returning to a changed world.

The biggest change, of course, was that his closest political ally, Lyndon Johnson, had now assumed the most powerful office in the world. As Johnson said so movingly to a joint session of Congress just five days after the assassination, "All I have, I would have given gladly not to be standing here today." But he was the President now, and he was taking on this most difficult office under impossibly difficult circumstances.

For one thing, he was a Texan taking the place of a beloved President who'd been murdered in Texas. It didn't take long for crackpot conspiracy theories to emerge, suggesting that Johnson — or his supposed cronies — had something to do with the assassination. (This theory had legs all the way into 2003, when a History Channel "documentary" repeated it. That program was about the worst kind of trash you can imagine, and the History Channel got so much heat for it, they had to apologize for having aired it.)

Another difficulty was that Johnson was inheriting a cabinet filled with Kennedy partisans. Kennedy had chosen Johnson as his running mate not because of any great shared vision, but because he'd needed a Southern conservative to balance out his ticket. The irony is that Lyndon Johnson would end up being a far more progressive president than anyone expected, ultimately pushing through many programs that Kennedy himself had struggled to get passed, as well as his own progressive initiatives such as the Voting Rights Act. But especially at the time, even though LBJ and Kennedy had shared a mutual respect and friendship, there was no love lost between Kennedy's people and their new President. And that was a situation Johnson found agonizing, as I saw firsthand one day out at the LBJ Ranch.

I'd met Johnson many times, but it wasn't until the Kennedy trip that he really got to know who I was. By then, I'd already helped guide Governor Connally through the legislative thicket of his first year in office and was seen as an up-and-comer in Texas politics. I'd traveled to Washington a couple of times for planning sessions, and met with both Kennedy and Johnson during those times, and this time I managed to make an impression. At Christmastime in 1963, about a month after Kennedy's assassination, I got further confirmation of that when President Johnson invited Governor Connally and me to the LBJ Ranch for a private visit.

Located in the Hill Country about 60 miles west of Austin, the LBJ Ranch was Lyndon Johnson's personal oasis. The stately white ranch house stood near the glittering Pedernales River, with juniper and oak trees dotting the land, and green pastures rolling far beyond that to the horizon. Johnson had all kinds of official events out at the ranch, but it was a rare privilege to get invited for a private visit. A state trooper picked up Connally and me in Austin, and drove us through a rainstorm to get there.

When we arrived, we started putting our raincoats on so we wouldn't get wet walking to the house. But Connally couldn't get his on, as his right arm was still in a sling, his chest and wrist not yet recovered from his bullet wounds. He'd had to get used to having Nellie do certain things for him, like tying his shoes, but he was too proud a man to simply accept his limitations. Irritated and impatient, Connally just jumped out of the car and made a run for it, and I followed him. The President met us at the door, and showed us into a sitting room, where we were quickly served coffee.

As exciting as it was to be there, I felt a little out of place. My God, this was the President of the United States and the governor of Texas having coffee — what in the world was I, a state representative, doing here? "Mr. President," I said, "Y'all may want to talk about some things, so I can just excuse myself —" and I started to get up.

"No, Ben," Connally interjected. "You sit down. I want you to hear this." I hesitated for a moment, and Connally said, "Sit down, Ben." I sat down.

Connally then turned his attention to LBJ. "Mr. President," he said, "you've got to fire Bobby Kennedy as attorney general." I mean, he got into it just that quick. No "How're you doing, thanks for the coffee," nothing.

Johnson reacted with disbelief. "Goddamnit, John, you must be crazy! His brother's been dead for one month. If I fire Bobby Kennedy, the liberals in the party will eat me for lunch! What in the hell are you talking about?"

"Now, listen," Connally retorted, "You're not hearing what I'm saying. I'm not saying 'Get rid of him.' I'm saying you've got to fire him as Attorney General. Give him some other job — I don't care if you name him secretary of state, or what." Here, Connally leaned in and pointed a finger. "But you have got to have an attorney general who guards your back and protects you every single day, or by God, you could get run out of office or worse. The attorney general is the only person in the cabinet who's got to be absolutely loyal to you, who'll fall on a sword for you. And Bobby Kennedy is not that man." But Johnson still wasn't buying it, and the two men continued to argue, sounding almost like an old married couple, while I sat there and sipped my coffee.

As Connally told it in his memoirs, he later advised Johnson to just fire Kennedy's whole cabinet and appoint his own. LBJ didn't take that advice — and he also never got a chance to shuffle Bobby Kennedy into another job, because Kennedy resigned as attorney general to announce his run for the Senate in 1964. But I never forgot Connally's argument that day at the ranch, or the passion he'd delivered it with, because it pointed up the continuing problem in the Democratic party of ill feeling between the liberals and moderates.

There was a jagged split tearing right down the middle of the party, and if anything, Johnson's ascension to the presidency had made it even more raw. And not only did Lyndon Johnson's and Bobby Kennedy's factions of the party distrust each other, the two men just plain didn't like each other. Soon enough, the ongoing battle between the two Democratic factions came to be symbolized by the deep personal animus between these two men.

The irony of all this is that, almost as soon as he became President, Lyndon Johnson picked up the banner that John Kennedy had carried — civil rights — and made it his own. In his November 27 address to Congress, just five days after Kennedy's death, he famously declared, "Let us continue" the work that Kennedy had started. He urged the Congress to act quickly on civil rights:

> First, no memorial oration or eulogy could more eloquently honor President Kennedy's memory than the earliest possible passage of the civil rights bill for which he fought so long. We have talked long enough in this country about equal rights. We have talked for one hundred years or more. It is time now to write the next chapter, and to write it in the books of law.
>
> I urge you again, as I did in 1957 and again in 1960, to enact a civil rights law so that we can move forward to eliminate from this nation every trace of discrimination and oppression that is based upon race or color. There could be no greater source of strength to this nation both at home and abroad.

And Johnson backed up his rhetoric with action. Kennedy had fought hard, but mostly ineffectually, for a civil rights bill. But Johnson was the arm-twisting, deal-making king of Capitol Hill, and he used every ounce of his legislative skill to pass a groundbreaking law, the Civil Rights Act of 1964, over fierce conservative opposition. Signed into law on July 2, 1964, the law made it illegal to, among other things, deny African Americans service in hotels, restaurants, and other public places on the basis of the color of their skin. Thanks to Lyndon Johnson, never again could a place like the Bearcat Grill in DeLeon legally refuse to serve a black man a hamburger.

Johnson's efforts in passing the Civil Rights Act of 1964 were truly heroic, as were his efforts throughout the rest of his presidency to fight for the rights of all Americans through his Great Society and further Civil Rights initiatives, including the historic Voting Rights Act of 1965. This is his greatest legacy — but it was one that he knew would ultimately damage the Democratic Party. As he told me one afternoon at the White House, when I was in Washington for a conference of legislative leaders, "Ben, I'm proud of these Civil Rights bills, but they're going to hurt the party in the long run." Over time, Johnson was proved right, as Southern conservatives, long a Democratic bedrock, slowly began deserting the party on the heels of advances in civil rights. This was the beginning of the massive shift that eventually put the South in solidly Republican hands.

LYNDON JOHNSON FOUND HIMSELF CAMPAIGNING FOR THE 1964 ELECTION practically from the moment he took over the Oval Office. I was up for reelection as well, but just like in 1962, I had no opponents, so there was plenty of time to work for the Johnson campaign and other races in Texas. I worked as hard as ever, and again felt like I'd made the big time when I got some special assignments up at the Democratic National Convention in Atlantic City, New Jersey. But I didn't keep my big head for long, as a couple of things happened that brought me right back down to earth.

This was my first Democratic National Convention, and I don't mind admitting that I was pretty excited to be there. Johnson was way ahead in the polls, the Democratic party was going strong in Texas and nationwide, and it really felt like our best days were ahead of us. When logistics coordinator Ted Connell asked me to go pick up Senator Eugene McCarthy at the airport, I was pleased — McCarthy was rumored to be on the short list to be Johnson's vice president.

When McCarthy got in the car, though, I soon realized why I'd been chosen for this task — no one else wanted it. Apparently, President Johnson had just informed McCarthy that he wasn't planning to pick him as VP, and McCarthy was in none too happy a mood about it. I can tell you that it was the longest, quietest car ride I'd had in a long time. But then things got worse.

I dropped McCarthy off at his hotel, and then parked the car in the nearest spot, down a nearby alley. I don't know what happened next, but that car either got towed or stolen, because nobody ever found it again. We'd gotten all these cars leased from a large auto dealer's association, and when they inventoried them at the end, my car was nowhere to be found. I just couldn't believe I'd managed to lose a whole car — and Ted Connell didn't make it any easier on me, teasing me that they were going to make me pay for it. He knew I didn't have anything like that kind of money, so he told me, "Don't worry, Ben, they'll probably wipe the slate clean if you just agree to spend a few days in jail." I knew better, of course, but sweating over a lost rental car still put a damper on what was otherwise a good time in Atlantic City.

My personal worries at the convention aside, the Democratic party was running stronger than ever in 1964. On election day, President Johnson beat Barry Goldwater in a landslide, winning 61 percent of the popular vote — the largest percentage ever recorded by a presidential candidate. Democrats picked up two seats in the U.S. Senate, and maintained a comfortable majority over Republicans in the House. In Texas, John Connally won reelection easily and the legislature remained solidly in Democratic hands, as the groundswell of support behind Johnson and Connally helped sweep out several Republican House incumbents. At that point, it looked like the Democratic party — led by Texas Democrats — was all but invincible.

But a closer look reveals that the cracks Johnson had foretold were already beginning to show. Goldwater might have managed to win only six states, but the ones he won presaged trouble for Democrats. One was Goldwater's home state of Arizona, but the other five — Louisiana, Mississippi, Alabama, Georgia, and South Carolina — were Deep South states. And of those five, four hadn't gone for a Republican presidential candidate since 1876. This was a clear message, and it marked the beginning of the South's eventual swing from Democratic to Republican.

There was one other big race in Texas that year, and it offered a blueprint for how we might be able to keep the party strong. It was the battle between Smilin' Ralph Yarborough and an up-and-coming Republican named George Herbert Walker Bush for Yarborough's senate seat.

George H. W. Bush, a son of former U.S. Senator Prescott Bush, was a 40-year-old millionaire in 1964. He'd made his fortune in the oil fields of the Permian Basin, and though he'd never run for office before, he'd gained some notice as the Harris County Republican Chairman. It was clear even then that the young, rich and handsome Bush had outsize ambitions, and he wasn't about to start at the bottom in elective politics — he went right for the U.S. Senate in his very first race.

I'd met Bush a couple of times and thought he was a solid, appealing candidate, though I'm not sure I would have predicted the kind of rise in politics he later had. He was just as polite as he could be, and he seemed to have a genuine desire to do something for Texans, rather than just winning to further his party's fortunes. His status as a latecomer to Texas (he was raised in Connecticut before moving to the state in his early 20s, following his service in World War II) might have damaged him in the polls, but he'd built up a solid oil business and had first settled with his young family in the unpretentious town of Midland, so voters seemed not to hold that against him.

If Bush had run that 1964 Senate race as a moderate, he might well have beaten Yarborough, who was about as far to the left as a state like Texas could tolerate. But for some reason, he instead pandered to the ultra-conservative crowd, alienating thousands of middle-of-the-road Texans in the process. He also wasn't helped by the fact that we already had one Republican senator in John Tower, and Texans weren't keen on having both senators be Republicans. What put the final nail in Bush's candidacy, though, was the fact that Lyndon Johnson stepped up and threw his support behind Yarborough, in spite of their ongoing personal feud.

Now, this might seem like an obvious thing to do — supporting your party's guy in a race against the other party's guy. But as we'd already seen with the Shivercrats in the '50s, and then again with John Tower's senate victory in 1961, that kind of intra-party support was never a given in Texas. In fact, Johnson's decision to back Yarborough proved highly controversial within the state party. John Connally was so mad about it, he wouldn't even speak to Johnson for a while.

But Johnson's decision was the right one, no matter the heat he took for it. It must have been galling for him, especially since Yarborough had so publicly snubbed him during the Kennedy visit. Johnson was nothing if not proud, and as thick-skinned as he tried to seem, he was highly sensitive to personal slights. But by throwing his weight behind Yarborough, he put the party's needs above his own — and the result was that instead of having two Republican senators in 1964, Texas had a Democrat and a Republican. The party ought to have learned a lesson from that election, but unfortunately, as would soon become obvious, it didn't.

In the meantime, I'd won a third term and was looking forward to the 1965 legislature, with Lyndon Johnson in the White House, John Connally as governor, and Byron Tunnell as Speaker of the House. This was a perfect lineup of my three biggest political allies and mentors — but it was soon to change.

IN JANUARY OF 1965, JUST A FEW DAYS BEFORE THE 59TH LEGISLATURE GOT underway, I went with Byron Tunnell and several fellow legislators up to State Representative Bill Heatly's ranch house, just outside Paducah in West Texas. We'd gone up for a day or two to choose committee assignments for the 150 House members and trade some political shop talk before the session opened.

On the first afternoon, we were in the middle of a meeting in Heatly's living room, papers strewn around and coffee mugs everywhere, when the phone rang. "Byron," said Heatly. "It's the governor, for you."

Tunnell left to take the call in a bedroom, and he was gone for a good 10 or 15 minutes. When he finally stuck his head out, he looked right at me and said, "Barnes, come here for a second." I went into the bedroom, and Tunnell shut the door.

"I've got some news," he said, "Ernest Thompson is leaving the Railroad Commission, and I'm going to take his seat." He paused for just a moment, then added, "I'm not going to be Speaker this session." But I barely even heard that last bit, because I was already halfway out the door, knowing what I had to do next. "Oh my God!" I fairly shouted. "I'm in! I've got to get to Austin!"

I must have looked like a crazy man, scrambling around and looking for my things as the rest of the group sat there, unaware of Tunnell's news. "Where's my stuff?" I blurted. "I've got to go!" Gradually, the others realized what was happening, and a couple volunteered to come back to Austin with me to shore up the votes I'd need to take Tunnell's place. "Let's go!" I said, and a carload of us headed off to the airport.

When we got to Austin, we hurried over to the Driskill Hotel to set up a "war room," with a bank of phones so we could let loose a barrage of calls to the other 149 members of the House. I needed a simple majority — 76 votes — to secure the Speakership, and I wanted to make damn sure it was wrapped up before anyone else could even think of running against me. Not only that, but I also wanted to win by a hell of a lot more votes than a simple majority. I already had more than a hundred "second pledges," and I wanted to win the Speakership unanimously, or as close as I could get to it.

The minute we got into the Driskill suite we started dialing phones. As soon as someone got through to a House member, I'd grab the receiver and start talking. "Listen, I need your vote. This is a chance for us to be Speaker — you're gonna be Speaker with me! We're all gonna be in this together! Come on and join me right now, pledge your vote!" It must have sounded like I'd lost my mind, but I never let anyone get a word in edgewise to suggest it.

We dialed those phones until our fingers were numb. For hours on end, we did nothing but call and strategize and count votes. After 24 hours, we had about 90 confirmed pledges. Soon, we were up to 120. Some of the members were wary about the whole second-pledge system that I'd started, fearing that it could lead to future abuses of power if political factions used it to maintain a perpetual grip on power. But in the end, we were able to persuade every House member but one to vote for me, in the interest of what we could do for Texas in the here and now.

And I'll tell you what, as much as I relished the chance to be the youngest Speaker since Reconstruction, what I really wanted was a chance to work with John Connally to help push Texas toward the future. Thanks to our treasure trove of oil and gas, Texas had been financially strong for decades. But that boom wasn't going to last forever, and it was high time we looked ahead, to what was coming next. Texas needed a new Constitution; a new focus on education, technology, and tourism; and new tax structures to help keep the state strong. I was young and energetic and ready to fight for those things, with the kind of optimism a 26-year-old has in spades. I couldn't wait to get to work with Governor Connally to make them happen.

And though we never talked specifically about it, it seems clear from Connally's moves that he wanted the same thing. Just about anyone would have jumped at the chance for the seat that he'd offered Byron Tunnell — despite its name, the Railroad Commission was one of the most powerful state commissions in Texas, because it regulated the oil and gas industry. The commissioners not only wielded tremendous power, but they also enjoyed the luxury of six-year terms. It was one of the most coveted appointments in the state — and Connally had made a point of choosing Byron Tunnell, intentionally opening up the Speaker's chair.

Much later, Larry Temple described Connally's thinking at that time. "Connally specifically wanted a change of leadership in the House. He didn't have any antagonism toward Byron at all — otherwise he wouldn't have put him on the Railroad Commission," said Temple. "But he thought that philosophically, Byron was not as progressive as he, Connally, wanted to be for the state. And Connally thought he wanted some things done in the legislature in '65 that would require some spending, particularly in higher education, and some changes to be made that he thought likely would not have been made under the Byron Tunnell regime.

"So, when the vacancy came along on the Railroad Commission, he thought it was very fortuitous situation, where he could put Byron in that commission, and open up the opportunity for Ben to be elected Speaker." But, as Temple says, "There are some people who would say John Connally got Barnes elected speaker. John Connally never thought that, never said that, and he never believed that. Did he open up the opportunity for Ben to get himself elected Speaker? You bet. He didn't get Ben a single vote. He didn't try to... but he appointed Byron intentionally for that to have the possibility — or the likelihood — of that occurring."

So it was that at age 26, I became the Speaker of the Texas House. Part of me was scared to death, but the other part couldn't wait to get started. My first day as Speaker, I stood in front of the House and was presented with a gavel the size of a sledgehammer, which Rep. Bill Dungan declared was symbolic of the "size of the state, the vote you received for Speaker, and the size of your new job." I swung that big old gavel down, and with a mighty bang started the next phase of my political life.

Chapter Five

The Johnson–Connally Wing and Business

ON JANUARY 4, 1965, JUST A WEEK BEFORE I BECAME SPEAKER, LYNDON Johnson stood in front of a joint session of Congress and announced his plan for a "Great Society." Johnson had just won the presidency by the largest margin in history, and in his State of the Union speech he gave notice: With the huge mandate he'd been handed, he wasn't planning just to muddle along as President. He was aiming to change the fabric of American society. At the time of his speech, with no American combat troops yet in Vietnam and the country not yet wrenched in two over the war, the mood coming out of the White House was one of optimism.

It was an exciting time to be in politics. Lyndon Johnson put all his energy into passing the groundbreaking programs — civil rights, the War on Poverty, the Great Society — that would mark him as one of our most visionary Presidents. Before he was done, he'd put dozens of transformational new laws on the books. Medicare, the National Endowment for the Arts, the Head Start program, the Clean Air Act — all these were initiatives under Johnson that have since become American institutions. Like the men who'd come to my family's farm 20 years earlier, bringing us the promise of electricity, Lyndon Johnson's government was once again in the business of improving ordinary people's lives.

I hoped to do the same thing in Texas. As Speaker, I was now one of the three most powerful politicians in the state, along with Governor Connally and Lieutenant Governor Preston Smith, who presided over the Senate. I'd never expected to become Speaker so quickly, but I jumped right into the job like I thought I knew how to do it.

First off, a few things needed to be done differently. I got rid of the old lottery system that determined which bills the House would consider, and instead appointed a new committee that would schedule bills according to their urgency. In the Texas Legislature, the Senate almost always got the credit for whatever good legislation got passed (or bad legislation that got killed), and I wanted to make the House more proactive than it had been. My first time meeting with the new Rules Committee chairman, I told him, "You know, we're not gonna come down this trail but one time. Let's don't sit over here and wait for the Senate — let's get out there and get some things done."

I also instituted something called the "Rule of Yes." When House members would ask me about introducing legislative initiatives, I always told them to go ahead and bring 'em on, unless it was something that seemed just absolutely worthless. I always felt like the House ought to decide for itself which bills to pursue, and my open-door policy had the effect of encouraging members to get off their butts and make something happen.

Finally, I opened up the Speaker's office to the media. There was a press room on the second floor of the Capitol, and reporters were always hanging around, trying to pick up any little tidbit they could. I decided to invite them to a weekly sit-down — every Monday morning, they could come to the Speaker's office and have a cup of coffee, and I'd tell them the plan for the week and answer their questions. Well, they just couldn't believe their luck — no Speaker had ever done such a thing before. They were so grateful, they not only fell over themselves thanking me but even gave me a prize: The Sigma Delta Chi "Friend of Journalism" award.

As the *San Antonio Express-News* reported when we opened the session, the 59th legislature was "faced with one of the heaviest and thorniest work loads in state history." We knew we'd have to wrestle with at least three big problems — education, the tax bill and redistricting. But it didn't take long to see which one Governor Connally planned to spend his time on.

Connally was absolutely fixed on putting Texas in the top tier of states in education. Even then, back in the '60s, he saw that technology would become the new engine of the U.S. economy, and he knew that Texas was lagging in that area. If we didn't make a move early toward the next economic boom, we'd get left behind.

The future aside, Texas also had plenty of problems in the here and now. Even though the state was financially strong, we still scored embarrassingly low in educational rankings compared to other states. We had one of the worst public school systems in the country. We lacked the kind of nationally-known, respected universities and colleges that states like California and New York had in abundance. Almost nine out of 10 of UT honor graduates left the state to go to graduate school. And faculty salaries at UT were lower than those at comparable institutions. Overall, we just didn't have the kind of focus and vision about education that would lead the state to excellence. But Connally was determined to change all that. And he turned to me to help him make it happen.

Connally knew that if we wanted to make improvements in education, we'd first have to convince the legislature to appropriate the money for it. This was easier said than done — the Texas legislature was a conservative, Southern body, not inclined either to rock the boat or to spend any more money than was necessary. As the newly-elected Speaker, I knew it was up to me to convey our vision for education, and wrest the votes we needed out of a reluctant group of representatives.

So I set about doing just that. I went from desk to desk in the chamber, explaining to my fellow legislators how the improvements Connally and I sought in Texas's educational system would benefit the state in dozens of other ways. Improving our education system would go a long way toward fixing other pervasive problems — social, cultural, and economic. The state could draw Research & Development money from all over the country and the world if we pushed our institutes of higher education to excel. We could ensure a stronger social safety net if we moved to take advantage of the coming wave of technology, rather than riding down agriculture and oil until they crashed. Connally was the first person I heard use the term "information age," and he rightly saw that there was a lot of money in it for Texas if we planned for its arrival.

This was the hallmark of Democratic initiatives in the mid-sixties: we understood the need to invest now, in order to reap bigger rewards later. You can't expect a garden to grow if you don't invest in the seeds, and that's just what we were doing. Tax bills are about the most unpopular form of legislation, but I made sure we pushed through a tax bill that would provide us the means to make the improvements we needed. And because of the education legislation we passed in the '60s, Texas had a seat at the table when the information age arrived at the end of the century.

Some of the legislation we pushed through seems obvious in retrospect, but it was contentious at the time. We raised teacher salaries, which the Senate — led by Lieutenant Governor Preston Smith, who was fast becoming my political rival — fought tooth and nail. We bumped up the state's fiscal support of the universities. And we started a program that served as a precursor to today's Head Start programs when we launched a pre-school English language program for Mexican-American kids. From kindergarten right up through Ph.D.'s, we worked to change the culture of education in Texas.

The most important education bill we passed during the 59th legislature was House Bill 1, which would create The Texas Higher Education
Coordinating Board to oversee and coordinate all the state's institutions of
higher learning. Just getting that bill through would have been an accom-
plishment in itself, but things got even more complicated when I had to go
up against one of my mentors — and one of the strongest supporters of
Connally's education initiatives — Frank Erwin.

In 1965, Frank wielded a certain degree of power in Austin — and he was
just as pugnacious as he was powerful. If he could get a bill passed in his favor,
that was good. If he could piss off a few hundred people doing it, that was even
better. But Frank had also taken me under his wing, teaching me the kinds of
things a green country boy from DeLeon needed to know if he was going to
succeed in the more sophisticated environment of the state capital.

In the three years since Frank and I had drunk that whiskey together at
Dolph Briscoe's ranch, he had won a variety of positions within the Democratic
party. First, he was chosen as chair of the Resolutions Committee at the 1962
state convention, then as chair of the state Democratic Executive Committee.
In 1964, he rose even higher, becoming Democratic National Committeeman
from Texas. But the job that reflected his true passion was one he got in 1963,
when he was named to the University of Texas Board of Regents.

The University of Texas was Frank's baby, and like any proud papa, he
fought like hell to get the best of everything he could for it. Over the next
decade, five years of which he spent as Chair of the Board of Regents, he would
succeed in raising state appropriations for UT from $40 million annually to
$350 million. He oversaw the expansion of the university's buildings by 16 million
square feet, and a rise in enrollment from 30,000 students to more than
77,000. But like an over-protective father, Frank sometimes went too far.

One night, Frank, Governor Connally's Chief of Staff Larry Temple and I
were in the Speaker's office drafting House Bill 1, which would create the
Texas Higher Education Coordinating Board to oversee and coordinate all the
state's institutions of higher learning. Frank was a big proponent of improving
higher education, of course, so he was for the bill — but only to a point. "This
is a great bill, Ben," he told me. "But let's put something in there making UT
exempt from a couple of those provisions." Much as he wanted the education
system improved, Frank was not the kind of man who was willing to give up
control of his own institution unless it was pried from his grip.

"No, Frank," I told him. "We're not gonna do that."

Frank raised his eyebrows a little bit. I suppose that, even though I was
Speaker now, he didn't expect I'd cross him so readily. And judging by the look

on his face, he didn't like it too much.

"Yes, we are gonna do it, Ben," he said, his voice even. "We're gonna have an exemption, and that's that. It'll be better for the university."

Now, Frank had a reputation for being a pretty persuasive sort. One famous story that made the rounds was about how he'd left an Austin drinking club one night and drove off the wrong way down a one-way street. A police car soon pulled him over, and after the officer looked at Frank's license, he said, "Mr. Erwin, didn't you see that arrow?"

"Hell, officer," Frank shot back, "I didn't even see the Indian!" He didn't manage to talk his way out of the ticket that night, but he did ultimately get out of the fine in court.

At any rate, Frank obviously thought he just needed to push me a little harder to get his exemption for UT. "Ben," he said, "We can't have people meddling in what the university's doing. Now, just settle down and write this thing up the way it ought to be."

"Goddamnit, Frank," I said, my temper finally flaring. "There is not going to be exemption! If we're going to do this thing right, UT has got to be a part of it. We can't ask all the other institutions to do it if it's not done equitably. Now, let's just get on with it."

Frank was stunned into silence for just a moment, but then he got mad. He stomped around a little bit, and shouted about how I was hurting the university, but I stood my ground — as I suspect he knew I'd do. In the end, we didn't write any exemptions into the bill, and Frank never made a fuss about it again. That was the first time I'd crossed him, and I didn't mean it as anything more than what it was — my firm opinion on what the best bill would be. But I guess it did serve notice that, no matter how many mentors I was gaining in my young political career, I wasn't going to be anybody's "Boy Friday" when it came to legislation.

Frank didn't hold that little disagreement against me, but when I faced a similar situation with another powerful Texan, it launched a feud that lasted more than 10 years. Over the years, a lot of people — including numerous political reporters in Texas — have asked what was the root of the feud between Bob Bullock and me. He and I had been close allies and pretty good friends, until all of a sudden it seemed he had nothing good to say about me, in public or in private. I've been asked many times what happened to cause that rift, but I never revealed it publicly — until now.

In 1965, the whiskey industry wanted to add an amendment to a House bill then under consideration. I don't remember all the details now, but the industry had hired Bob Bullock to lobby the House for the amendment. Bullock knew that, because the amendment wasn't relevant, or germane, to the bill, it wouldn't normally be considered. So he came to ask me to put it up for consideration anyway, in my capacity as Speaker. He made it clear that he'd receive a healthy fee from the whiskey industry if he could just get that amendment up for consideration.

The amendment didn't seem germane to me, but just to be sure, I checked with the House Parliamentarian, who agreed that it wasn't. Bullock kept pushing me to include it, though, so I went to a higher authority — I asked a sitting Supreme Court justice what he thought. He said the same thing the Parliamentarian had: this amendment shouldn't be considered with this bill.

Now, the truth is, I've never been averse to helping friends. But this was a different case. Bullock was asking me to do something that didn't warrant serious consideration for any reason other than because he, my friend, had asked for it. And that wasn't something I felt comfortable doing. When I told Bullock so, he was furious. He just couldn't believe I wouldn't do what he wanted.

Bullock had walked into my office that day as a friend, but when he walked out, he wasn't — and wouldn't be again until more than a decade later, when we were both older and wiser. From that point on, he went as hard against me politically as he could. I couldn't believe his reaction was so strong to something that seemed so minor, but Bullock was never one to do things halfway. I'd find out the hard way just how effective that could be a few years down the road, when Bullock would turn the full force of his political power against me in a crucial, and bruising, election season.

———

BY THE TIME THE 59TH LEGISLATURE ENDED IN THE SUMMER OF 1965, JOHN Connally was riding high as the most popular and effective governor Texas had seen in years. The fact that he'd been in the limousine with President Kennedy in Dallas, and had survived near-fatal gunshot wounds, made him a mythic figure in the eyes of many Texans. He stood tall as one of President Johnson's closest confidants. And at age 48, he was as confident and charismatic as he'd ever been. At that moment, John Connally held the state in the palm of his hand.

During his first term, Connally had mostly just been feeling his way around. But in his second term, with one legislative session under his belt and me in the Speaker's office, we teamed up to push through all kinds of legislation. And after we'd get a bill passed in the House, I didn't just sit back and wait to see what the Senate would do — I went on over to the senators' offices and lobbied them to pass it too. Previous Speakers hadn't really done that, but I wasn't too concerned about precedent. All I cared about was getting my bills made into law, and if that meant jawing with a bunch of mossback senators and horse-trading support for their bills, I was more than happy to do it.

My efforts in the Senate were met with consternation by Lieutenant Governor Preston Smith. Even as early as 1965, we were shaping up to be political rivals, and he flat didn't like the way Connally and I worked the legislature to our advantage. As the *Houston Chronicle* later put it, "Smith watched helplessly during the 1965 session as the proud Senate was humbled time after time by the Barnes-led House... The animosity between Smith and Barnes grew after the session ended in 1965 as it became clear to Smith that Barnes also was shooting toward the governor's chair."

Now, I don't mean to come off like I was the resident genius in the Capitol building, or that nobody on Earth could have done things the way I did. But the truth is, John Connally and I just worked well together. We shared a vision for Texas, and it was our great good luck to have entered politics at about the same time. As the months went by, our working relationship got more and more streamlined, and we also worked to solidify relationships with the business interests that would help us keep the Democratic party strong for years to come.

With Connally's power at its peak, there was one question on everybody's mind as the dog days of summer ended in 1965. Would Connally run for a third term in 1966? Or would he feel like he'd made his point, and just ride off into the sunset?

Connally played it close to his vest that fall, and even I didn't know what he planned to do. As 1966 began, though, he had to make a decision, as the primary was just five months off. It was time we got together to sort it out, so State Democratic Executive Committee Chairman Will Davis called a meeting at a roadside motel in Amarillo, Texas, where the state Democratic executive committee was meeting.

I'll tell you what, with all the egos in that meeting room there was hardly any space to breathe, but at least we were going to find out once and for all who was doing what. Preston Smith kept making noises like he was going to run for governor, regardless of what Connally did. Of course, if he'd announced that, and then Connally had run, Smith would have been trampled by him in the primary. Nobody really believed he'd run against Connally, but Smith was the kind of man who felt the need to bull around like he was the one making all the decisions in the room.

Connally loved to control the moment, and when we invited the press into the meeting room for his announcement, I knew he'd wait until the last possible moment to reveal his plans. And he did. He talked about Texas, about the legislature, about education, about his favorite place to get barbecue — about anything and everything except what everybody was there to hear. Then, toward the end of his speech, he made his announcement: he'd decided to run for a third term.

That room erupted in more whooping and hollering than the stands at a UT football game. Even a few journalists applauded, and Connally just stood up there and drank it all in. A lot of people would later argue that Connally's passion for politics waned after he'd been shot in Dallas, but anyone seeing his face that day could tell that he was energized by his decision, and by the reaction it had garnered.

I was excited, too. With Connally staying in place, and Smith running again for lieutenant governor, I was planning to run again for Speaker — and I fully expected that in the 60th legislature, in 1967, we'd be able to continue passing groundbreaking legislation for Texas.

With our political lineup set, Texas Democrats went into the summer of 1966 feeling optimistic. Once again, I didn't have any opponents in my House race, and no one was running against me for the Speaker's chair. So although my predecessors as Speaker would have taken that time to go home and earn some money, I turned the Speakership into a year-round job, spending the summer working on some political initiatives of my own. I put on the first conference ever held in the U.S. on dyslexia and learning disabilities, a topic that to that point had never really been discussed in public. We arranged for about a thousand people to take part, and were amazed when nearly 3,000 showed up. There was a real hunger for information, and I was proud to help bring the subject out in the open.

I did a lot of traveling that summer, including a trip to Peru in which I tried to drum up interest for "Hemisfair," a project that the city of San Antonio was planning for 1968. The idea was to set up a World's Fair-type gathering that would celebrate Latin American culture in Texas, giving us a permanent cultural center and drawing tourists to South Texas. In fact, on my trip to Peru, I felt embarrassed that I couldn't speak any Spanish, and I became convinced that Texas public schools ought to offer mandatory Spanish classes. This was a radical idea in the sixties, and back in Austin I took my share of ribbing for it. As one pundit sniped, "It's a good thing the Speaker didn't go to Japan."

I also went up to Washington, D.C. a couple of times, visiting with President Johnson in the White House and getting involved with political groups like the National Legislative Conference, the Council of State Governments, and the National Conference of Legislative Leaders. I was eager to get involved with national governance organizations, both to get Texas in the forefront and because I could learn a lot from how my fellow legislators in other states did things. I got elected to the executive committee of the National Legislative Conference that summer, and took my place in the ranks of up-and-coming young legislators. By now I was 28, and more than just an overgrown boy, but I still was running at 100 miles an hour. My party and my state were flying high, and I was right up there with them.

Then came August of 1966, and a couple of events that brought us all back down to earth again. That was a hard month, and it started with the very first day.

———

I WAS SITTING AT MY DESK IN THE SPEAKER'S OFFICE JUST BEFORE 1 P.M. ON August 1, 1966, when phones all over the Capitol building, including my own, suddenly started ringing. I don't remember who first called with the news, but what they said was chilling. Somebody had gone up to the observation deck of the Texas Tower and was shooting at people on the ground.

This would turn into one of the most tragic days in the history of not only the University of Texas, but of Texas itself. The Texas Tower was a 307-foot bell tower that had stood since 1937 as a proud symbol of the university. From the top, you can see all of Austin, including a majestic view of the Capitol, just a mile or so to the south. But on the morning of August 1, a man named Charles Whitman went to the top with a footlocker full of guns, and once there he started firing on innocent people down below.

Governor Connally was out of the country, and Lieutenant Governor Preston Smith was out of town. I got on the phone with Frank Erwin and Colonel Garrison of the Texas Department of Public Safety, and the three of us conferred on what to do next. We talked about whether it would be feasible to have a helicopter or small plane fly close enough for a police sharpshooter to take out the gunman — and as Frank and I later learned, a small-engine plane did circle the area, with a policeman inside trying to fire on Whitman. When Whitman began firing back, however, the plane was forced to retreat.

In the absence of the governor and lieutenant governor, I was the highest-ranking political figure in Austin, and after I hung up the phone with Colonel Garrison, I decided someone from state government needed to be at the Tower to help make critical decisions. Frank Erwin and I headed for the network of utility tunnels that branches out beneath the UT campus, and we were able to walk underground all the way to the Tower's base. By the time we got there, the killing spree had mercifully ended.

Whitman's shooting spree lasted a little more than an hour and a half, but a couple of police officers finally made it up to the observation deck and waited for their moment to take him out. When Whitman saw them he opened fire, but they stood their ground, hoping to get a clear shot without losing their own lives in the process. In the end, the officers — Ramiro Martinez and Houston McCoy — were able to shoot Whitman, and nearly two hours after the horror began, it was finally over. Whitman had killed 16 people (one of whom died a week after the shootings), and he'd wounded 31 more. The tragedy shook the university and state to the core, and I guarantee you, it shook me too.

The Texas Tower shootings were nationwide news that summer. Charles Whitman had perpetrated the worst mass killings ever by a lone gunman on American soil, and he'd done it at a time when the country was already getting more and more jumpy. By the summer of 1966, American involvement in Vietnam was increasing, violent clashes over civil rights were intensifying, and the painful memory of John Kennedy's assassination was still fresh in everyone's minds. The optimism of the early part of the decade was gradually giving way to the anxiety of the late '60s.

In Texas that summer, there was also growing unrest among the thousands of migrant workers who labored in the state's farms and fields. Many of them worked at near-starvation wages — 50 cents an hour or less — under terrible conditions. South Texas in the summer is so hot, the corn practically pops right on the stalk, and these workers were out in the fields for 10 or 12 hours a day, seven days a week, picking melons under the blazing sun. So when a labor union organizer named Eugene Nelson made his way down to the Rio Grande Valley, it didn't take him long to stir things right up.

Nelson first called on the workers to strike, but soon he had the idea of starting a march, which was a surefire way to get more press attention. Under Nelson's direction, a little band of migrant workers, labor organizers and church workers set off from Rio Grande City on the Fourth of July. They only meant to go as far as San Juan, 50 miles down the road. But when they arrived there after four days or so of marching in the dusty heat, a few of them decided they ought to keep going. Very quickly, they made a plan to march another 400 miles right into Austin itself, with the aim of arriving at the Capitol on Labor Day and demanding a meeting with the governor to talk about minimum wage laws.

All through July and August, the scraggly band had marched northward. They numbered anywhere from 15 or 20 full-time marchers to a couple hundred when sympathizers joined them in the bigger towns. They got press coverage the whole way, and Ralph Yarborough got himself in the papers too when he flew down from Washington to join them for a day. As an extra poke at Connally, Senator Yarborough even sent a telegram to be read at a rally the marchers held in Connally's hometown of Floresville.

As the marchers got closer to Austin, Connally realized that their demands to meet with him on Labor Day could cause him some trouble. For one thing, Connally wasn't the kind of man who responded well to "demands" that he do anything, so he wouldn't ordinarily have been inclined to agree to a meeting. And even if he had been, the fact was, he had long-standing plans to be out of Austin on Labor Day. But if the marchers got all the way to Austin after two long, hot months and Connally wasn't there to meet with them, he knew there would be demonstrations or worse. He fully expected that by the time the marchers got to Austin, they'd have attracted students, labor activists, and all other manner of hangers-on who'd like nothing more than to stir things up right in Connally's back yard if they could do it.

On August 31, with the marchers nearing New Braunfels, just 50 miles outside of Austin, Connally and I talked about what we ought to do. I was scheduled to be in Dallas on Labor Day, so neither of us would be in Austin when the marchers arrived — but neither of us thought it would be right to leave them no one to meet with. So we decided to go ahead and meet with them right then. We'd drive down to New Braunfels, hear their concerns, and tell them face to face that we wouldn't be in Austin when they arrived.

Like any spur-of-the-moment plans, this one wasn't as well thought out as it could have been. The first mistake we made was the biggest one: Governor Connally, Attorney General Waggoner Carr and I jumped into the governor's limousine to make the drive. Somehow, none of us realized that pulling up beside a ragtag group of tired, hot, dirt-poor marchers in a shiny, black, bullet-proof Lincoln Continental might send the wrong message. We must have looked like the fat-cat bankers come to toss a penny at the hungry masses. I hate to think about it, even now.

We caught up to the marchers just off Interstate 35, and the three of us stepped out of the air-conditioned limo in our suits and cufflinks. A few reporters had gotten wind of our plans, and had raced ahead to be there when we arrived, so unfortunately, the whole scene was recorded for all posterity.

Things started off well enough, as we walked down the line of 50 or so marchers, shaking everybody's hand. Then Father Antonio Gonzales, one of the march's leaders, offered Connally an olive branch, telling him the Latinos loved and respected him.

Connally responded that he knew and appreciated that, and he told Father Gonzales that he didn't need to put on a whole march to come and see him — that he could come anytime. The exchange was very friendly, and if we'd just stopped right there, everything would have been just fine. But when the conversation continued, it got worse.

Connally began talking about all his initiatives aimed at helping the Mexican community — Head Start, schools for migrant workers, and the like. "We have attempted to do everything we know how to do," he said, before going on to warn Father Gonzales about the rest of the march. "As governor," he said, "I'm aware of the fact that things can get out of hand in marches, as they have elsewhere in the U.S., and that's the last thing we want in Texas." He went on to say that he wouldn't be in Austin on Labor Day, but that even if he would have been, he still wouldn't have met with the marchers there.

That didn't sit too well with anyone. Connally had a way of appearing somewhat high-handed, and his cool assurances didn't go down very easily with the ragged band of exhausted marchers. As Labor leader Hank Brown later said of our little group, "They made an ass of themselves." And the reporters seemed to agree. It was not our finest hour.

This episode didn't cause any irreversible damage to Connally's career or reputation, but it definitely caused some fallout for the Texas Democratic party. At the time, Attorney General Waggoner Carr, who'd gone with us to New Braunfels, was in the middle of a tight race against Republican John Tower for his U.S. Senate seat. For Carr to win, he'd have to cull support from both liberals and conservatives in the party. But after New Braunfels, Father Gonzales announced that he expected most Latinos to vote for Tower. "I would say the great majority will vote for Tower," he told reporters, "not because they like Tower's position, but because they would like to have a two-party system, and as a protest against Connally."

That was bad enough, but on top of it, Ralph Yarborough was again doing his best to split the party. Under pressure, he publicly announced that he would indeed vote for Carr — but he made a point of adding that he certainly couldn't bring himself to do anything more than that for Carr's campaign. Liberals across Texas acted on that information exactly as Yarborough knew they would, by not only refusing to support Carr, but even organizing against him. Liberal state Senator Babe Schwartz made a valiant effort to get his wing of the party back into the fold, telling a reporter from the *Fort Worth Star-Telegram* that liberals were sending their party down the road to disaster, but his words went unheeded. As Schwartz would later remark in wonderment, "Liberals hated the conservatives in the Democratic party beyond their comprehension of hating a Republican."

Once again, the Texas Democratic party was devouring itself. Two years later, Father Gonzales would publicly apologize for having urged support of Tower in the '66 election, but by then it was too late. Carr lost the election by 200,000 votes, and Tower continued to be the cornerstone of the Republican presence in Texas politics.

⸻

DESPITE THE NEW BRAUNFELS INCIDENT, CONNALLY WAS NOT AS DIVISIVE A Texas Democratic politician as it might have seemed. In fact, the opposite was true. As a September 20, 1966 *Wall Street Journal* article described in great detail, John Connally was actually the force that kept the state's Democratic party from splintering, and who helped keep the Republican party from gaining ground. This was the most extraordinary achievement of the Johnson-Connally era in Texas politics — and it was one I hoped to build on even after these two Texas giants retired.

The article is worth quoting at length, as it so perfectly summarizes the political trends under Connally:

> [Connally] has slowed Texas' drift toward becoming a Northern-style two-party state... and has preserved at least a while longer the firm control of the conservative Democrats...
>
> "He's halted the trend far more effectively than anyone else could have," asserts a Texan now working in the White House. "He's set back the liberals and Republicans a decade."...
>
> By appealing to all segments of the electorate and sometimes taking liberal actions along with conservative ones, Gov. Connally has established a political consensus here far broader than anything [President] Johnson has achieved nationally. Rank and file voters seem so pleased with his performance that sniping from liberal or Republican leaders simply does not register...
>
> ...As governor, Mr. Connally has built his consensus partly by keeping conservatives happy with his stands on national issues, opposing Medicare, federal aid to education and 'right to work' repeal. On the state level, he has stood firm against a minimum wage law, and aided by a sales tax started by his predecessor and by the long economic boom, has gotten by with only modest tax increases of his own.
>
> However, as an adroit politician who recognizes the population shift to urban and suburban areas, Mr. Connally has been liberal enough to win many rank and file voters of moderate or generally liberal leanings. He has increased

state support of education, strengthened health programs, raised welfare levels and teacher pay and enlarged water development programs. New and expanding industries have kept employment high, helping the governor with poorer voters.

Through carefully selected appointments, he has strengthened himself among Negroes and Mexican-Americans. He has used his popularity to consolidate his power and has made the governor's office into a power center. He has groomed ... Texas House speaker Ben Barnes as a possible heir, and with Mr. Barnes' help, has enacted his legislative program with minimum fuss.

If there was one thing that Texas Democrats did well in the '60s — and one thing that today's struggling Democratic party ought to emulate — it was creating this bridge between conservative business interests and progressive constituencies. Lyndon Johnson, John Connally and I were considered "conservative" Democrats by the party's liberal wing. But all three of us pushed through dozens of progressive laws. We made it possible to enact progressive legislation while ensuring it was politically and socially acceptable for the business community to support the Democratic party. As a political formula, it was — and still is — a sure winner.

Connally picked his battles carefully. He focused on progressive measures as part of a larger economic strategy, rather than as ends in themselves — a strategy he called "progressive but prudent." He fought for better education for all Texans, not just because he wanted to improve people's lives but because he knew it would strengthen the state economically. He and I pushed to create a tourism board, not simply because we wanted to show off the state, but because we knew it was becoming easier and more financially beneficial to pick a tourist than a bale of cotton.

The Johnson-Connally wing of the party also cultivated a group of powerful businessmen, many of them based in Houston, and encouraged their involvement in initiatives aimed at strengthening the state. This group would get together on a Friday night to talk politics, play cards, and drink whiskey, and I'll tell you one thing — they were every bit as focused on improving the state as they were on their own businesses. They exercised true civic duty, planning for the future of not only Houston but Texas as a whole, and it was thanks in large part to their efforts that Texas moved into the technological age as smoothly as it did.

This is another element of the party's strength that we've lost today: we need to find and cultivate business leaders who care about more than just profits, and who'll work with us to improve the state. In the '60s in Texas, we had a group of business leaders who were more than happy to sit down in a room with Gov. Connally and me to figure out how to raise the money we needed to make improvements in state programs. Those men and women would sit with us for hours, devising ways to tax themselves so we could continue to improve the state. They weren't afraid to take a hit now for improvement later, and their efforts are a big part of the reason why we were able to effect such dramatic improvement in the social and civic life of Texans.

Today, by comparison, we've seen a rash of companies that are focused only on profits — no matter the damage they do to the state, their stockholders or anyone else. Too often, corporations' involvement in politics is limited to campaign donations for their favorite politicians, rather than the needs of the state's residents. If there's one thing we need today in Texas, it's a focus from our political and business leaders on the future of the state, rather than the future of their own party or company.

Both Lyndon Johnson and John Connally were focused on technology and education as the ticket to the future strength. Most people have forgotten it now, but Lyndon Johnson was one of the visionaries behind NASA in its early days. In 1960, he was appointed Chairman of the National Aeronautics and Space Council, and he also was one of the most vocal proponents of sending a man to the moon — a mission that would have fizzled out after Kennedy's assassination if Johnson hadn't continued pushing for it. Johnson also fought to get the Manned Spacecraft Center, later renamed the Lyndon B. Johnson Space Center, located in Houston.

Getting the space center for Houston meant tremendous economic development for Texas. The U.S. government, alarmed at the advances the Soviet Union was making with the Sputnik program and manned space flight, was ready to pour funding into our space program. Suddenly, there was money for contractors, scientists, and Research and Development — all areas that would boost the state's economy and technological significance. With Texas slowly moving away from its agricultural roots, and unwilling to put all our eggs in one basket with the oil and gas industries, Johnson and Connally pushed for Texas to take the lead on what Connally called "the information age."

As Speaker, I got religion on the technology issue thanks to three of the principals at Texas Instruments, who took me on an eye-opening trip up to Massachusetts. They took me to see Harvard and the Massachusetts Institute of Technology, and set up meetings for me with the presidents of those universities. I began to understand then what it meant for a state to offer both world-class educational institutions and a sense of possibility about the future. "Mr.

Speaker," one of the TI founders told me, "we're running the risk of never having another Texas Instruments emerge in our state, because we're just not investing in the brainpower. Texas has got to graduate more engineers and scientists, and create excellence in higher education, or we're in trouble." I'll tell you what, that trip made me a believer, and from then on I made a point of putting funds in the appropriations bills to foster technology and improve higher education in Texas.

So it was that, under the Democratic party's leadership, Texas began the turn toward technology that would help keep the state strong beyond the oil boom. Companies like Ross Perot's Dallas-based EDS and Texas Instruments flourished during the '60s, and our education initiatives began turning out more scientists and engineers within the state.

The result of our initiatives was that individual Texans found their lives improving, while the health of the state overall improved too. The *Dallas Morning News* summed it up in an editorial endorsing Connally for governor in 1966:

> The News' strong and continued support of Gov. Connally is based primarily on the fact that the governor, Lt. Gov. Preston Smith, House Speaker Ben Barnes and others aligned with their philosophy and leadership have created a favorable political climate for the steady advancement of Texas...
>
> We are one of the few states in America operating in the black; that, plus the favorable tax rate, helped Texas to rank second only to New York in the attraction of new industry (1963-66) and expansion of existing facilities (1,000 new plants since Connally took office in January, 1963)... We have the nation's finest highway and road system — 65,818 miles...
>
> Those who vote Republican on Tuesday against these conservative Democrats are voting to weaken this political climate and the type of state government that is lifting Texas to higher levels of achievement...

On election day in 1966, the Democrats ran as strong as ever, though a few scattered Republican victories poked through like straggling flowers in the desert. John Connally won reelection with more than 70 percent of the vote, but three Republicans won seats in the Texas House, and one Republican won election to the Senate, breaking a drought that had stood since Reconstruction. And John Tower defeated Democrat Waggoner Carr to retain his U.S. Senate seat.

Two other Texans won their first seats in 1966. George H.W. Bush, fresh off his loss to Senator Ralph Yarborough in 1964, won himself a seat from

Houston in the U.S. House of Representatives to launch his political career. Also in Houston, a woman more or less unknown outside her district became the first African American to win a seat in the Texas Senate since the late 19th century. Her name was Barbara Jordan.

Chapter Six

Vietnam, Civil Rights, and the Texas Air National Guard

IN JANUARY OF 1967, THE TEXAS DEMOCRATIC PARTY CELEBRATED ANOTHER year of big election wins with the traditional "Victory Dinner" in Austin. For $25 a plate, people could come have a steak dinner, hear Anita Bryant sing, and laugh as comedian Cactus Pryor poked fun at all the politicians. Four thousand people showed up, and flush with support, we got ready to head right into the 60th Legislature.

Although Barbara Jordan had been elected to the Senate, and I was across the rotunda serving as Speaker of the House, I sought out her political friendship right away. She'd lost in the Democratic primaries in 1962 and 1964 before finally winning her seat in 1966, but she'd already made ripples in Austin, thanks to her booming voice, obvious intellect, and eloquent speaking style. Though she made the news at first because of her unique status as a black woman senator, it wouldn't take her long to prove she was no fluke.

One of three daughters of Ben and Arlyne Jordan, Barbara grew up in a household that put a premium on hard work. She'd spent her childhood in one of Houston's poorer wards, but her father, who was a warehouse laborer before later becoming a Baptist preacher, worked to provide his family with a stable home life. Barbara took her work ethic from her father, and she excelled in Houston's public schools before graduating with honors from Texas Southern University. She then got her law degree from Boston University, and came back to Houston to open up a law practice.

Barbara was an imposing presence, a heavy-set woman who projected just about the highest degree of self-confidence you could imagine. Anyone growing up black in Texas during the '40s and '50s had to put up with being treated like a second-class citizen, yet Barbara always carried herself like she belonged absolutely anywhere she chose to be. From the very beginning, I knew her success in the legislature would ultimately be good for Texas, so I was determined to help give her the tools she'd need to succeed. As the only woman among 30 men — and the only state senator who couldn't get into private political watering holes because of her race, her gender or both — she was going to need the help.

At the very beginning of the session, I invited Barbara to come over to the House side and sit with me up on the dais. From there, I could point out various legislators on the floor and tell Barbara what she ought to know about each one. She'd sit up there with me, nodding her head as I whispered little tidbits of gossip, political stories, or strategies. She knew she was getting a one-of-a-kind crash course, and I could look at her and tell she was absorbing everything I was saying. I also told her most of what I knew about each of her fellow senators, and gave her suggestions how best to deal with them.

Barbara also became a regular at the evening sessions I held in the Speaker's apartment, located right in the Capitol building on the House side. Like Sam Rayburn's old "Board of Education," I liked to have legislators over for a few drinks and political talk in the evenings. At first, I just wanted to make sure Barbara was included. But soon it was obvious to everybody that she was fitting right in — I guarantee you what, that woman could hold her own with anyone when it came to drinking scotch and swearing a blue streak. That wasn't all we did in those sessions, of course, but like any bunch of men in Texas, it's fair to say our company wasn't a place for anyone with delicate sensibilities. Barbara loved it. For all her lofty oratory and regal bearing, I never heard anyone guffaw as loudly at a dirty joke as Barbara Jordan did.

Barbara was aligned with the party's liberal wing, but even from the beginning she took care to court the conservatives and moderates as well. She shocked her fellow liberals by befriending Dorsey Hardeman, an ultra-conservative from San Angelo who was one of the craftiest and most powerful senators in Texas. No one could quite believe it when Barbara began joining Hardeman for the occasional strategy session over whiskey, but she always placed her political needs above any personal feelings — an extremely useful skill that precious few politicians have. If I'd admired her for her perseverance in winning her seat, I now understood that Barbara was going to be a formidable politician in her own right, no matter where she came from or who she was.

In the meantime, on the House side, I continued to push for legislation I thought would help Texas — some of which was more progressive than what John Connally was willing to support. He and I still worked as closely as ever, but on certain issues we just had to agree to disagree. And as time went on it became clear that, despite his mostly forward-thinking views on education, civil rights and the future of Texas, Connally still held to some stubbornly conservative views — and he never appeared concerned in the least about who they might upset, a trait that would cost him political capital more than once.

One issue we disagreed on was the minimum wage bill. Texas needed a law that would protect the kind of workers we'd met on that dusty road outside New Braunfels in August of 1966, and I was determined to pass a bill in the House to set that in motion. Now, minimum wage legislation had never been a big issue of mine, and hardly anyone thought it could be passed in Texas anyway. But about two months after the New Braunfels incident, I'd traveled down to the Rio Grande Valley to have a look at the working conditions for myself, and during that visit I got converted to the cause.

I met with Bishop Humberto Medeiros down there, since the Catholic clergy in South Texas had been very involved in that summer's strike and march. Bishop Medeiros and I must have stayed up half the night talking about the hardships those workers were facing every day. He told me honestly that he didn't think a minimum wage of $1.25 an hour would make a whole lot of immediate economic impact — but then he said the words that convinced me it was worth pursuing anyway. "The one thing the law would do," he told me, "is send a message to these workers. For once, they would know that someone in Austin cared enough to look out for them. That's never happened before."

I suppose it sounds corny today, but I came away from that late-night meeting with a real determination to pass that legislation. I don't deny that I've got an ego, or that I enjoyed the power plays of the political game, or that I was as cynical in some ways as anyone in politics ends up being. But every once in a while in my career, there were moments when I truly remembered why it was that I got into politics. It's the same feeling I had looking up at the Capitol building the first time I went to blow the whistle on the Health Department scandal, or that I'd had way back when I read *Les Misérables* in high school — a sudden sense that you want to do something that really matters.

When I got back to Austin, I told my aides and colleagues I was going to pass a minimum wage bill. And all of them thought I was crazy. They told me I might as well just spend the time banging my head against a wall, as the effect would be the same. As it turned out, the bill was harder to pass than I thought — but that was due mostly to a committee chair who decided to go into hiding rather than deal with it.

Liberal Representative Honore Ligarde of Laredo sponsored the bill, which would establish $1.25 an hour as the state's minimum wage. I sent it down to the Labor Committee for a hearing, but committee chairman Gene Hendryx decided he'd rather just not hold that hearing, thank you very much. He knew I'd have a fit if he said that straight out to me, though, so instead, he just disappeared from the Capitol for a few days.

I don't know where he went, but I do know where he was found, thanks to a persistent reporter who tracked him down a few days later. The reporter sat down with Hendryx at the Forty Acres Club, and over a stiff drink asked him, "So, where you been, Gene?"

"I'm hiding from that goddamn Barnes!" Hendryx replied. "He wants me to call a hearing and pass out this minimum wage bill, but I ain't going to do it." It wasn't exactly a shining example of democracy in action — and it also didn't work. Hendryx ended up holding the hearing a few days later, and the debate was on.

Despite the fact that we started out with almost no support for the bill, I started a full-on campaign of fast talking and arm twisting. I worked my butt off and spent a lot of political capital trying to get that bill passed, even though most of my political allies, including Governor Connally, the moderate Democratic establishment and the business community, all hated it. Even my own father — who'd never said a word to me about my career since my election back in 1960 — offered the only direct comment he'd ever make about my involvement in politics. One afternoon when I was home in DeLeon for a visit, he looked at me and said, "Son, these peanut farmers down here don't like that bill at all."

"Well, I know, Daddy," I told him. "But it needs to be done. This is something I've got to do."

And we did it. We passed that minimum wage bill in 1967, and although it died in the Senate, I'm as proud of that victory as of anything I did as Speaker — and even though we couldn't get a law out of it, we did eventually get a $1.60-per-hour minimum wage law passed in 1969, when I was lieutenant governor. In that session, Barbara Jordan and I worked together to get it passed in the Senate — one of many times she and I would team up to try and push Texas toward the future.

———

BY NOW IT WAS CLEAR TO JUST ABOUT EVERYBODY THAT I WAS AIMING FOR higher office. For one thing, I'd turned the Speakership into a full-time job, working the political angles all year round. During the 18-month period between the end of each Legislative session (in odd-numbered years) and the next election day (in even-numbered years), most Speakers had traditionally gone back to their home districts, where they worked at second jobs and prepared for their reelection campaigns. But I spent my time traveling all over Texas to meet with constituents, all over the country for legislative conferences, and up to Washington to meet with President Johnson and other national leaders.

Yet, although I dedicated full-time hours to being Speaker, I did have a few business interests on the side. The annual salary for a representative in Texas was just $4,800 a year, so pretty much every legislator had a second job. I'd gotten to know several prominent and successful businessmen, including a hotel and construction entrepreneur named Herman Bennett, and I'd been invited to take part in several business ventures — invitations I'd gladly accepted. Any partnerships had to take into account the fact that, initially at least, I didn't have a lot of cash to put up front into the ventures. That's probably what set a few tongues to wagging in Austin.

The way it worked was this: Bennett would bring me into a partnership for a particular business or investment. In lieu of my putting cash into the venture, he'd spot me the money up front. For the investments that paid off, he would deduct the amount I owed him before doling out any dividends to me. Now, this was obviously a favorable arrangement for me. Bennett fancied himself my mentor, and he desperately wanted me to go into business with him as soon as I got out of politics — in fact, he kept urging me to go ahead and get out, so we could "make some real money together." But there was nothing illegal about what Bennett was doing, nor did he take any interest in legislation or political business in Austin.

My business interests were never a secret, and they weren't particularly out of the ordinary, but as my political profile rose it was probably inevitable that some people would try to stir up concern about them. A few negative stories about me started popping up during the 1967 session, speculating about how much money I'd been making and offering backdoor insinuations that I was receiving favors because I was Speaker. Ultimately, there was no fire to the smoke, and so apart from the occasional grumblings reported in the press, nothing ever came of it. But I do believe that those first few stories planted seeds that would later sprout into real trouble for me.

For the moment, however, I just kept my head down and kept working hard. For a young man from DeLeon, my position offered a chance to see things and meet people I'd never have thought possible — and I'll tell you what, I enjoyed every minute of it. From meeting cabinet members and Senators out at the LBJ Ranch, to hobnobbing in Houston with the Apollo astronauts, to having drinks in Austin with the likes of Willie Nelson and Ray

Price, I was having the time of my life. And there were plenty of funny, interesting, and just plain strange stories that went with the territory.

While I was Speaker, for instance, I'd worked hard to kill a couple of wiretapping bills. This was another of those issues that John Connally and I disagreed on — he kept telling me how important wiretapping was for law enforcement, and I kept telling him it would open the door for potential abuses. I fought hard against Connally and his allies on those bills, and when I managed to get them killed, I earned myself an unexpected admirer in the process: Jimmy Hoffa. He walked into the Speaker's office one afternoon, stuck out his meaty hand and said, "I want to shake the hand of the bravest man in America! As long as you're running, the Teamsters will be there for you!"

During the 60th Legislature in 1967, we also had plenty of national political figures come to Austin. Vice President Hubert Humphrey, Attorney General Ramsey Clark, and Secretary of State Dean Rusk all addressed joint sessions of the Legislature, and their visits were rounded out with barbecues out at the LBJ Ranch and dinners in Austin. As Speaker, I got to take part in all the events, and I tried to make the most of my time with these influential men. I also took every opportunity to spend more time with President Johnson, both on these trips and up in Washington.

There were a few funny episodes with famous visitors, too — like the time I met Congressman Wilbur Mills at the airport just before he was scheduled to give a speech. It was apparent that Mills, the chairman of the House Ways and Means Committee, had enjoyed a couple too many drinks on the flight down, so I spent the next 20 minutes walking him around the airport and pouring about a gallon of coffee in him, trying to sober him up. He might have been one of the most powerful men in Washington, but I led him around that airport just like a little child that day, helping him walk it off.

Another time, I had to scramble around to find comedian Bob Hope a masseuse in Brownwood, where he'd come to do a benefit for a university. Not surprisingly, there were no professional masseuses among the town's 18,000 or so citizens, and nobody had told us in advance that Hope would need one. So when he turned to me on the ninth green of a golf course and said, "When am I gonna get my massage?" I suddenly had visions of having to spend hundreds of dollars flying someone in because Bob Hope's shoulders were tired from the nine holes of golf we'd just played. But luckily, someone remembered about a housekeeper living down in the flats who knew a thing or two about massages, so I sent someone down in a car to fetch her. I never told Bob who she really was, and to tell the truth, he seemed to think she did a pretty good job.

But the funniest story was when my friend Chill Wills, a character actor in

Hollywood westerns, convinced me to meet with his speech coach to cure my bad manners and down-home DeLeon drawl. I flew to Los Angeles and went to one lesson, feeling a little silly but knowing that I probably did need some polishing — especially if I wanted to run for higher office. That evening after the lesson, I went to Chill's house to pick him up for dinner. While I was waiting in the living room, the doorbell rang. "Go on and get that!" Chill yelled from the bedroom. So I opened up the door, and there stood John Wayne.

I'm not often tongue-tied, but I didn't know quite what to say when the most famous actor in America was suddenly standing right there in front of me. I didn't have to say much, anyway, because right then Chill came blowing out of his bedroom, saying, "Howdy, John — you ready to go out on the town?" With that, the three of us hit the streets of L.A. for a night of dinner and drinking that I don't believe has ever been matched in history. I have never in my life seen anyone put away more whiskey than Chill Wills and John Wayne that night — those two drank like men dying of thirst. And by the time we straggled back to Chill's house at about 4 a.m., I knew I'd be hurting the next day.

Sure enough, when I woke up the next morning, my big old red-headed noggin felt like it was about to explode. When I went to the speech coach for my session, she took one look at me, shook her head, and said, "Ben, go on home and come back when you're not hung over." Well, that was all it took. I went straight to the airport, got on a plane, and flew home to Austin. And that was the extent of charm school for me.

DESPITE THE FAILED ATTEMPTS TO POLISH MY IMAGE, BY THE END OF 1967 I'D managed to raise my profile in national Democratic circles. In August of 1966, I was elected to the executive committee of the National Legislative Conference. In March of 1967, President Johnson named me as one of 26 members of the Advisory Commission on Intergovernmental Relations, a national board charged with studying relations among local, state and federal governments. And in July of 1967, I was voted president of the Southern Legislative Conference — the youngest person and first Texan to receive the honor.

These appointments only served to intensify the seemingly unquenchable thirst I had for politicking. I had no intention of simply being a figurehead in these organizations; right away I started plotting how to use my new positions to further the political causes I cared about. Unfortunately, one of the biggest issues I fought for at that time was a position I'd come to regret later. Throughout 1966 to 1968, I traveled around the country urging support for President

Johnson's policies in Vietnam.

I supported American involvement in Vietnam for a couple of reasons. For one thing, I believed in it on its merits. At that time, with the Cold War raging, the USSR beating us in the space race, and mainland China having converted to Communism, it really did feel like the world was becoming a battlefield between two warring ideologies. The theory of the "domino effect" felt real to me — if we didn't stop Communist expansion in Asia, then who would?

Like many of my fellow Democrats, I also wanted to support President Johnson. After the Civil Rights legislation passed, this was his biggest, most controversial issue as President, and he needed all the help he could get in drumming up support for his policies. He'd started his presidency with a mountain of goodwill, but by 1967 it was eroding quickly as more and more Americans became disillusioned over Vietnam. It was obvious that the war was beginning to tear the country apart, but Johnson's advisers pressed him to continue sending troops, and he put his trust in their judgment.

Johnson believed — and by extension, so did I — that we were giving our fighting forces the means to win that war. It wasn't until later that I realized how badly he'd been misinformed by the very men who should have been looking out for him.

A couple of times when I was at the White House, President Johnson invited me to join him down in the situation room. Once, I listened as Robert McNamara and General Westmoreland told him, "More troops, Mr. President. We need more troops to win this thing." I saw firsthand how much Johnson agonized over sending boys into battle. And I knew that his greatest desire was to fight battles on the home front, making better the lives of ordinary Americans rather than messing around in an unpopular war half a world away. Lyndon Johnson was a bull of a man, as strong and politically savvy as anyone I've ever known. But his anguish over the conflict in Vietnam caused him greater pain than I've ever seen another person bear.

I came to feel terrible regret over my actions in promoting the war. I'd traveled all over the country, making speeches and pushing for support of American involvement. I'd faced students and other protestors as they shouted, heckled, and threw things. Once, at the University of Texas, I stood in the back of a flatbed truck, shouting to be heard when all of a sudden a cup came flying out of the crowd, hitting me and spilling liquid all over my shirt. It was urine. After that happened, I just felt disgusted at the students who were protesting the war and railing against their President, and I'm sorry to say I lost some of my objectivity about them. In speeches, I began praising organizations like the Boy Scouts and ROTC students, while railing against the "beatniks and peaceniks" — thereby adding my voice to those that were dividing the country rather than healing the growing rift.

In my new leadership roles, I pushed for the national legislative bodies to adopt official resolutions supporting the war. When Robert Kennedy's supporters nearly succeeded in killing a pro-war resolution I'd pushed through the Southern Legislative Conference, I lobbied harder than ever to get it revived. When the National Legislative Conference tried to reverse a similar resolution, I managed to shoot that down too. I spent more political capital than anybody even knew I had in trying to stir up official support for President Johnson's Vietnam policies.

Day by day, week by week, month by month, America became more and more divided. All of a sudden, it felt like the whole country was being consumed by rage. I think the depth of it took nearly everybody by surprise — after all, ever since the start of World War II, we had been more or less united against foes both internal and external. We'd had a long period where Americans stood together — to fight the Nazis, to help rebuild Europe, to fight the new nuclear threat from the Soviets. But starting in the early 1960s, there was a series of events that created a lot of anger and frustration in America. I was too close to things to really see it at the time, but in the years since, I've thought a lot about how we got to the point we did in 1968, where the very notion of our united states started to break down.

I believe a lot of the anger and frustration stemmed not just from Vietnam, but from other events as well, such as the Cuban Missile Crisis, the assassination of John F. Kennedy, and — most especially — the upheaval caused by Johnson's push for civil rights. Lyndon Johnson had exhibited immense courage in pushing for the Civil Rights Acts the way he did. He felt like he only had a certain amount of time to do it, and by God, he was determined to get it done. He knew it would hurt the Democratic party in the long run, and he'd made his peace with that — but I don't believe he ever thought it would result in the kind of immediate national upheaval that it did. In fact, I believe he thought the opposite: that his civil rights legislation would have a calming effect.

He believed that because Martin Luther King Jr. and Ralph Abernathy were telling him so. The Civil Rights movement was the watershed social movement of the 20th century, and thanks to Dr. King, it was for the most part a non-violent one. But it still stirred up a lot of unrest and scattered violence across the country, and Dr. King and Rev. Abernathy kept pressing President Johnson to pass more legislation to calm things down.

As President Johnson told me in 1965, "King keeps telling me, 'Pass the Civil Rights Act, and we'll be able to get people off the streets.'" But in the end, even after Johnson put his presidency on the line to pass civil rights bills, the unrest only increased. And as protests over the Vietnam war grew, those two movements began to meld. The Vietnam war was, after all, a race and class issue too, because of the inequity of the draft. One of the things that pained President Johnson more than anything was the fact that the people who were now railing against him — the youth, the poor, and minorities — were the very ones whose lives he'd been working so hard to improve.

If Lyndon Johnson hadn't realized at first how divisive and destructive the fight over Civil Rights could get, he certainly must have after he received an envelope from the FBI in the White House one afternoon. Inside was an audio tape, and when the president played it, he was as shocked as he could be. When I came to Washington shortly after he received it, he decided to play it for me, too.

I'd come to the White House at Johnson's invitation, but instead of meeting him in the Oval Office, where I'd normally go, I'd been sent up to the residence on the second floor. The president met me there "I want you to hear something, Barnes," he told me. "You're not going to believe this." We walked into his bedroom, sat down, and he punched the "play" button on a tape recorder. And he was right — I couldn't believe what I was hearing.

It was a recording, obviously made in secret, of Martin Luther King Jr. in what I will only describe as a very compromising situation. There were voices of a couple of women on the tape, as well as that of another man. I literally could not believe that I was sitting in the White House, in the company of the president of the United States, listening to an embarrassingly intimate tape of the greatest civil rights leader in our history.

President Johnson wasn't playing the tape for prurient reasons. I think he just couldn't believe the lengths the FBI — and specifically, J. Edgar Hoover — would go to in an effort to discredit and threaten Martin Luther King. Hoover, who for my money is the lowest, most dirty-pool man in 20th-century American politics, was sending a message not only to King, but to President Johnson as well. The president was not a man who was easily intimidated, but I had to wonder what effect Hoover's proud display of blackmailing tactics might have on him. All he said to me was, "I want Hoover to destroy this tape, and all the copies of it."

I left the White House that day amazed at the lengths that some people in Washington would go to in an effort to bring down their political enemies. Little did I know that, soon enough, I'd gain firsthand experience of it.

PUSHING SO HARD FOR SUPPORT OF THE VIETNAM WAR WAS A MISTAKE I'LL always regret, but there was another, more personal mistake that I regret even more. In my capacity as Speaker of the House, I helped a couple dozen or so young men — boys from political families, some from wealthy families, and even a few Dallas Cowboys football players — avoid service in Vietnam by pulling strings to get them into the National Guard. I'm embarrassed to say that, at the time, I really didn't think much about it. And I didn't think about the young men who'd have to go fight in the war because someone else was getting their rightful place in the Guard.

One afternoon, a man named Sidney Adger called my office in the Capitol. Sid was a successful oilman from Houston who knew a lot of people in politics, and he and I had been friends — not close, but friendly — for a couple of years. He was better friends with George H.W. Bush, the Texas Republican who'd won election to the U.S. House of Representatives in 1966. And it was the Bush family he'd come to see me about that day.

Sid asked if I'd mind doing a favor for the congressman. He said that Bush's 21-year-old son, George W. Bush, was about to graduate from Yale, which would end his student deferment and make him eligible for the draft. Sid knew that, as Speaker of the Texas House, I was in a unique position of power — he knew I could make a call for Bush and recommend him for a spot in the Texas Air National Guard. There was a long waiting list of young men trying to get into the Guard, but if I could help Bush jump ahead in line, it would ensure that he wouldn't get sent to Vietnam.

Now, I'd known the elder George Bush for a few years, and in fact, a lot of people at that time expected us to run against each other for the U.S. Senate in 1970. Some people saw us as the two young up-and-comers of our respective parties — so there wasn't an immediately obvious reason why I'd want to do him any favors. But I looked at it as a simple political favor of the kind that might one day pay back a dividend or two. And I'm embarrassed to say that I really didn't think anything more of it than that.

So I made a call to General James Rose of the Texas Air National Guard, and recommended that they give the younger Bush a spot in the Guard. And just like that, George W. Bush jumped ahead of boys less fortunate than himself — boys with no political strings they could pull — to avoid service in Vietnam. I can't say for sure whether General Rose gave Bush his spot solely because of my call, but I don't doubt at all that it had an effect.

Nearly four decades later, during George W. Bush's 2004 campaign for reelection to the presidency, I appeared on an episode of *60 Minutes* to answer questions about that meeting and phone call. I told Dan Rather, who conducted the interview, exactly what I've just written here — which is exactly what I'd said all along, the very few times I'd ever spoken publicly about it. When the show aired, Republican political operatives and Bush family loyalists had a field day attacking me and claiming my recollections were false. So once and for all, in this book, I want to make a few things absolutely clear.

First, George H. W. Bush did not contact me personally to ask for this favor — nor have I ever once claimed that he did.

Second, Bush family friend Sid Adger did contact me, and asked specifically for me to help get George W. Bush a spot in the National Guard to keep him out of Vietnam. Did Adger do this at the request of the Bush family? I don't know, and have never claimed to know. It would seem a little strange for Adger simply to have done it on his own, but I don't have any knowledge of anything different.

Finally, I did make the call to the National Guard on George W. Bush's behalf, and he did jump ahead of others in line. Considering how many young men were on the waiting list at that time, there is absolutely no way Bush could have gotten into the Texas Air National Guard so quickly unless he had special help. All those who claim that Bush got into the Guard without having any strings pulled on his behalf are just flat wrong. Those are the facts.

When I agreed to appear on CBS's *60 Minutes* in October of 2004, I'd never spoken to any journalist about my involvement in getting Bush into the Guard. But I'd recently been caught on camera talking about the Guard issue at a rally for John Kerry in Austin, and that tape had aroused a whole raft of rumors and speculation. I felt like I needed to set the record straight, and I knew and respected Dan Rather, so I agreed to do an on-camera interview with him. Over the objections of many friends and political allies, I opened up on national television, knowing that I'd get hit by a barrage from Republicans no matter what I said — and that barrage did come. But it wasn't half as bad as the fusillade that brought down Rather and his associates after they aired another segment during the show that relied on apparently falsified documents.

Dan Rather is a good man and a fine journalist, but it's clear CBS made some mistakes in airing that segment. What's more unfortunate, though, is the fact that the uproar over the documents obscured the much more important issue: Did George W. Bush really serve his full time in the National Guard? I believe it's clear that he didn't. And I also believe that, regardless of whether he fulfilled his service or not, he acted shamefully in letting his millions of dollars worth of pilot training go absolutely to waste, just because of his personal whims.

For a man like George W. Bush, who would later make such a prideful show of his military experience, it was bad enough that he took advantage of family connections to avoid service in Vietnam. But then, after learning to fly in the Texas Air National Guard — at a cost to U.S. taxpayers of hundreds of thousands of dollars in training — he let his pilot's certification lapse because he refused to take a routine physical. This was exceedingly unusual, to say the least — why and how could a young officer simply decide he wasn't going to fly anymore, after taking advantage of all that training? Some speculate that Bush refused to take the physical because he was afraid it would show evidence of drug use. I don't know anything about that, but I do know that he wasted a lot of money and time — and a place in the Guard that could have gone to someone who took his responsibilities more seriously.

In the months leading up to the 2004 election, hundreds of journalists and political operatives tried to find evidence that Bush had not fulfilled his duties in the Guard. To date, no one has been able to find a definitive "smoking gun" — a document that proves Bush shirked his duty. And yet, I believe it's clear that Bush didn't fulfill his duties in the Guard after he transferred to Alabama to work on a political race. Bush's presidential campaign staff spent months trying to dig up evidence that he'd gone to his Alabama Guard meetings — but the only real "proof" they produced was that Bush had a dental appointment one day on the base. They couldn't even produce a single credible witness who could remember seeing Bush at the base on the many weekends he was supposed to be there. During the Vietnam conflict, any serviceman who missed more than three National Guard meetings was automatically supposed to be deployed to Vietnam. The fact that nobody in Alabama remembers seeing him report for meetings strongly suggests Bush missed a significant number of meetings.

Now, I didn't get into all that on the *60 Minutes* show, because I wanted to stick to what I knew 100 percent to be true. I've never changed my story on the issue of helping Bush get into the Guard, and I never will. Anyone who suggests otherwise is simply not telling the truth.

With all that said, I want to make clear how ashamed I am of what I did. I thought at the time that I was simply doing political favors, but as I got older, I came to realize I'd been playing God. For every privileged boy like George W. Bush that I helped, another young man was shipped to Vietnam. In the years since, I've wondered about the fates of those anonymous men, who were possibly killed or injured in Vietnam because of the strings I pulled. No one should have that kind of power, and I'll always be sorry that I used it in the way I did.

ABOVE: *The Texas of my youth, in the 1940s and '50s, was a place where family farms were still plentiful and high school football was king.* OPPOSITE TOP: *John Connally's election as Texas governor in 1962 launched the most productive and important alliance of my political career. During Connally's three terms as governor, we worked to try and push Texas toward a future beyond agriculture and oil.* OPPOSITE BOTTOM: *President Johnson knew how to earn a young politician's loyalty. I was just 25 years old, about to start my second term in the Texas House of Representatives, when I received this telegram from the White House.*

WESTERN UNION

TELEGRAM

W. P. MARSHALL, PRESIDENT

1201 (4-60)

The filing time shown in the date line on domestic telegrams is LOCAL TIME at point of origin. Time of receipt is LOCAL TIME at point of destination

DA12 RA030   1963 DEC 16 AM 8 54

R WA018 GOVT NL PD=THE WHITE HOUSE WASHINGTON DC 16=

ARRANGEMENTS COMMITTEE FOR BEN BARNES DINNER=

CARE I F BAY BROWNWOOD TEX=

I SALUTE BEN BARNES, ONE OF THE MOST OUTSTANDING YOUNG

LEGISLATORS IN THIS HOUR OF TEXAS HISTORY. I ADD MY WARM

CONGRATULATIONS TO THOSE OF HIS FRIENDS WHO HONOR HIM

TONIGHT IN BROWNWOOD=

LYNDON B JOHNSON.

OPPOSITE TOP: *In 1965, at age 26, I was elected the youngest Speaker of the Texas House since Reconstruction days. Here, I'm pictured at the Speaker's desk in 1967.* OPPOSITE BOTTOM: *As Speaker of the House, I had the privilege of getting to know political luminaries who came through Austin such as Secretary of State Dean Rusk, shown here addressing a joint session of the Legislature in 1967.* ABOVE: *After I became Speaker, I began spending more time with President Johnson. Here, he and I shake hands after a 1966 meeting in the Oval Office.*

PREVIOUS SPREAD: *At the 1965 unveiling of President Johnson's portrait in the Texas Capitol, I joined Lieutenant Governor Preston Smith (in glasses) and Governor Connally (right) in welcoming the President.* OPPOSITE TOP: *Vice President Hubert Humphrey, flanked by Governor Connally and me, addressed a joint session of the Legislature in 1968, the year he ran against a resurgent Richard Nixon for the Presidency.* OPPOSITE BOTTOM: *Christian evangelist Billy Graham offered frequent spiritual counseling to President Johnson during the Vietnam years. He also officiated at Johnson's funeral service in 1973.* ABOVE: *General William Westmoreland, shown here at the 1969 dedication of the Douglas MacArthur Academy of Freedom, pushed President Johnson to send more troops to Vietnam, leaving the president in an impossible position as the war intensified.*

OPPOSITE TOP: *As Vice President, then as President, Lyndon Johnson pushed for Texas to have a place in the growing field of space exploration. At a 1971 NASA event, Rep. Jake Pickle and I chat with Neil Armstrong, the first man to set foot on the moon in 1969.* **OPPOSITE BOTTOM:** *As an ambitious young statewide politician, I began getting some notice from national organizations and press outlets. Here, I'm pictured as one of the U.S. Jaycees' "Ten Outstanding Young Men," in a group that includes Jesse Jackson (front row, second from left), football player Gale Sayers (front row, second from right) and future Senator Jay Rockefeller (top row, third from right).* **ABOVE:** *At the 1968 Democratic National Convention in Chicago, the chaos on the streets was nearly matched by chaos in the convention itself. Here, Governor Connally huddles with a group of delegates as I get some input from two others at top left.*

ABOVE: *Barbara Jordan gained notice for being an African American woman in the Texas Senate, but she was no fluke. She was a formidable politician and a strong ally during my time as lieutenant governor.* OPPOSITE TOP: *George H. W. Bush and I were both expected to run against Ralph Yarborough for his Senate seat in 1970. I opted to run for lieutenant governor instead, and Bush ultimately got beaten by Lloyd Bentsen — a devastating loss that could have left his political career in tatters.* OPPOSITE BOTTOM: *Molly Ivins once wrote that the Texas Legislature was "the finest free entertainment in Texas. Better than the zoo. Better than the circus." Here, Sen. J. P. Word and I talk on the Senate floor in 1971.* FOLLOWING SPREAD: *At the dedication of the LBJ Library and Museum, Lyndon Johnson warmly shakes the hand of President Nixon, who at that moment was working to bring down the Texas Democrats any way he could.*

'DON'T MIND US—WE'RE JUST STANDING AROUND LOOKING SUSPICIOUS'

OPPOSITE TOP: *Frank Erwin, John Connally, Lyndon Johnson and I sit on the dais at the dedication of the Lyndon B. Johnson Library and Museum in 1971. Erwin, who became the most powerful non-politician in Texas, was an early mentor of mine.* OPPOSITE BOTTOM: *By the time British Prime Minister Harold Wilson, flanked by Lyndon Johnson and me, came to Austin in May of 1971, the Sharpstown scandal was rocking the Texas Democratic party.* ABOVE: *Lady Bird Johnson, shown with me at an Appreciation Dinner in 1970, is one of the most gracious and kind-hearted people I've ever known. During the difficult later years of Lyndon Johnson's presidency, she had a calming effect on him that was obvious to anyone who saw them together.* FOLLOWING SPREAD: *On Primary night in May of 1972, friends and advisers gathered around as I wrote my concession speech. Pictured from left to right are Bob Armstrong, Julian Read, Bob Strauss, George Christian, Ralph Wayne, me and Gaylord Armstrong.*

OPPOSITE TOP: *(left to right) Wayne Gibbens, John Mobley, Howard Rose, Larry Temple and Mike Myers were invaluable advisers to the Johnson-Connally wing of the party.* OPPOSITE BOTTOM: *Despite the fact that the Bush family wasn't too happy with my decision to appear on 60 Minutes and talk about the National Guard issue, I've always had a fine relationship with George H.W. Bush. Here, we shake hands at a mid-90s event for Rudy Giuliani, who's pictured at center.* ABOVE: *Bill Clinton won the presidency with a smart blend of moderate and progressive policies, credibility among Southern voters, and a campaign style that emphasized what Democrats were for rather than what we're against — all keys to revitalizing the Democratic Party today.*

Chapter Seven

Money, Marbles, and Chalk

IT WAS A TUESDAY NIGHT IN EARLY OCTOBER OF 1967 WHEN JOHN CONNALLY called a group of us down to the governor's mansion for a meeting. His third term as governor was almost halfway through, and now he had to decide whether to run for a fourth. Connally hadn't tipped his hand yet, but I knew he was leaning against running — though I still hoped we could convince him to change his mind.

A few weeks earlier, I'd revealed my plans to run for lieutenant governor in 1968, even though some had urged me to wait and see what Connally decided first. A contingent of Democrats wanted me to run for governor if Connally opted out, but I thought it wiser to go ahead and announce for lieutenant governor, for a couple of reasons. For one thing, I didn't want it to seem like I couldn't make a decision without Connally. Despite the fact that I'd bucked him often enough in legislative matters and had established my own place in state government, my political opponents still tried to paint me as little more than Connally's protégé. One even put out a mocking campaign slogan for my 1968 race: "Vote for the Barnes that John built."

I also hoped that if I went ahead and announced for lieutenant governor rather than governor, Connally would feel compelled to run again — if for no other reason than to defeat Preston Smith, who'd already declared for the governor's race. Connally and I had both bumped up against Smith on numerous issues, and neither of us felt he had the kind of vision Texas needed. If Connally ran, he'd beat Smith easily — but if not, Smith would be the front-runner.

The final reason I decided to go ahead and announce for lieutenant governor was that I was still only 29 years old, and I didn't want to push too far too fast. I was proud of having earned my House seat and the Speakership, but I was also very conscious of not seeming too politically ambitious, fearing it would turn voters away. I did want to run for governor or maybe U.S. Senator at some point, but there was plenty of time for that. The most important thing to do now was to keep building on the moderate-business alliance that Lyndon Johnson and John Connally had done so much to develop.

But despite my hopes that Connally would run again, he told us at that Tuesday night meeting that he was leaning strongly against it. He was concerned that Bobby Kennedy might win the presidential nomination over Lyndon Johnson in 1968, which would put him in the awkward position of having to run in tandem with a national candidate whom he disliked both personally and politically. He also was just plain tired from his five years in office. Because of our Constitution, the Texas governor's office is far less powerful than those of most other states, and Connally had gotten fed up with having to rely on others to get legislation through and make changes in the state government.

And there was another reason why Connally was leaning toward not running. Ever since that day in Dallas when he and Kennedy were shot, I think he'd been reevaluating — maybe not even consciously — his life and career. I've never had a near-death experience, but I'd imagine that anyone who goes through one spends some serious time thinking about his place in the world. And in the summer of 1967, Connally enjoyed a rare opportunity to get away from everything and think about things more than usual.

He'd been invited by ABC television to go on a six-week safari in Africa, where he and other celebrities would be filmed hunting exotic game for a show called *American Sportsman*. So off he went into the African bush with the likes of Bing Crosby, comedian Phil Harris, and *The Fugitive* actor David Janssen. For an avid hunter like Connally, tromping around in the jungle for weeks on end, tracking and shooting elephants, buffalo, gazelles, and leopards, was the chance of a lifetime. For the first time in years he truly got away from everything, and when he came back, he was in a more introspective frame of mind than I'd ever seen him. In fact, as I later learned, he'd made his decision not to run again while on that safari.

In the week following Connally's meeting at the mansion, a lot of people tried to convince me to change my mind and run for governor, but I just didn't feel like it was the right thing to do. To end any speculation, I made my official announcement for lieutenant governor exactly a week later, at a press conference in a room just off the House chamber, with my wife, Martha, at my side. Ever since news of Connally's late-night meeting had leaked to the press, Austin was awash in rumors that he'd been trying to convince me to run for governor. My continued insistence that I wouldn't switch was seen by a lot of people as further evidence that, although I was a close ally of Connally's, I was far from being simply his protégé.

It would be another month before Connally made his official announcement that he wasn't running, and plenty of people in Austin still believed he would change his mind. It wasn't out of the realm of possibility, but I'd seen something in John Connally's eyes that night at the mansion, and it seemed like this time his mind was really made up.

Though front-running Democrat Preston Smith was also in the moderate-conservative mold, the liberal Democrats and Republicans in Texas were as thrilled as they could be that Connally would at last be gone. He was the man who'd kept the moderate core of the party in a position of strength, and with him stepping down, both the left and right were just about hyperventilating at their newly brightened prospects. If there was anything I'd learned from my association with Connally and Johnson, it was the value of keeping the party core strongly allied with business, and I knew it would soon be time for me to step up and try to fill the void Connally was leaving. It was a daunting task, and there was no guarantee I'd have the same kind of success, but I was determined to try.

At Christmastime that year, I got the best encouragement possible. I'd been invited to a dinner party at Judge Homer Thornberry's house in Austin, and when I got there I found myself in the company of President and Mrs. Johnson and their closest friends and advisers in Austin. Their daughter Luci and her new husband, Pat Nugent, were there, as well as J.C. Kellam, who managed their radio and TV stations, and Donald Thomas, who was a business partner of Johnson's. Frank Erwin was there, too, and we all ate and drank into the evening, talking about politics and the future of Texas.

Toward the end of the evening, as the party was breaking up, President Johnson pulled me aside. "Ben," he said, "I want to tell you something. I don't know what's gonna happen, or what decisions you're gonna make in the years to come. But I want you to know one thing." Here, the President leaned in close, as I'd seen him do a hundred times with others. "I want you to know that I'm for you — money, marbles, and chalk."

Well, I'd never heard that particular phrase before, but I never forgot it. This was the first time that Lyndon Johnson had been so specific about his support for my political career, but it wouldn't be the last.

THREE MONTHS LATER, ON THE EVENING OF MARCH 31, 1968, I SAT WITH Frank Erwin and a few legislators in the Speaker's apartment watching President Johnson give a televised speech about Vietnam. Looking at his drawn face, it was obvious that the recent events at home and abroad had really taken a toll on him. In the four years since I'd first started getting to know him, I couldn't help but notice how the lines in his face had deepened, and how tired his eyes were, especially when he was talking about this most painful subject.

The president was trying to put a positive spin on the situation, revealing that he'd given orders to ratchet down the number of attacks on Vietnam in hopes that this would compel the North Vietnamese to come to the table for talks. He announced the appointment of Averell Harriman as his personal representative for any negotiations, and reiterated that we were ready to send our "representatives to any forum, at any time, to discuss the means of bringing this ugly war to an end."

But this optimistic beginning was followed by the grim realities of the kind that continued to haunt the President. A few moments later, he revealed that the Joint Chiefs of Staff were urging him to send 13,500 more troops to Vietnam, and that the war effort would require $2.5 billion more in the current fiscal year and $2.6 billion in the next. As he looked into the camera and delivered this difficult news, I found myself wondering how he was holding up as he prepared to launch into a politically difficult reelection campaign.

Then he started on a new tack. At first, it wasn't clear exactly where he was going with it.

> Fifty-two months and 10 days ago, in a moment of tragedy and trauma, the duties of this office fell upon me. I asked then for your help and God's, that we might continue America on its course, binding up our wounds, healing our history, moving forward in new unity, to clear the American agenda and to keep the American commitment for all of our people.
>
> United we have kept that commitment. United we have enlarged that commitment.
>
> Through all time to come, I think America will be a stronger nation, a more just society, and a land of greater opportunity and fulfillment because of what we have all done together in these years of unparalleled achievement.
>
> Our reward will come in the life of freedom, peace and hope that our children will enjoy through the ages ahead.
>
> What we won when all of our people united just must not now be lost in

suspicion, distrust, selfishness, and politics among many of our people.

Believing this as I do, I have concluded that I should not permit the Presidency to become involved in the partisan divisions that are developing in this political year.

At that last line, I sat up in my chair, suddenly aware of the possibility that something extraordinary was about to happen. You could have heard a pin drop among us as President Johnson went on to speak the words that stunned the whole nation.

With America's sons in the fields far away, with America's future under challenge right here at home, with our hopes and the world's hopes for peace in the balance every day, I do not believe that I should devote an hour or a day of my time to any personal partisan causes or to any duties other than the awesome duties of this office — the presidency of your country.

Accordingly, I shall not seek, and I will not accept, the nomination of my party for another term as your president.

None of us could believe what we'd just heard. No matter how trying the last few years had been, and no matter how frustrated I knew President Johnson was, I never imagined he'd simply take himself out of the running in 1968. Politics was that man's life — so removing himself from politics seemed akin to admitting his life was over. All I could think was that this was bad news for Texas, for the Democrats, and for the country, although I suspected that deep down, it must have also been something of a relief for the President and his family.

Not long after President Johnson's speech, the phone in my apartment started ringing. It was John Connally, and he wanted us to come down to the Capitol to talk about what had just happened. So Frank Erwin, State Executive Committee Chairman Will Davis, and I headed down to the Capitol, and for a couple of hours we met with Connally and a few others and talked about what we ought to do next.

Johnson's announcement immediately changed everything about the game, both nationwide and in Texas. Nobody relished the idea of Bobby Kennedy running away with the nomination in Johnson's absence — but we also feared that a deep split over the Democratic nomination might ultimately have far greater consequences than just on the 1968 race. With Johnson stepping aside, we also realized that Texas would, for the first time in decades, lack a national leader of his or Sam Rayburn's stature in Washington. And with

Connally stepping down at the same time, we needed to ensure that Texas Democrats would continue to have strong leadership to push the party into the future.

At the meeting in the Capitol that night, we talked about whether Connally should be named Texas's "favorite son" presidential candidate as a way of stemming the expected tide of support for Bobby Kennedy's candidacy, as well as uniting the state's Democrats, even just temporarily, under one candidate. We also talked about whether we should push for Connally as a Vice Presidential candidate on a ticket with Hubert Humphrey, the Presidential candidate of choice for Democratic moderates and conservatives. President Johnson's announcement would, we knew, give even more hope to Texas Republicans than Connally's had, and we were anxious to minimize any boost they might get from it.

The reality was, Texas Republicans had been biding their time until Johnson and Connally were gone — and they'd never been shy about saying so. In July of 1967, before either man had yet bowed out of politics, Republican state Senator Henry Grover had practically foamed at the mouth while talking about the possibilities for his party when those two were gone. "Texas, like most states of the South and West, is going Republican," Grover told a group of party supporters. "The only thing that keeps Texas Democratic is that President Johnson is from Texas." A former Democrat himself, Grover evoked a groan from the audience when he talked about the Democrats nominating either Bobby Kennedy or Vice President Humphrey in Johnson's stead. "That makes conservative Democrats groan just as much as you — don't think it doesn't," he said.

Two months before Johnson's announcement, syndicated columnists Rowland Evans and Bob Novak had also offered their unvarnished view of where Texas might be heading without Connally at the helm. In January of 1968, they wrote that conservative "Tory" Democrats had been hit by "paralysis," and suggested that "the strong possibility is a transfer of power in Austin next year to a Republican or — much worse from the Tory viewpoint — to liberal Democratic Senator Ralph Yarborough as governor." They went on to speculate that President Johnson had "abandoned" Connally, not urging him to run again in part because Johnson was "well aware of the governor's problems among [Mexican voters], whose power has been swelling."

Now, that prognostication, like so many offered up by journalists or columnists supposedly "in the know," was wrong. Johnson and Connally had in fact had several private conversations about their respective 1968 races, and Connally was one of the very few who'd known all along that the president was thinking of stepping aside. There was no feeling on Johnson's part that

Connally's relationship with Hispanic voters might hinder his race in 1968, partly because Johnson was already thinking he wouldn't run again. But it was unfortunately true that Connally's relationship with minority voters in Texas — both Hispanics and African Americans — had suffered in recent years. And soon enough, Connally would make remarks that would exacerbate those strains even more.

April 4, 1968, four days after Johnson's announcement, was a day packed full of campaign events for me. I drove down to Richardson for an early breakfast, then on over to Dallas for a mid-morning coffee meeting. That day's schedule included a luncheon, the official opening of my Dallas campaign headquarters, and a reception held by the Democratic party's precinct chairman. It would have been a normal day of campaigning — except for the unthinkable thing that happened just after 6 p.m. that day.

While I was making a speech in Dallas, Martin Luther King Jr. was shot to death on the balcony of the Lorraine Motel in Memphis, Tennessee. I got word of the assassination at the precinct chairman's reception, but I just couldn't believe it was true. There had been numerous terrible incidents in the struggle for civil rights, from the Birmingham church bombing in 1963, to the murder of three activists in Mississippi in 1964, to the shooting of James Meredith in 1966. But this was just impossible to fathom. The leader of the civil rights movement, the man who'd consistently preached non-violence and had given hope to millions of Americans, had been gunned down in cold blood.

Right away, I knew we needed to reach out to the many Texans who would be devastated by this news. The next morning I made a statement, just before heading back to Austin.

> My sympathy goes for Dr. King's wife and family. It was a terrible tragedy which adds more complications to our heavily burdened country. I hope all Americans regardless of race, creed or color will strive to follow the words of Dr. King, who continually advocated non-violence — all realizing that change and progress must come from the framework of the Constitution and laws of this country.
>
> Never before has there been a greater need for all Americans to work together with united spirit for greater opportunities for all Americans and for a greater respect for law and order.

Not long before I made my statement, John Connally was making unscripted remarks to the press in Weslaco. When I later heard what he said, I was just about struck dumb. There was one bit in particular that got people across the country — but especially African Americans — completely riled:

> Much of what Martin Luther King said and much of what he did, many
> of us could violently disagree with, but none of us should have wished him
> this kind of fate...
> He contributed much to the chaos and the strife and the confusion and
> the uncertainty of this country, but whatever his actions, he deserved not the
> fate of assassination.

I'll tell you what, this was about as tone-deaf a statement as anyone could possibly have made. For Connally to take a tragic moment like this and twist King's legacy around to make him seem little more than a rabble-rouser, and possibly even partly responsible for his own shooting, was more than I could comprehend. Connally later tried to back off his comments, but it was too late. He'd made his statement, and it didn't reflect well on him or on Texas.

This was one of several incidents that fed into the perception that John Connally was prejudiced. The perception had started early, when Connally opposed several of President Kennedy's civil rights initiatives. In mid-July of 1963, Connally had given a televised speech in which he objected to Kennedy's Civil Rights Act, on the grounds that it would infringe on the rights of those who own private property. And when Lyndon Johnson became President, Connally objected to one of his first civil rights initiatives — an anti-discriminatory housing bill that Connally thought was politically toxic. As Connally wrote in his memoirs, he and Johnson "[argued over] his social legislation, not the merit or justice of it, but the volume and speed with which these acts landed on states ill-prepared to process them."

That statement says a lot about John Connally and the decisions he made on sensitive issues. The truth is, Connally was capable of looking at legislation with a cold, hard eye, and judging it based on its political timing as much as its merits. When he met with that group of hot, dusty, tired farmworkers outside New Braunfels that day in 1966, he didn't see a group needing special attention — he saw a group wanting him to do something that he wasn't prepared to do for anyone, no matter who they were. He wasn't going to be in Austin on the day they wanted, so he simply told them he couldn't meet with them, and that was that. It didn't occur to him at first — nor did it occur to any of us — that it might look bad to present that message the way he did. At the time, we all felt we were handling that meeting in the most equitable way possible — by not treating the marchers any differently than we'd treat anyone else.

Connally said and did things that were hurtful and tone-deaf, and he took positions that would be unthinkable among politicians today. But there was another side of him — a side that showed itself in actions rather than words. When Connally was governor, he appointed over three thousand non-white candidates to state positions — more than all of the previous Texas governors combined. And his many education initiatives were aimed at raising the bar for all Texans, minorities included. Hispanics and blacks voted consistently for Connally over his Republican opponents, partly because he really did walk the walk.

One prime example came when Connally appointed Rev. C. A. Holliday, a prominent African American minister, to the Board of Corrections. There had never been a black person on the prison board, and a couple of state senators — including Barbara Jordan's "friend," Dorsey Hardeman — didn't like the idea too much. They started making noise about blocking the appointment, but Connally's response was swift and certain. "If you bust him," the governor told them, "I will appoint another black, and another, and another" until the legislators approved. John Connally put his political capital on the line, and that was all it took — the Senate approved Rev. Holliday by a solid majority. That, to me, is far more representative of John Connally's attitudes than the unfortunate comments he made about Martin Luther King.

———

THE YEAR 1968 WASN'T EVEN HALF OVER, AND ALREADY THE COUNTRY WAS suffering more upheaval than we'd seen in decades. The presidential election was up for grabs, one of the greatest civil rights leaders in history had been murdered, and cities all over the country had erupted in flames and rioting as anger over the assassination was violently unleashed. The news from Vietnam just kept getting worse, and as spring slid down into the first heat of summer, it felt like everyone was wondering the same thing: what could possibly happen next?

In the very early hours of Wednesday, June 5, we found out. At around 12:15 a.m., just after he'd claimed victory in the California Democratic primary, Robert Kennedy was gunned down in the pantry of the Ambassador Hotel in Los Angeles.

I'd spent the previous evening watching my six-year-old daughter, Amy, perform at a dance recital in Austin. It was a rare, brief respite from politics, and to tell the truth I felt a little relieved at having an early night for a change. I was dead asleep when my phone rang with the news. And I have to say, the disoriented feeling I felt had nothing to do with having been waked up suddenly, as it lasted well into the next day.

We'd just opened a special session of the Legislature — a rare occurrence in an election year — but as the sun came up that Wednesday and Senator Kennedy clung to life in a Los Angeles hospital, we knew we couldn't just go on with business as usual. Many of the legislators driving in to the Capitol for a day's work found out about the shooting on their car radios, and it was a somber group that assembled in the chamber that morning.

I made a short statement to the press, offering my sympathy to Ethel Kennedy and the rest of the family, and expressing concern that violence against our leaders seemed to be becoming commonplace. I closed by saying, "We hope and pray for Senator Kennedy's complete recovery," which at that point still seemed possible, if not likely. But Kennedy held on for just 24 more hours before dying on the morning of June 6.

Now, I will admit that I'd never had any particular affinity for Bobby Kennedy. He was a sworn political foe of my two closest political allies, and I believed that his brand of liberalism would ultimately prove damaging to the Democratic party. While I admired many of the stands he took — and agreed with many of them myself — I felt like he was too focused on the pure ideology of his positions, rather than the political reality of how to keep the party strong enough to be able implement them. But, his assassination was one of the great tragedies of the times. One thing Bobby Kennedy shared with his brother Jack was the ability to make Americans feel hopeful, and that was something we sorely needed in the darkening days of the late 1960s.

With Bobby Kennedy dead, the national Democratic party was thrown into tumult. Kennedy's victory in California on the night he was shot had all but ensured he'd be the nominee, and now the presidential race was left without the leaders of both the party's moderate wing and its liberal wing.

Connally and I moved immediately to make sure the Texas Democratic party wouldn't suffer similar disarray. We were helped by the fact that our slate for the fall elections had been settled back on Primary Day in May, when Preston Smith had beaten Eugene Locke and Waggoner Carr to win the nomination for governor, I had won the nomination for lieutenant governor, and Crawford Martin had won for attorney general. None of us was expected to face particularly strong Republican candidates in the fall, so it was clear that our party's grip on the statehouse would continue.

John Connally was a lame-duck governor, but he had no intention of relinquishing power in the state convention — or, for that matter, in the upcoming Democratic National Convention in Chicago. He was absolutely determined to control the state party's actions in the months leading up to the November elections. That might have been a tall order for a man of lesser charisma than Connally, but he never even entertained the thought that he wouldn't be the one pulling the strings, right up until the last day of his governorship.

The state convention opened in Dallas's Memorial Auditorium on Tuesday, June 11, just five days after Kennedy's death. Right away, Connally moved to establish his dominance. Over the scattered objections of the party's liberals, he pushed through the "unit rule" resolution that would allow him to control the Texas delegation's votes at the upcoming national convention in Chicago. Under the unit rule, all of Texas's 104 votes would go to the candidate who won the majority of the votes — if, say, Hubert Humphrey won 60 votes and the liberals' favorite, Eugene McCarthy, got 44, then all 104 would go to Humphrey. The benefit of the unit rule was that the bigger block of votes would give Texas more clout in the nomination process. The drawback, as liberals saw it, was that it "disenfranchised" them from having their votes count for their candidate.

In getting the unit rule passed, Connally also guaranteed that he'd be voted the "favorite son" candidate on the first ballot, if he so chose. This would ensure that Texas wouldn't have to commit to its true choice until the second ballot — giving the state even more clout as the nomination race heated up. These were classic political maneuvers to put the state in a position of strength, and Connally pulled them all off with aplomb. The unit rule was to stay in effect until Connally himself chose to release the delegates, making him the undisputed ringleader.

As soon as Connally got the unit rule passed, the liberals immediately began grumbling that it was undemocratic. But Connally was unbowed. Texas delegations had been operating under the unit rule for more than a hundred years. And as Frank Erwin put it to a reporter, "There's nothing unusual or sinister in this procedure. The state's influence [in Chicago] will be greatly increased."

Now Connally took steps to solidify his grip on power even more: not only would he help pick the 104 delegates Texas would send to the national convention, but he also engineered the selection of a close ally, Dallas lawyer Bob Strauss, to replace Frank Erwin as Democratic National Committeeman. All this happened in a matter of hours, and every time Connally's name was mentioned from the podium there were rousing cheers throughout the crowd, leavened by a smattering of boos.

A handful of liberals, seeing how badly they'd been outflanked, staged a walkout right at the end of the convention, after all the issues had been voted on. But even that was ineffectual — most of the other delegates, including some of their fellow liberals, didn't even realize they'd left. They went down to the Baker Hotel for a half-hearted session in which several speakers denounced Connally for everything from his position on Vietnam to his remarks following Martin Luther King's assassination. But their "rump convention" didn't detract in the least from the ovation that Connally was receiving back at the auditorium.

With a finely tuned sense of showmanship, Connally made a grand entrance just as the convention was winding down. The crowd went crazy as he stood at the podium, drinking it all in. He saw his "favorite son" status "not as a place of aspiration and ambition," he told the cheering crowd, "but rather as a point for the articulation of the basic principles that have made this nation great and good." With that, we were ready for Chicago.

Chapter Eight
The National Nervous Breakdown

THE AUTHOR DAVID HALBERSTAM ONCE WROTE THAT, IN 1968, AMERICA WAS "on the verge of a national nervous breakdown." If that's the case, then the three days of the Democratic National Convention in Chicago was the time we just about fell right over that brink. There had never been a convention quite like that one, and hopefully there never will be again. And not surprisingly, a whole lot of the uproar — inside the convention walls, at least — had to do with Texas.

Lyndon Johnson's withdrawal and Bobby Kennedy's death had left the national Democratic party in disarray. And now, eight years after Sam Rayburn had warned me to stop him at all costs, Richard Nixon was roaring back into the national scene, running strong against Ronald Reagan and Nelson Rockefeller in the race for the Republican nomination. At the Republican National Convention in Miami on August 8th, Nixon surged ahead to win the nomination, completing an amazing comeback from his loss in the 1962 California governor's race. In his acceptance speech, Nixon pledged to bring "an honorable end to the war in Vietnam," hitting at the Democrats right where we were most vulnerable.

The war was tearing America apart, and it was driving a wedge down the heart of the Democratic party as well. Our moderate wing felt like we needed to support President Johnson and provide continuity in existing national policy. The liberal wing wanted to denounce the war, period. With the war already so unpopular among most Americans, we knew we had our work cut out for us if we wanted to sell our presumptive candidate, Vice President

Hubert Humphrey, to the American voters. After all, Humphrey represented the face of an administration that had steadily lost popularity as the news from Vietnam grew grimmer. Add to that the fact that Humphrey, while as decent and honorable a man as you'd ever find in politics, was proving to be a wishy-washy candidate, and we knew we might be in trouble.

Humphrey's nickname was the "Happy Warrior," and he had an upbeat personality that won him a lot of supporters. But especially in contrast to President Johnson, Humphrey just didn't have the kind of sharp political sense he needed to have during those uncertain times. At that moment, we needed someone who'd step up and grab hold of the party by the scruff of its neck, like John Connally had done in Texas during our state convention. But Humphrey was either too nice of a man or too uncertain of himself to do it.

Humphrey knew he couldn't win the presidency without Texas — not just our electoral votes but our political support as well — so he worked hard to get our state's Democrats on board with his campaign. He made some effort to win Connally over, but it was already clear to him that Connally wasn't thrilled with his candidacy, and that the two men were too different to form much of a bond — political or otherwise. So Humphrey turned his attentions to me.

Just two weeks before the convention, Humphrey came to San Antonio and asked me to meet with him for a private breakfast. He was staying at the Hilton Palacio del Rio, so I made my way there early on the morning of Saturday, August 10th, and went up to his hotel room, where we wouldn't have to worry about being overheard.

Humphrey and I sat down in his suite, and I told him that, at a recent meeting of the Southern Legislative Conference, I'd gotten an earful from state leaders about how George Wallace, who was campaigning on a segrega-tionist platform for the American Independent Party, was running strong enough to be a threat. They believed Wallace might even win a few states, unless the national Democrats toughened up their stance on issues that mattered to conservative Southerners — things like law and order and a clamp down on the violence that had exploded in American cities.

Humphrey took all that in, then steered us to a theme I already knew well: he wanted me to head up his campaign in Texas. He'd made his first overtures a month or so earlier, and my response then had been noncommittal. I wanted Humphrey to win, of course, but the political calculus of joining his campaign was complicated. In the long run, I felt like it would be better for the party and for Texas if I kept a united front with Connally — especially because I knew Connally didn't want me to head up Humphrey's Texas campaign. In fact, the whole situation between Connally, Humphrey, and me was threatening to get a little sharp-edged, with Humphrey misplaying his hand by continuing to try and win me over, away from Connally. At our breakfast meeting, for example, he urged me to act as a floor leader at Chicago. I won't deny that I was pleased to have been asked, but this was another political minefield I didn't want to get stuck in.

By the end of our meeting that morning, Humphrey hadn't gained anything he wanted, and I was, if anything, feeling even worse about his candidacy than I'd felt going in. The next week, on a flight down to Florida in advance of a National Legislative Conference Meeting, I told a reporter — off the record, or so I thought — that Humphrey needed to "shape up," or he ran the risk of losing the support of Texans such as President Johnson, Governor Connally, and myself. The reporter printed my comments, and I got some flak over them, but the substance was true. If Humphrey was going to have a chance of winning against Nixon, there were certain stances he absolutely had to take. And as it turned out, a big part of the convention was the behind-the-scenes story of our battling Humphrey to take them.

The week before the convention opened on August 26th, I told Humphrey I couldn't agree to head up his campaign in Texas. I also responded publicly to his request that I serve as floor leader, by referencing the relationship between Humphrey and Connally. As I told a reporter, "I'm a delegate committed to John Connally as a favorite son candidate for President. I have no other role to play. If Governor Connally and Vice President Humphrey get together, it could change my situation." I had absolutely no intention of acting as a maverick and adding further disarray to the mess the party was already in. As we'd all soon see, things were perfectly capable of getting messier on their own.

———

LIKE AT ANY POLITICAL CONVENTION, MUCH OF THE REAL WRANGLING IN Chicago took place not in front of the cameras, but in the days leading up to all the pomp and ceremony. Relations between John Connally and Hubert Humphrey were getting chillier by the hour, as the Vice President seemed to be planning an end-around designed to thwart Connally politically. On the Wednesday before the convention, Humphrey had released a letter saying he favored abolishing the unit rule — despite the fact that he'd earlier promised Connally it would stay in effect. Connally was furious at this double-cross, but Humphrey was doing precious little to mollify him.

On top of that, we learned that the platform committee was thinking about inserting softer language into the Vietnam plank — things like an unconditional bombing halt and unilateral cessation of U.S. combat actions. At this, Connally went absolutely crazy. He'd been scheduled to go up to Chicago on a specially chartered "Texas Chief" train on August 23, with a whole group of Texas Democratic delegates, but with this new development he knew he couldn't wait. He flew immediately up to Chicago to try and urge the platform committee back into a more moderate stance on Vietnam.

On Thursday, August 22nd, Connally spoke in front of the committee, offering up the kind of clear vision and sharp, soaring rhetoric that Humphrey had so far seemed incapable of summoning himself. "It is cruel and evil," he told the committee members, "to encourage or promote hope of peace without tangible assurance of achieving such peace. These are strong words, I know, but these are times for strong words... Whether we like it or not, we are the leader of the free world. We are the bulwark of liberty. We cannot evade our responsibilities in Vietnam or elsewhere." His ended his speech with a plaintive appeal to support President Johnson in the Vietnam plank. "I would implore this committee," he said, "to write a plank which supports the determined fight of this Administration to preserve not only our own freedom, but to help provide the opportunity for freedom for peoples everywhere." When he finished, the committee members jumped to their feet and gave Connally a standing ovation.

Connally's intervention certainly had an effect on the committee — but so did an event on the other side of the world. On August 20th, just two days before Connally's speech, Warsaw Pact military forces had invaded Czechoslovakia, putting an end to the "Prague Spring" and bolstering Connally's argument that the U.S. needed to stand strong in the face of continuing Communist aggression. Connally's words, coupled with the television images of Soviet tanks rolling through Prague, were all the committee needed to push through a tougher Vietnam plank. Though the full convention would still have to vote on both possible planks, Connally had won the first of many skirmishes in Chicago.

While all this was going on, I was down in Miami for the annual meeting of the National Legislative Conference. I'd just been elected president of the organization, and one of my goals during the meeting was to push through yet another resolution on Vietnam. Though I later came to regret having pushed so hard for pro-Vietnam resolutions, at that time, with the presidential election in the balance, I believed then — and still believe — that the Democratic party needed to show a united front to run strong in the fall. That would offer us our only hope of Humphrey beating Richard Nixon, who was at that point running solidly ahead of Humphrey in the polls.

There's just no easy way to sum up the very complicated relationship between the Vietnam war, the Democratic party, and the elections of 1968. If we hadn't become so mired in the war, Democrats could have run on a plat-form extolling all the strides President Johnson had made in improving lives of ordinary Americans, making civil rights a reality, and competing with the Soviet Union in the space race and Cold War. We could have offered a message about keeping Americans safe at home, and of keeping the nation economically strong. But Vietnam thrust a dagger right through all that. There would be no winners in that conflict, and the end was nowhere in sight. Yet it was clear that we couldn't simply abandon the President, and abandon the tack that the party had taken over the past few years, without losing a moderate voting segment that we desperately needed.

In many ways, this was just a larger version of the ongoing struggle we'd been facing in Texas. The only way we could win was by keeping the moderates and lib-erals together — but that task was proving more complicated than herding cats.

Connally might have won his first battle in Chicago, but there were more to come. Still angry over Humphrey's about-face on the unit rule, he now threatened to withdraw the Texas delegation from the convention altogether. Humphrey and Connally both knew that Humphrey had enough votes to secure the nomination — unless, that is, something extraordinary took place. And John Connally was the kind of man who could arrange for such an extraordinary event. As the battle over the unit rule heated up, it seemed he might do just that.

A couple of days before the convention started, Frank Erwin announced to the Rules Committee that the Texas delegation might well nominate Lyndon Johnson if the unit rule was abolished. Governor Connally seconded this bombshell, telling reporters that "there is a growing sentiment to make that nomination, period." This, of course, caused no small amount of consternation — for about 24 hours, anyway, until President Johnson himself shot it down when he told a reporter, "I am not a candidate for anything, except maybe the rocking chair." In fact, in a very unusual move, Johnson wasn't even planning to attend the convention. Considering the reception Texans were destined to get in Chicago, the sad truth is, he was probably better off staying at his ranch.

The Rules Committee voted 18 to 3 to recommend abolishing the unit rule — but the battle was not yet lost, as the committee scheduled a full floor vote on the issue for the first night of the convention. And there was even more in store for us when the committee heard a request by liberals that the Texas delegation be refused our place at the convention because we supposedly didn't adequately represent Mexicans and African Americans. The committee turned down the request, but the liberals appealed and won the right to a floor vote on that issue, too. So even before the convention began, we knew that Texas was going to be in the middle of just about everything — the rules and seating votes, the Vietnam plank vote on Tuesday, and ultimately the nomination vote on Wednesday.

With so much at stake, John Connally now played another high card on Humphrey when he threatened to arrange a "favorite son" revolt by the Southern states if Humphrey didn't respond to Texas's concerns. Connally still had the power to deny Humphrey the first-ballot nomination by urging Southern states to vote for their own "favorite son" candidates. And Humphrey had to know he wasn't afraid to do it.

Down in Miami, where I was still at the NLC meeting, a couple of reporters asked me about the growing fracas in Chicago. They knew I was in regular contact with Connally, and that I'd know exactly what he was trying to do. So I told reporters the facts. I said that Humphrey couldn't win the election without Texas, and if he hoped to do it, he'd need to take a strong stand in support of Johnson and his Vietnam policies. "I'm concerned about how active Johnson will be in the campaign if Humphrey takes an anti-administration position on Vietnam," I went on. "If Humphrey continues making dovish statements and takes [liberal candidate Eugene] McCarthy for his running mate, he'll make it much more difficult for the Texas Democratic leadership to support him, and make it much more difficult to carry Texas in the national election." It's hard to overstate just how important Texas was going to be for Humphrey in the election — but I wasn't sure that Humphrey himself understood that quite yet.

On Sunday, August 25th, at Dallas' Love Field, I boarded a flight — dubbed the "Texas Favorite Son Charter" — with several dozen other Texas delegates for the trip to Chicago. We arrived in the early afternoon to find a passel of journalists there to greet us. Because I was co-chairing the Texas delegation with Connally, the reporters singled me out right away for questions about his relationship with Humphrey — all of which I answered with noncommittal observations about our goal of better party unity, so as not to stoke further the fires that were already growing.

When our group of delegates got to the Conrad Hilton Hotel on Michigan Avenue, I couldn't believe what a ruckus was going on already. The convention hadn't even started yet, but there was chaos everywhere. The hotel had been overbooked, and frustrated delegates were crowded around the front desk, demanding rooms for themselves. Rooms with only one bed were crammed with four and five delegates — and those who found themselves without rooms couldn't even call other hotels because there was a telephone strike going on in Chicago. To make things even worse, most of the city's taxi and bus drivers had gone on strike as well, creating even more of a mess in the streets.

Hundreds of protestors had already descended on the city, and many of them had stationed themselves in Grant Park, just across from our hotel. You couldn't come into or out of the Conrad Hilton without encountering a mob of screaming, spitting demonstrators, and they definitely weren't shy about getting right up in your face. At one point during the convention, I nearly got in a fight when one long-haired young man lunged at me to try and rip my delegate badge off my jacket. At another, a mob of protestors surrounded our car outside the hotel, blocking us in.

When they started jumping on the bumpers and rocking the car like crazy, back and forth, my aide Nick Kralj reacted in true, if unexpected, Texas style. He pushed his way out of the car and whipped out a pistol he'd brought with him from home. "Everybody move back!" he shouted, holding the gun high above his head. "This car is moving through!" I'll tell you what, those people parted like the Red Sea. From the looks on their faces, I don't believe they'd seen anything like that before.

We'd scheduled a caucus for the Texas delegation on the evening of Sunday, August 25th, the day before the convention opened. The meeting would take place up on the 8th floor, where we'd established our headquarters and where Connally's and my suites were located. Because we'd been warned about the phone strike that was wreaking havoc across Chicago, I'd brought down a bunch of walkie-talkies with me, so we were able to keep in touch with each other and with our delegates at all times.

At the two-hour caucus meeting, it was clear to everybody that Governor Connally was still burning over Humphrey's unit rule double-cross and his weak stance on Vietnam. He told us he still intended to have his name placed in nomination as Texas's "favorite son," thereby denying Humphrey our votes on the first ballot. Withholding our 104 votes wouldn't be enough to deny Humphrey the nomination, but it would certainly send a message. And if Connally was so inclined, he could still urge other Southern states to do the same, which could indeed add up to enough votes to thwart Humphrey on that first ballot.

What happened next was one of the finer moments the Texas Democratic party had enjoyed in recent history. Despite the legacy of friction between our state's liberals and moderates, and despite the fact that some delegates were put off by Connally and his views, the full caucus vowed to stick with Connally — no matter whether the unit rule was officially abolished or not. They had committed to go with the governor as a favorite son, and by God, they were going to do it for the good of Texas. In that room, at that moment, Texas Democrats demonstrated the kind of unity that we desperately needed the whole party to share.

Now, with his delegation in hand and the convention opening the next evening, Connally knew it was time to confront Hubert Humphrey face to face.

━━━━━━━

ON THE AFTERNOON OF MONDAY, AUGUST 26, JOHN CONNALLY AND I MET with Humphrey in his suite on the 25th floor of the Conrad Hilton. We were joined by Humphrey's convention manager Larry O'Brien and Texas Democratic Party Chairman Will Davis. Typical of Connally, he didn't waste any time on pleasantries before getting right to what was on his mind.

First, he chastised Humphrey for having yanked the rug out from under Texas in recommending the unit rule be scrapped. "We came into this convention under the unit rule," he said, his voice even, "and we held our state conventions under the unit rule. And we're not going to change the rules in the middle of the game."

Second, he told Humphrey he needed to get a handle on what was happening outside the convention hall. The hippies and protestors who had gathered in Chicago were creating a huge uproar — and the convention hadn't even started yet. There was a feeling that things were already out of control, and the tepid response from Humphrey, the party's leading figure in President Johnson's absence, made it seem like no one was at the wheel. "You've got to get up and speak for law and order," he told Humphrey, "or we'll never get over this convention."

Connally had started off the meeting using a firm but civil tone of voice. But the more he poked at Humphrey for his failures of leadership, the hotter he got. The problem was, Connally didn't just want to tell Humphrey what he ought to be doing differently right here, right now in Chicago — the truth is, he wanted him to be a different kind of candidate altogether. Connally was the quintessential executive personality, the kind of man who made firm, quick decisions and who wasn't afraid to hurt feelings or make enemies if it got the job done. As Jake Pickle often described him, he was "sometimes wrong, but never in doubt!" And being that kind of man, he simply couldn't abide watching Humphrey, the party's presumptive nominee, waffling back and forth and letting himself be blown about by the winds of circumstance. Connally saw a weakness and indecision in Humphrey that threatened to cripple the Democratic party, just when we needed to band together as strongly as we could.

About a half-hour into the meeting, when the discussion turned to Humphrey's waffling on the Vietnam plank, Connally absolutely let loose. I'd seen him angry many times before, but this was ferocious — his face reddened and the veins on his neck popped out as he lit into Humphrey about his disloyalty to President Johnson. "You're turning your back on the man who got you this far!" Connally roared. "You wouldn't even be in Chicago if it weren't for Lyndon Johnson!"

Humphrey just sat there and took it, which only served to make Connally even angrier. He launched into an absolute barrage, and Humphrey continued to sit passively, his face pale and sweat dotting his brow, looking near tears. As Will Davis later told one of Connally's biographers, "The tonguelashing [Connally] gave him ... was an epic... He orally spanked that man as hard as I've ever seen anyone chastised. He either strengthened Hubert's backbone, or gave him some, or scared him half to death."

Toward the end of the meeting, Humphrey told us he'd fix the mistake he'd made in urging abolishment of the unit rule. He said he'd officially oppose changing the rules for this convention, and make that known to the other delegates prior to their vote on the convention floor. He also reiterated his support for the tougher Vietnam plank Connally had won from the Platform Committee. All in all, Humphrey essentially capitulated on just about everything Connally wanted from him. We left the meeting with mixed feelings — happy that we'd turned Humphrey around on a couple of things, but still worried that we had a candidate who seemed like he could be swayed by whoever managed to speak to him last. And as we'd soon learn, even when Humphrey promised us something, that didn't mean it would happen as we expected.

A few hours after that meeting, at 6:30 p.m., the convention officially opened at the International Amphitheatre, down by the Chicago stockyards. This was the evening when the delegates would vote to either seat the Texas delegation (and the Georgia delegation, which was also under fire) or accede to the liberals' complaints and deny us our place in the hall. Connally and I expected the seating vote to come earlier in the evening than the unit rule vote, for a simple reason. If we won the seating vote first, our delegation would not only be granted its legitimate place, but we would then officially be bound by the rules of the 1964 convention — which recognized the unit rule as legitimate. This was an obscure little piece of rulemaking, but Connally and I both understood that it offered Humphrey a way to ensure we got exactly what he'd promised us. And so we expected him to make sure it would happen that way.

But instead, to our surprise, convention organizers called for the Rules Committee votes first. This meant that if the delegates voted to abolish the unit rule, the whole convention would be subject to that stricture — no matter what happened with our delegate seating vote. Once again, Connally felt double crossed by Humphrey. And his anger only rose when Humphrey offered no more than a token, too-late effort to convince the delegates to vote for keeping the unit rule. He'd promised us he'd fight for us, but all he did was send his aides into the hall about an hour before the vote to pass around a letter. He'd later claim that he didn't realize they planned to hold the vote so soon, but that was hardly a consolation. He'd either done it purposefully, or he didn't know what was going on at his own convention — neither of which was a particularly encouraging prospect. A disgusted Connally told reporters, "This has to have serious repercussions against the nominee in November, whoever he is."

Now, it may seem like all this back-and-forth over convention rules is just a lot of silliness. In the grand scheme of things, you might argue that in the face of serious issues like Vietnam and the clashes between the police and protestors outside the convention walls, these kinds of battles were unimportant. But the thing was, they pointed up to more serious problems with Humphrey and his campaign. At every turn, we got more evidence that the lines of communication and the level of leadership within Humphrey's campaign were completely inadequate. These rules fights were merely the obvious symptoms of a larger affliction.

At any rate, faced with this sudden debate and vote on the unit rule, we sent Tom Gordon of Abilene up to speak in favor of keeping it. He hadn't even finished uttering his first sentence when you could hear the boos start echoing through the hall. This was the first time — but by far not the last — that a Texan would find himself booed during the convention.

Despite Gordon's admonishment that the convention was "changing the playing rules in the middle of the ball game," the delegates quickly abolished the unit rule by a voice vote. John Connally, however, had no intention of abiding by a rule change he felt was unfair. On the very next issue, a roll-call vote on another rule, Connally stood and thundered, "Mr. Chairman, Texas — voting under the unit rule — casts 104 votes no!" This pronouncement was met by more boos, and the anti-Texas sentiment of the convention grew even deeper.

A couple of hours later, we found out just how deep that sentiment was. We knew we'd still have to face a vote on seating our delegation, but neither Connally nor I had been worried about the outcome. The liberals' objection was politics as usual, and we knew it would have been very unusual to deny us our seats based on such a complaint. But as the clock ticked past midnight and the delegates began casting their votes, we suddenly realized the tally would be much closer than we'd thought. With reporters surrounding Connally and me on the floor, Connally admitted, "I didn't think it would be this close, but I had never tallied the vote."

In the end, we won the vote 1,368 to 955, and as the first day of the convention wound down at around a quarter to three in the morning, the Texas delegation was bloodied but unbowed. President Johnson had sat up watching the televised battle at the LBJ Ranch, with Lady Bird at his side. As soon as the clock had struck midnight, it was his birthday, and although the first day of the convention had offered precious little in the way of gifts for him, I knew he was hoping for a much greater gift on Tuesday or Wednesday. It was a hope he dared not reveal publicly, but one that anyone who knew him well had seen in his eyes over the past few months. He desperately wanted to be drafted by the convention to run in November — and what better day to do it than on Tuesday, August, 27, his 60th birthday?

When Lyndon Johnson had taken himself out of the race during his March 31 speech, he'd done it for good reasons. The presidency had weighed heavily on him — his health wasn't good, he was tired, and the prospect of continuing to wrestle with the Vietnam conflict loomed like a specter over a potential second term. His father and grandfather had both died relatively young, and he had real doubts that he would live to see the end of another four-year term. He'd also hoped that his withdrawal from the race would serve to activate the Paris Peace Talks, perhaps ultimately bringing an end to the conflict that had dogged his presidency.

President Johnson didn't really want to run again, and he certainly didn't want to serve four more years. But there's no doubt that he wanted to be asked. For all of his legendary brusqueness, his sometimes-coarse manner, and his brash displays of political power, he was far more thin skinned than most people realized. The simple truth was, he wanted his party to want him — he wanted to be needed.

There were rumors that the President might make a surprise visit to the convention on his birthday, but as we gathered in the amphitheatre for the Tuesday session, he instead made his way from the ranch to Austin for a private birthday gathering. No matter how much he desired it, Johnson must have realized that there was no chance the convention would try to draft him. In fact, pretty much the opposite was happening — at this point, just about any mention of Johnson's name was greeted by boos and hissing throughout the hall.

I didn't believe that drafting President Johnson would have been a good idea, but it tore me up to see how he was being treated in that convention hall. This was a man who'd given his all to his country, who'd overseen the greatest advances in civil rights since Abraham Lincoln, and who'd done more for ordinary Americans than any President since FDR. No matter what people thought of him personally, Lyndon Johnson was a man who truly cared about giving Americans a better life, and he'd put himself on the line time and time again to prove it. Yet here was his own party, booing and hissing him like he was some kind of criminal. It was, and remains, one of the most egregious insults ever perpetrated on an American President by his own party.

At the front of the convention hall, Anita Bryant sang "Happy Birthday" to the President, and the delegates responded with restrained applause. And this was as good as it would get for LBJ on Tuesday, as the vote on the Vietnam plank — the vote that could ultimately vindicate him — was pushed back to Wednesday at the urging of liberal delegates. The debate and vote on Vietnam would precede the first ballot for the presidential nomination.

Before Tuesday was over, though, John Connally would offer a gift to Hubert Humphrey. For days, he'd been holding his "favorite son" nomination over Humphrey's head, but now that Humphrey had come around on the Vietnam plank, Connally was ready to release his delegates. Texas, South Carolina, and Tennessee all released their delegates on Tuesday, ensuring Humphrey would win the nomination on the first ballot.

The next day, during the vote on the Vietnam plank, the Texas delegates once again showed their unity. Without the unit rule binding them, our delegates were free to vote how they liked — and it was no secret that several of them intended to vote for the more liberal, minority Vietnam plank, rather than the plank Connally had pushed through with the Platform Committee a week earlier. But Connally and I talked to each delegate — and to other states' delegates as well — and urged them to support Johnson. "Let's go into this with a united front," I told the Texas delegates. "Let's do this for the President."

There was an hour of argument for each plank, and then the vote on whether to adopt the minority plank. At our urging, every single Texas delegate agreed to vote in support of President Johnson. So when the time came to record our state's votes on the liberal plank, Governor Connally was able to bellow with great pride, "Texas casts 104 votes no." Like they'd done during our Sunday night caucus, the Texas delegates had swallowed their differences and banded together. For President Johnson, this was at least a salve to the wounds he'd suffered during the convention so far. When the vote was counted, the majority plank had been adopted 1,567 to 1,041.

With the passage of the more moderate Vietnam plank, we'd pretty much accomplished what we'd set out to do in Chicago. Humphrey easily sewed up the nomination on the first ballot later that evening, and then the only thing left was for him to choose his running mate. Even though President Johnson had withdrawn from the race, the Democratic party had at least chosen his Vice President as its candidate, and had adopted a moderate Vietnam plank in keeping with his policies. These choices would not only help preserve Johnson's legacy, but more importantly, they'd give us a better chance of winning against Nixon in November.

———

SHORTLY AFTER THE END OF THE CONVENTION, HUBERT HUMPHREY PAID a visit to Houston. It was a short trip, notable mostly for the fact that nobody in Texas Democratic politics seemed to take any notice of it at all. This was Humphrey's first visit to Texas as our party's presidential nominee, and nobody even made an effort to meet with him — not John Connally, not Preston Smith, not Ralph Yarborough. Humphrey's performance in Chicago had left a bitter taste in everyone's mouth, and just two months before the election, it appeared he was a pariah in our state.

I was the only Democratic statewide official who agreed to meet with Humphrey on that visit. I went to his hotel in Houston, and during our meeting he asked me how in the world he should deal with Connally. Humphrey understood that he'd need the full support of Connally, Johnson, and the rest of the Texas Democratic establishment to win the state in November — and he also understood that he was far from having it. He was even unsure of what he should do about President Johnson's lukewarm support, and asked my advice on that, too. "Do you know what the President is thinking?" the Vice President asked me, his face betraying the kind of plaintive uncertainty that had driven Connally so crazy in Chicago.

"Just stick to your guns, and campaign like you expect to win," I told Humphrey. "The Texas Democrats will come around." And I wasn't saying that just to buck up Humphrey — I knew everybody would get behind him sooner or later. I understood why Connally felt the way he did, but Humphrey couldn't win without Texas, and no matter how disappointed Connally might have been in Humphrey as a candidate, we needed him to win in November. For my part, I wasn't just thinking about preserving party unity — I was also remembering that warning Sam Rayburn had given me about Nixon eight years before. Rayburn had urged me to stop Nixon at all costs, and, at this point, the best way I could do that was by helping Hubert Humphrey win. So that's what I intended to do.

As September gave way to October, Connally did indeed come around and start campaigning for Humphrey, as did the rest of the state's prominent

Democrats. In late October, less than two weeks before the election, Connally, Preston Smith, Ralph Yarborough, and U.S. Representatives Henry Gonzalez and Jim Wright all made appearances with Humphrey in various cities across Texas. Humphrey's numbers started to rise, and despite the competition from George Wallace's third-party bid, it began to look like he might win the state, after all. And if he could win Texas, it wasn't a stretch to imagine he could win the election.

But unfortunately, Richard Nixon had a very dirty trick up his sleeve — one that involved Texas's own Senator John Tower. It was insidious almost to the point of treason, and to this day it's still not widely known about. A handful of top Democrats found out about it just days before the election, but unfortunately we couldn't do anything about it.

Six days before the election, on October 31st, President Johnson ordered a halt to U.S. bombing in North Vietnam — a precondition the South Vietnamese had demanded before agreeing to participate in scheduled peace talks. Johnson's hopes were riding high for the peace talks as our last, best chance to end the war, and, as an aside, he also knew that any progress he made would help Humphrey. But unbeknownst to Johnson, Richard Nixon had been working with John Tower and an associate of his, a woman named Anna Chennault, to lobby the South Vietnamese behind the President's back. Chennault was in communication with South Vietnamese President Nguyen van Thieu's regime, and on Nixon's orders, she convinced them to thwart Johnson's peace talks prior to the election.

So it was that on November 2nd, just two days after President Johnson's pledge to stop the bombing, Thieu announced he wouldn't be coming to the talks. This was a real blow to President Johnson and Humphrey both, but what was truly amazing about it was that Richard Nixon had glibly interfered with United States policy in a time of war, for nothing more than his own political gain. Of all the nasty campaign tricks Republicans have ever pulled — the Willie Horton ad campaign against Michael Dukakis, the Whitewater clamor against Bill Clinton, the Swift Boat attacks against John Kerry — none had the distinction of wantonly interfering with U.S. foreign policy. What Nixon did was dangerous, unethical, and most likely illegal.

Lyndon Johnson found out about the interference a few days before the election, when he received a surreptitiously made tape of one of Chennault's conversations from the FBI. Word spread quickly among a small group of Humphrey's advisers, and a fierce debate arose as to what, if anything, he should do. I'd been told about the Chennault affair too, and in one of the last conversations I had with Humphrey before election day, I urged him to blow the whistle on Nixon. "If people knew that Nixon did this," I told him, "there'd be enough backlash to put you over the top."

At that point, Humphrey said something that I'll never forget. "I can't do that, Ben," he told me. "If I do, then what happens if Nixon wins? He'll have no credibility. He won't be able to govern. It'll be bad for the country."

I'll tell you what, Humphrey's decision to stand pat was the most decent thing I'd ever seen a politician do. Humphrey — in stark contrast to Nixon — was thinking not just of himself and his political ambitions, but of what was best for the country. No matter how frustrated any of us had been with Humphrey in Chicago or thereafter, I was reminded again at that moment of what a true patriot and honorable man he was. He possessed an essential decency that's all too often missing in politics — a decency his opponent clearly lacked.

On Sunday, November 3rd, just two days before the election, we held a giant rally for Humphrey in the Houston Astrodome. It was scheduled at the same time as a Dallas Cowboys football game, and a whole lot of skeptics thought there was no way we could pull Texans away from their television sets long enough to come to a political rally. But we rented hundreds of yellow school buses, we brought people in from all over the state. We got Frank Sinatra to come and perform, and both Lyndon Johnson and John Connally made appearances. Fifty-eight thousand people showed up — reportedly the largest political crowd Humphrey had ever faced — and the whole thing was televised. Humphrey got the crowd going with a rousing speech, and as I stood watching him I thought, *We might win Texas yet.*

In fact, on November 5th, Hubert Humphrey did win Texas, by just under forty thousand votes — the only Southern state that he won. His victory in Texas wasn't enough to push him over the top, though, as Nixon beat him by less than one percent of the popular vote in one of the closest presidential races in history (though Nixon won the electoral vote 301-191). Republicans also gained net seats in both the U.S. House and Senate, although Democrats still maintained comfortable majorities in each.

I was proud of how Texas Democrats had pulled together in the end. But as Richard Nixon prepared to assume the highest office in the land, and Lyndon Johnson and John Connally got ready to step down from elective office, it was obvious that a lot of things were about to change — both in Texas and across the country.

Chapter Nine

'Big Word, You'd Better Carry Me Across'

THERE'S NO QUESTION THAT THE EVENTS OF 1968 MARKED A TURNING point for the Democratic party nationally. Four years earlier, in the elections of 1964, we'd seemed almost invincible. President Johnson won the election by the biggest margin in history, and Democrats gained net seats in both the House and the Senate. And on the heels of Kennedy's assassination in Dallas, our elected officials had enjoyed the good will and wishes of the vast majority of Americans. But by the end of 1968, much of that good will had begun to erode.

The two main factors behind this change of sentiment were civil rights and the Vietnam war. With regard to Vietnam, considering the advice and information he was given, I don't believe there was much President Johnson could have done to improve his situation. But the fight for civil rights was a different matter. Johnson certainly didn't have to push so far so fast — but the fact that he did is testament to his courage, strength and sense of justice. Lyndon Johnson knew that his efforts to push through civil rights legislation would ultimately damage the party, but he also knew it was the right thing to do. And unlike so many of today's politicians, he chose to do what was right, rather than merely what might bring him or his colleagues more votes.

Nixon, on the other hand, had blatantly stirred up racist sentiment in the South in an effort to win votes. His "Southern Strategy," cooked up with the help of Texas's own John Tower, was a cynical, purely partisan strategy that called for slowing the pace of desegregation, kowtowing to Southern Republicans and conservatives, and choosing a reactionary running mate. Thanks in part to this strategy, Nixon did win every Southern state but Texas

— and the Republican party had found its new playbook. This basic political strategy — divide and conquer, using the rawest, most emotional issues in American life as a bludgeon and wedge — is the same strategy Republicans continue to use today, unfortunately to great effect.

Like John Tower's 1961 Senate victory that opened a crack in Texas's Democratic wall, Nixon's 1968 triumph in the South seemed to open up a world of possibilities for Republicans. For more than a century, the South had been reliably Democratic. It was more or less given that certain states would go for Democrats, and our national strategy had always taken that into account. But now, it appeared that all bets were off. Was this a one-time thing, or was it the beginning of a real shift? As the tumultuous year of 1968 came to a close, nothing seemed certain anymore.

Along with the Republicans' newfound confidence, the Democratic party faced other looming problems. With Humphrey's defeat and Lyndon Johnson's retirement, Democrats lacked a unifying presence at the top of the party. The destabilizing rift between liberals and conservatives threatened to grow wider. And we didn't have a clear strategy for winning back Southern voters. In the wake of the elections, pundits across the country declared that the Democratic party was in a "state of shambles."

Yet despite these ominous clouds, Texas still offered glimmer of hope. Even though Connally and Johnson would soon be gone, a slate of moderate Democrats had won in November: Preston Smith as governor, myself as lieutenant governor, and Crawford Martin as attorney general. We also bucked expectations by retaining huge majorities in the state House and Senate, and the ties between state Democrats and the business community continued to remain strong. Nobody doubted that we'd feel a void in Texas once Johnson and Connally were gone, but we had the basic structure in place to continue the progress they'd started. And at age 30, now the youngest lieutenant governor ever elected in Texas, I hoped to help build on that tradition.

I'd won what seemed to be a pretty clear mandate on November 5th, when I surpassed both Johnson and Connally to become the largest vote-getter in Texas history. With nearly 2 million votes, I'd also managed to become the first statewide candidate to win every single county in Texas. I'd outpolled Humphrey by more than half a million votes and won several hundred thousand more than any other Democrat in the state.

Now, I'm not relating all this to tell you how great I was or how wonderful my victories were. My point is this: I'd spent the eight years of my political career working both sides of the fence in Democratic politics, and I had staked plenty of political capital on the kinds of progressive initiatives liberals held dear. I'd invited legislators of all persuasions to have drinks and talk strategy. And I'd cultivated contacts and support in the business community and made sure they felt involved and engaged in what we were trying to do for the state. I'd fought for tax bills, and explained to the people of Texas why it was important to pay for initiatives that would strengthen Texas in the long run. The result was clear on Nov. 5th, when people across the state voted in record-setting numbers to elect me as their lieutenant governor.

All I'd done was taken what my political mentors Lyndon Johnson and John Connally had taught me and pushed it to the next level. To my mind, being a Democrat didn't have to be an either-or, liberal-or-moderate proposition — it just seemed natural to me to work with both sides, and take the best of what each had to offer. When liberals turned against conservative Democrats to vote for their Republican opponents, I couldn't understand it. When conservative Democrats tried to shut the liberal minority out of the legislative process, I knew it was counterproductive. It didn't seem like rocket science to me then, and it doesn't today. The lessons we learned during those years in Texas can help the Democratic party start winning again — but more importantly, they can help lead to a more efficient, thoughtful, and fair way of governing for both parties.

———————

WITH JOHN CONNALLY GONE, THE SPOTLIGHT NOW FELL UPON GOVERNOR-elect Preston Smith and me as we got ready for the inauguration and opening of the legislature in January of 1969. Unfortunately, a silly incident started off the year by stoking tension between us.

Preston Smith prided himself on being an unpretentious, salt-of-the-earth type. He was a former theater operator in Lubbock, the seventh of 13 children who'd grown up in a small community called Corn Hill. He liked to answer his own phones, and more often than not preferred to drive his own car rather than ride in the Lincolns provided to statewide officials. His hair was always carefully combed, and he wore heavy black horn-rimmed glasses that gave him a professorial look. His only known extravagances were the polka-dot bow ties he liked to wear with his dark suits.

I liked Preston, but we often seemed to find ourselves clashing over one thing or another. It seemed there was a little bit of competitive feeling on his part — even though I was twenty-six years younger than he was, I was already in a position to challenge him in coming elections. He'd announced his intention to run for another couple of terms as governor, and a lot of people expected I'd run against him at some point, so he might have felt like he ought to keep me at arm's length. At any rate, he didn't like the fact that I seemed to attract press attention, even though I was lower on the totem pole than he was. It would be far too strong to call what we had a "feud," but there was definitely a bit of a raw feeling there.

In the weeks leading up to the inauguration, I took a trip to Las Vegas and paid a visit to singer Robert Goulet, who I'd gotten to know on earlier trips out there. I never was shy about introducing myself to people, and I'd become friends with a few performers in Vegas — Elvis Presley, Vic Damone and Wayne Newton among them. On this trip I asked Goulet if he wouldn't mind coming to Texas to perform at the inauguration. He told me he and his wife, entertainer Carol Lawrence, would be happy to do it for no charge.

Back in Austin, when I mentioned this to Preston Smith, he raised his eyebrows, cocked his head, and said, "Who is Robert Goulet?"

Well, I'll admit that I found that a little surprising. Goulet might not be as much of a household name now, but at the time, he was one of the biggest stars on Broadway, in movies, and in the recording industry. In 1960, he'd originated the role of Lancelot in the first Broadway run of *Camelot,* starring with Richard Burton and Julie Andrews in the performance that first gained him national fame.

"He was the star of *Camelot,*" I told Preston. "He played Lancelot."

"What's *Camelot?*" the governor-elect replied.

Now, this would have been a completely forgettable conversation, except for two things. One is, I made the mistake of mentioning it to someone else in Austin, and because it was a funny story, word quickly spread. Then, Preston vetoed my choice, telling me he'd rather have country music stars like Glen Campbell and Jimmy Dean perform than this Robert Goulet person. So I had to call Goulet, embarrassed, and rescind my invitation. The story made the papers, getting things off to a little bit of a rocky start.

And Preston was destined to get even more agitated, as I started getting more press attention when the legislative term started. In February, *Newsweek* magazine named me one of the "Top Five Men Moving into Political Leadership for the Next Decade," along with Jay Rockefeller, Julian Bond, John Danforth, and Don Riegle. The next month, I made a trip to Washington, where I met with DNC chairman Fred Harris and Ted Kennedy (although my visit with Kennedy was notable mostly for the fact that the driver got lost, and delivered us to his house so late that Joan Kennedy met us in her bathrobe). On top of all that, I was still active in all the national legislative conferences — and the more I did, the more I wanted to do. Looking back, I don't know when I ever found time to sleep.

That spring, the *Wall Street Journal* did a front-page story on me called "The Heir Apparent." The paper took note of the bridge I'd been trying to build between the moderate and liberal Democrats in Texas:

> Mr. Barnes is a rarity in this politically turbulent state.
>
> Here, where the liberal and conservative wings of the dominant Democratic party still wage bitter, unrelenting warfare, Mr. Barnes currently enjoys support from both groups. His natural power base is the conservative oil-business-financial complex that supported ex-Gov. John Connally and Lyndon Johnson before him.
>
> ... Mr. Barnes has won substantial liberal support by solidly backing such programs as a state minimum wage and improved antipollution laws. Perhaps prematurely, he is regarded as the man who just might do the near-impossible: Unite the emerging Texas left with the old conservative wing.
>
> Last fall the Texas Observer, a liberal journal published every two weeks, concluded that Mr. Barnes 'has become, perhaps in ways Lyndon Johnson never did, in Texas, the consummate consensus politician.' Declares a liberal state senator: 'I wouldn't be a bit surprised to see Ben Barnes someday as Vice President or President. I think he's got Lyndon Johnson's characteristics and abilities better than Lyndon has.'

Now, that last line was probably just somebody trying to say something interesting enough to get their quote in the paper, but I couldn't help but be pleased with that kind of coverage. On the other hand, a few paragraphs later, the paper mentioned the issue that was starting to dog me a little bit more, the more my visibility increased.

> [S]ome critics question how Mr. Barnes — whose parents are of modest means and whose annual public salary since 1960 never has exceeded $4,800 (the lieutenant governor's pay), plus expenses — already has become modestly wealthy, with a clear potential of eventually becoming quite wealthy. The answer, apparently, is through a series of transactions that rarely involved any real financial risk to Mr. Barnes or any substantial outlay of his capital.
>
> Mr. Barnes recently put his net worth at '$25,000 to $35,000... maybe $5,000 or $10,000 more.' These figures, however, hardly suggest the scope of his present investments. Among them are an interest in a prospering construction firm, 20% interests in two Texas radio stations, 50% of a 36-unit apartment building, 25% of a planned shopping-center venture, a 12% inter-

est in a Holiday Inn franchise (Mr. Barnes recently sold similar interests in two additional franchises), part-ownership of farms totaling 790 acres and a small interest in a Bolivian tin-mining project.

... Mr. Barnes's financial growth got its initial impetus when Herman Bennett, principal owner of a Brownwood, Texas construction firm, granted him an option to acquire up to an 11% interest in the firm under extremely beneficial terms.

... Says Mr. Bennett of his relationship with the lieutenant governor: 'I grew up with Ben Barnes, and we've just been friends for a long time. Our business association has nothing to do with politics, and I never ask him for anything.' Pressed to comment on the generous arrangements to finance Mr. Barnes's stakes in the ventures, he adds: 'I guess I'm just a very liberal fellow.'

Nobody ever suggested I was doing anything illegal, and nobody ever found a reason to comment on my business dealings other than because they were "interesting." The truth is, Herman Bennett never did ask me for anything — apart from occasionally nagging at me to get out of politics altogether and become his business partner. Herman was obviously grooming me to partner with him whenever I did get out of politics, even though, at the time, I had no intention of getting out. But in the meantime, it just seemed to make people uncomfortable that a statewide politician — especially one who'd grown up in modest circumstances, in a little town like DeLeon — might also have an active and successful business life on the side, even if serving in the Legislature was a part-time job with part-time pay.

I didn't like the fact that my business dealings drew comment in the press, but I always figured it was nothing more than a minor headache. As lieutenant governor, there were bigger things to worry about — like the $300 million shortfall that was facing the 61st legislature as we convened in January of 1969. And I'd be tackling it with just about the most hard-headed, independent-minded bunch of senators you could imagine.

In Washington, D.C., the House of Representatives has a reputation for being full of colorful characters, while the Senate — the "most exclusive club on Earth" — is supposedly a stately, accomplished crowd that takes itself very seriously. Whether that's true or not is a subject for another book. But I can tell you that in the Texas Senate that I presided over as lieutenant governor, there were more eccentric, unpredictable, and flat crazy characters than you'd find in any novel. And they were blessed with Texas-sized egos to boot. As Franklin Owen once said of his fellow senators in an earlier legislative session, "They remind me of 31 pissants on a log floating down the Mississippi River, and every one of them thinks they're steering the log." That sentiment still held true in the 61st legislature.

We had A.M. Aikin Jr., a courtly, distinguished gentleman from Red River County who never deigned to utter a curse word, instead spitting out the phrase "Jot ding!" whenever he got riled. We had a dozen or more liberals, including stocky, bull-headed Babe Schwartz and "Good-time Charlie" Wilson, a very able state legislator who gained fame for his legendary drinking and skirt-chasing before launching a secret decade-long battle as a U.S. Representative to funnel aid to Afghan rebels fighting against the Soviets in the 1980s. We had Barbara Jordan, who was taking Texas politics by storm with her legislative skills and ability to fit in with the "good old boys." And we had a few hard-drinking senators who made it hazardous to consider any legislation after lunch, when they'd often wobble back to the chamber and fall asleep in their chairs.

The question was, how could I get the Senate working together well enough to pass the legislation Texas needed to move into the future? Because the Senate operated under super-majority rule, the dozen or more liberals had enough votes to block any legislation they didn't like, whether on its merits or just to tweak Governor Smith or me. I knew had my work cut out for me, so I jumped right in with a first move some of the old-time Senate moderates found shocking.

When I was doling out the committee assignments, I did something nobody had done before: I appointed a few of the liberal Democrats to key committees. Not only had previous lieutenant governors never done such a thing, they often wouldn't even recognize liberal senators on the floor to do something as simple as move to adjourn! I don't know whether it's because I was younger than all the senators, or because I figured I'd have an easier row to hoe politically if I kept good relations with them, but I made a vow early on to treat each senator with respect, and to work with them whenever I could.

But not everyone thought that was such a good idea. When I named liberal Senator Babe Schwartz to the finance committee, A.M. Aikin was so mad, I thought he'd have a coronary. "Jot ding, Ben!" he shrieked at me. "You're going to ruin us! What in the devil are you doing?" Aikin was practically shaking, he was so angry — he just couldn't believe I'd bring the liberals into the tent like that. But I knew I had to deal with the liberals if I wanted to get my programs passed, and beyond that, I knew they deserved a place at the table. Besides, as Babe Schwartz himself soon found out, there was another good reason for putting him on a committee.

"Ben gave me a job that kept me too busy to be as much trouble as I wanted to be," Schwartz said later. "I had a choice: I could spend my time scheming against Ben, or be on the finance committee and gain the benefits of associating with other members and coalescing with more people. So I chose to make a little less trouble. That was a stroke of genius on Ben's part — I was so busy I didn't know which way was up."

With the committee assignments in place, we got right into the business of legislating. And one of the first things I did was to pull Barbara Jordan aside and ask for her help on a new bill.

"Senator Jordan," I said, "I'd like for you to draw up a new bill. I want to have a single bill that will strike down every previous segregation law this body has ever passed." I don't remember what she said in response, but I do know it didn't take her long to do it. And just like that, we teamed up to strike down years of segregation legislation.

Well, that didn't sit too well with the segregationists in the Senate, or with the average Texans — and there were still a lot of them — who harbored racist sentiments. A letter I got that same year from a constituent named J.F. Cleaver betrays the attitude that was still sadly prevalent during that time:

Dear Mr. Barnes:

It is widely believed that you could be U.S. senator. You certainly have much prestige and influence. Only someone with vim, courage, industry could make the record you have made: heartiest congratulations to you. You come from a prosperous section, and have what it takes.

Why should not legislation be passed outlawing de-segregation? In schools where de-segregation was introduced, moral and intellectual standards deteriorated substantially. There is one solution: continued segregation. Do you want our children to be forced into contact with bastards? 80% of negroes are illegitimate. You are reasonable and courageous enough to face facts. Results of comprehensive tests show that negroes do not have mental capacity on a level with that of the ordinary human. They have by far the worst crime rate: do you want our youngsters to be thrust into contact with potential criminals? Is it not our duty to provide wholesome environment? "As the twig is bent the tree's inclined."

Unless wicked de-segregation is proscribed, the nation is doomed.

DISCRIMINATION forever.

With best regards,

J.F. Cleaver

I'm not sure what you could say to someone with those kinds of views to change his mind, but in my reply I tried to find common ground somewhere. Today, as I look at this letter, I'm reminded at how different the times were, and how far we've come since then:

Dear Mr. Cleaver:

Thank you very much for your letter stating your support for the return to segregation in our nation's schools. Your opinions on this matter are interesting and I appreciate your bringing them to my attention.

The Supreme Court has ruled that segregation is unconstitutional and must be abolished. The State of Texas must, so long as she remains a member of the Federal system, obey the United States Constitution and, therefore, cannot legalize segregation.

While I understand your concern that forcing white children to go to school with black children will corrupt their moral, intellectual, and social standards, I would suggest that such has not been the case in areas where schools have long been integrated. I would also point out the availability of private schools for those children whose parents wish them to remain separated from children of different races.

Your continued support is most encouraging and very much appreciated.
Sincerely yours,
Ben Barnes

———

AS THE SESSION PROGRESSED, SENATORS ON BOTH SIDES CAME TO REALIZE that they'd have a hard time pigeonholing me. I was still nominally part of the moderate-conservative wing, but for any given issue, I tried to take my position on the merits rather than on any kind of party blueprint.

The Tort Claim Act was one example. That vote came down to a 15-15 tie, with one senator skipping the vote. He'd apparently committed to both sides, and rather than have to actually pick one, he just didn't come to work that day — a common strategy for senators wanting to avoid a vote. With the count at 15-15, I'd have to cast a vote to break the tie.

Just about everyone in the chamber expected that I'd vote against the Tort Claim Act, in the interest of Texas businesses. But I'd had an off-the-record conversation with Chief Justice Bob Calvert of the Texas Supreme Court and had asked him outright whether Texas needed this bill or not. When he told me we did, I made up my mind. At the last minute, I voted "aye," passing the bill by a 16-15 count.

I'll tell you what, there were some shocked faces in that chamber — and none more shocked than the lobbyist for the Texas Municipal League, who was up in the gallery watching the proceedings. You could smoke in the Capitol building then, and he had a big old pipe in his mouth that just fell right down onto the Senate floor the minute he heard me say "aye." He burned a hole in the Senate carpet — though he really would have rather have burned it in my butt that day.

As the spring progressed, House Speaker Gus Mutscher and I tried to sort out the $300 million shortfall by passing a one-year spending bill, with nominal tax increases, to get us temporarily back on track. Texas had always had two-year appropriations bills, and I felt it was high time we switched to one-year bills, which were more accurate and easier to plan for. But Governor Smith would have none of it, and he promptly vetoed the bill. So, as the regular session ended, we'd made no progress on making up the shortfall, and it looked like we might have to institute a state income tax — something absolutely nobody wanted. The state's finances were just in a mess, and now we'd have to call a special session to make a plan for the next two years.

What happened next doesn't rate among the finer moments of the Texas Legislature, though the fallout wasn't as dire as the press made it out to be at the time. In fact, the biggest fallout was that the Legislature's bumbling on the issue helped stoke resentment of the political crowd in Austin — the kind of resentment that would ultimately cause a lot of trouble in the 1972 races.

Preston Smith called for the first special session to convene on July 28th, just five weeks before the state's new fiscal year on Sept. 1st. This wasn't much time to get a major tax bill together, so I knew we'd have to scramble. In Texas, tax bills normally have to originate in the House — but this time around, the House passed the buck, sending the Senate nothing more than a caption. Now it was up to us to formulate and pass a tax plan to dig Texas out of its hole.

Two senators had tax-plan ideas. Charlie Wilson, a liberal, wanted to institute a corporate tax, and Tom Creighton wanted a new sales tax on groceries, beer, and liquor. I didn't think either tax was a great idea, but at this point the state needed the money however we could get it, so I called Wilson and Creighton into my office in the Capitol for a little meeting.

I handed each man a sheet of paper and said, "All right. The first to come back with 16 signatures for his tax bill, that's the one we're gonna run with." And off they went, in a race to see who could get the signatures first.

When Creighton came back with 16 signatures, the decision was made. And though I knew changing the sales tax to include these items would be a tough sell to the Texas voters, more than half the other states in the union had similar taxes — and the bottom line was, Texas needed that money. Still, to soften the blow, I called for a provision stating that any household making less than $25,000 could receive all those taxes back at the end of the year.

Even though Tom Creighton had gotten the signatures, I wanted to make absolutely sure those 16 senators would truly vote for the tax when the time came. So I gathered them all one evening in the living room of the lieutenant governor's apartment, and as they stood there in a little group, I said, "Now, listen. You all have been telling me I've got your votes. Well, now it's time to step up and prove it."

I drew an imaginary line in the carpet, and faced the senators again. "Every one of you that's going to vote for this bill, I want you to step across this line."

The senators looked at each other and chuckled, remembering the story of the Alamo, where William Barrett Travis famously drew a similar line in the dirt. Slowly, one by one, each senator stepped across the line, until only one was left: my good friend Ralph Hall, who was reclining in a wing-tip chair, his feet draped lazily over the edge. Ralph knew the tax vote would cause some grumbling among voters, so, with a pained look on his face, he turned to Senator J.P. Word and said, "Big Word, you'd better carry me across!" — mimicking the words of an ailing Alamo soldier named Jim Bowie, who'd asked his fellow soldiers to carry his cot across Travis's line in the dirt.

Everybody laughed, but with Ralph across the line, we had our 16 votes. And I'd already checked with House Speaker Gus Mutscher, who'd promised me he had the votes we needed to pass the food tax in the House. So, despite the mess Preston Smith had left us in, I felt pretty confident that we'd figured out our solution to the tax problem.

That's when the trouble started. When the bill came up for debate on the Senate floor on Friday, August 22nd, the liberal senators started what became a 27-hour filibuster. They'd have to filibuster right through to Monday the 25th to defeat the bill, but that wasn't their plan. As Senator Babe Schwartz later said, "We wanted to filibuster until we knew every newspaper had gone to bed on Sunday morning. That meant the headlines would say: 'Senate filibusters food tax' rather than 'Food tax passes Senate,' which would have been the case." They were trying to rile up ordinary Texans against the food tax — and boy, did they succeed.

That Sunday after the papers came out, angry telegrams and telephone calls started pouring into the Capitol — from Dallas housewives, university students, church groups, and everyone else in Texas, it seemed. Yet the 16 senators who'd stepped across that line stood strong, and the bill passed in the Senate.

But when the House reconvened on Monday morning, Speaker Gus

Mutscher was facing a very different political climate than when he'd made his earlier promise to me. In the House galleries, opponents of the tax waved placards that said, "Vote No on Ben Barnes' Bread and Bean Tax!" and "Milk for the Babies Comes Before Beer for the Boys!" Then an anonymous caller phoned in a bomb threat to the Capitol, sending everybody out into a driving summer rainstorm. This also happened to be the time of year when swarms of crickets descend on Austin, so the people who evacuated the building ended up crunching across the thousands of crickets underfoot. It was like the tax bill was bringing on the apocalypse.

Inside the Capitol, Gus Mutscher crumbled quickly. Despite the popular revolt against the bill, I think he'd still have been behind it — except for the fact that it called for taxing beer as well as groceries. Mutscher was very close to the beer lobby, and their chief lobbyist, Homer Leonard, was in Mutscher's ear all day Sunday and Monday, urging him to kill the bill. In the end, Mutscher succumbed, going back on his word to me. Following his lead, the House voted 147 to 0 to kill the bill.

Well, I just couldn't believe Mutscher had folded like that. Texas was at a fiscal crisis point, and the Senate had managed to come up with a workable solution. I didn't want to levy a sales tax on groceries and beer, either — but I knew the alternative was far worse. In the end, Texans got slapped by much higher property taxes, which have ultimately taken more money out of their pockets than our proposed food tax would have.

I was so angry at Mutscher, and at beer lobbyist Homer Leonard, that I called the Senate into session right after the House vote on Monday afternoon just to make a public statement. Leonard was there, up in the gallery, and I turned and pointed right at him — something that was never done in the chamber. "We are gonna pass that tax bill," I said, "and it's gonna include a bar-relage tax on beer. If I have to stay here until snow falls on the Capitol lawn, we're gonna pass that beer tax." We did it, too — and that barrelage tax ultimately cost the beer companies a whole lot more than the sales tax would have. They deserved no less for having interfered in a self-interested way that was so damaging to the state.

Preston Smith's initial veto of the one-year bill that Mutscher and I had passed, followed by Mutscher's crumbling on the food tax bill, gave the press a juicy storyline for the week. One editorial cartoon showed Smith, Mutscher, and me all playing quarterback, with a tax football being hiked and one of us saying, "Can anybody think of a play?" Smith got loudly booed the next weekend when he went to the Cowboys-Oilers professional football game to flip the coin. And editorial writers had a field day suggesting we'd bumbled our way through the special sessions. As one paper put it: "The most likely beneficiary is the Republican party of Texas. GOP leaders already are pointing to the tax fiasco as evidence that all is not well in the Democrat-dominated statehouse." If that was true, we'd find out soon enough, as the 1970 elections were just a year away.

Chapter Ten

Strange Bedfellows: Connally, Nixon and George H. W. Bush

IN THE FALL OF 1969, WITH THE 61ST LEGISLATURE FINALLY AT AN END, political writers turned their attention to the next year's races. Nothing less than the future of Texas Democrats in the era following Johnson and Connally was at stake, and everybody seemed to have an opinion about it. Now that I had one term as lieutenant governor under my belt, plenty of pundits figured I'd want to run for something else — either for governor against Preston Smith, or for the Senate against Ralph Yarborough.

At the time, I had good reason to think I could win either office. A poll taken in April had shown that I'd beat either Smith or Yarborough in head-to-head elections by about 10 percentage points. I hadn't hidden the fact that I wanted to move up the political ladder, and so for the rest of the fall, editorial writers and cartoonists had a great time speculating on what I might do. Ralph Yarborough and Preston Smith were both expected to run again, so, as far as anyone knew, I was one of only two possible wild cards in those races. The other was George H. W. Bush.

After losing to Yarborough in 1964, Bush had won election to the U.S. House of Representatives from his Houston district in 1966. As the son of former Senator Prescott Bush and an up-and-coming young Republican, he was treated very well by his elders in the House, who handed him a seat on the powerful Ways and Means committee — the first freshman Congressman to receive that honor. Bush was smart, polite, and well liked among both his fellow representatives and his constituents. In fact, nobody had even filed to run against him in 1968, which was pretty much unheard of then for a Republican in Texas.

Just about everybody expected Bush to take on Yarborough again, now that he had two terms in Congress under his belt. If I chose to run against Yarborough and then beat him in the primary, that would pit me against Bush in November. A lot of moderates in both parties weren't too keen on that idea, feeling like Bush and I were similar politically and that it wouldn't help either of our careers to wage a bruising race against each other. A few Democrats even worried I might actually lose to Yarborough, and they didn't want to see my career derailed so early — at the time, I was still only 31 years old.

But I wasn't afraid to face either Yarborough or Bush, who the newspapers had dubbed the "glamour boy" of Texas politics. I'd already faced him down once, in a debate in front of the Texas Medical Association. It wasn't exactly a friendly crowd for me — for one thing, it was in Bush's home territory of Houston, at the Shamrock Hotel. For another, Bush and I were debating Medicare and Medicaid, two of President Johnson's groundbreaking programs, and the doctors assembled for the debate weren't terribly well disposed to someone who was ready to sing the praises of those programs. I believe Bush thought he'd whip me pretty good that day, but I managed to rise to the occasion in front of his home crowd — enough to where the *Houston Chronicle* wrote a positive editorial about my performance. Bush probably realized then he'd have to run a hell of a race to win if we got into it in 1970.

For his part, Ralph Yarborough was just as paranoid as usual about whether I'd run against him — and I'll admit that I fell prey to the temptation of further provoking his paranoia that September. Ralph's supporters in Dallas were throwing a big Appreciation Dinner for him on the evening of September 25th, and, while they'd invited me, nobody really expected I'd come, especially since I hadn't yet announced whether I'd be running against Yarborough the following year or not.

Well, it turned out that I happened to be in Dallas to make a speech that day anyway, so I decided to drop by the Yarborough dinner at Memorial Auditorium afterward. When I walked in, the 2500 people in attendance were listening to remarks by Congressman Earle Cabell. By the time I made my way to the head table, about half of those people had started buzzing among themselves, almost drowning poor Earle out entirely. Reporters pushed their way to my table, asking me why I'd come and whether I'd be speaking, and Ralph just sat there stony-faced, watching all the hubbub. This was the kind of thing that drove both him and Preston Smith crazy, and I knew it. It wasn't my most dignified moment, I confess. And, I'm further sorry to admit, I did enjoy it.

I was invited up to the podium to speak, and I couldn't resist another little poke. "I want to thank [event organizer] Mr. Nasher for letting me be publicity chairman for this event," I said, as laughter rippled through the crowd. "Senator Yarborough," I continued, turning toward Ralph, "if I knew I'd get this much publicity, I'd come to all your events." But after I'd had my fun, I gave a rousing speech in praise of Ralph, telling the crowd that "the Democratic Party has a very fine warrior in Senator Ralph Yarborough — and Texas has a very fine citizen, a very fine senator in Ralph Yarborough."

Ralph's supporters didn't know whether my showing up meant I wasn't going to run against him, or that I'd just pulled off the most brassy dinner appearance in recent memory. In fact, I hadn't decided yet what to do, though I did understand that running against Ralph in '70 would leave a bitter taste in the liberals' mouths — and I had no interest in alienating any liberal Democrats. I'd spent too much of my 10 years in politics trying to bridge the gap with liberals to risk putting them off now.

ONE AFTERNOON A FRIEND OF MINE, BARRY SILVERMAN, WAS VISITING WITH me in the lieutenant governor's office when, all of a sudden, the big wooden doors to the hallway just busted wide open. Barry knew I'd gotten death threats during the months I'd spoken out in support of Johnson's Vietnam policies, and less than a year had passed since the assassinations of Martin Luther King and Bobby Kennedy, so he was in a nervous frame of mind. When he whipped around and saw a couple of tall men wearing dark suits burst into my office, he just about dove under my desk.

Barry turned back in time to see me jump up and head for the door, and, as he told me later, he thought I was about to try and outrun them. He was still sitting there, looking wild-eyed, when I said to him, "Barry, if you'll stand up, I'd like to introduce you to President Johnson."

Lyndon Johnson was back in Texas, living at his beloved ranch, but he'd occasionally drop by to see me and talk politics — with, of course, a couple of Secret Service agents in tow. He always took an active interest in what I was doing and what my plans were, though he never flat out tried to tell me what he thought I should do. Even though he was out of politics, he still had greater insights into what was going on in Texas than just about anyone in Austin, and the fact that he rarely ventured away from the ranch made his visits all the more meaningful. I valued our talks together more than I think he ever knew.

In mid-October of 1969, President Johnson invited me to come up to the penthouse atop his television station in Austin to discuss my plans for 1970 and beyond. He felt, like I did, that it would be a mistake for me to anger the liberal establishment by running against Yarborough. "You'll kick his ass good if you do run," Johnson told me, "but you'll be forever marked as a Southern conservative, and the Texas liberals will never forgive you for beating their champion."

If I ran for governor, on the other hand, I'd be going up against someone more conservative than me: Preston Smith. This was clearly what President Johnson thought I ought to do, not only because it would be more helpful to my political career in the short run, but because it could have an even greater impact down the road. Lyndon Johnson was the ultimate political strategist, and he desperately wanted Texas to continue to play a major role in national politics long after he was gone. I believe he had very high hopes for me — in fact, he'd soon make them known in a very public way — and the simple truth was, he knew it was easier for a governor to be a serious candidate for President than a senator or congressman. And especially after the Democrats' loss of the South in 1968, a Southern governor would have an even better chance — as we'd all see in 1976, when Georgia's Jimmy Carter won the nomination.

Now, I don't mean to suggest that Lyndon Johnson was trying to groom me for the presidency. And I certainly wasn't planning my political career with that goal in mind. But especially since his retirement, President Johnson had taken to expressing increased confidence in what he thought I could do. Whether this was mere wishful thinking on the part of a Texan who cared deeply for his state and its place in American politics, I can't say. Maybe he was just trying to encourage me and get me to think in terms of greater possibilities for my own political future. He never pushed me to do one thing or another. But just as he'd told me back in 1967, when he'd said he was for me "money, marbles, and chalk," I knew the President was behind me — and that was certainly a powerful feeling as I moved ahead in my political career.

In the meantime, the Republican swing that had started with the 1968 elections appeared to be continuing. In November of 1969, Virginia and New Jersey, the only two states that hold gubernatorial elections in odd-numbered years after presidential elections, both elected Republican governors. New Jersey hadn't had a Republican governor since Alfred Driscoll was elected in 1949 — and Virginia, the linchpin of the South, hadn't elected a Republican governor since 1869.

The two elections shared a couple of similarities. In both states, President Nixon was popular. But, more ominously, in both states the Democratic party was badly split between moderate / conservatives and liberals — in fact, one hundred prominent Democrats in Virginia's capital of Richmond had declared their support for the Republican candidate in the days leading up to the election. It didn't take a political genius to see what this might portend for Texas if we weren't careful to keep the party together.

As soon as those elections were over, all kinds of pundits jumped on the bandwagon to predict the demise of the Democratic party, in Texas and elsewhere. John Tower, himself a former Democrat, declared that he expected the legions of Johnson-Connally Democrats in Texas to convert to the Republican party. He told the *Dallas Times-Herald* that conservative Democrats were "demoralized" and that they saw "no influence for anyone from the South in the Democratic party in the future."

I believed Tower was wrong about the party's future, but I'll admit that I was concerned about its present. My fear was that we were veering too far to the left, rather than keeping a steady course down the center. "The thinking of the party at this time is almost entirely of putting together northern-type liberals," I told a UPI reporter. "There's not a single strong spokesman for the South, Southwest, or West. If the party continues going the way it appears to be going, it will be very hard for the South and for Texas." Thirty-five years later, it's amazing to look at those words and realize how true they remain today.

After being down and out for so long, Texas Republicans were almost indecently excited about their prospects in 1970. Dallas County Republican chair Tom Crouch started telling reporters that Republican Paul Eggers would win the governorship, George Bush would win the Senate race, and Republicans would in 35 seats in the House in 1970. There was a wave coming, and, by God, Texas Republicans were gonna ride it.

Syndicated columnists Robert Novak and Rowland Evans further stoked the fires by reporting in mid-November that "Big Texas Money" was switching allegiance from conservative Democrats to Republicans, and in December they declared that the national Democratic party was broke, with debts of "$8 million to $8.5 million." As usual, both columns blew the party's problems out of proportion — but it certainly wasn't helping us to have reporters now jumping on the bandwagon about how terrible things supposedly were.

This was a critical time for the Democratic party, and no matter how much I wanted to plot my own political course, the needs of the party had to come first. I don't mind admitting that I would have loved to run for governor or senator in 1970, and I believe I'd have won either race. The *Lubbock Avalanche-Journal* even jokingly editorialized that I ought to be allowed to have both offices, to "save taxpayer money." But in the end, that wasn't what was best for Texas Democrats at that moment in time.

In late November, Lloyd Bentsen came to see me in my office. Bentsen had built himself an impressive career since serving in the Army during World War II. He'd worked as a lawyer and county judge in the Rio Grande Valley, then won a seat in Congress in 1948. Bentsen served three terms before getting out of elective politics and starting a financial holding company in Houston. Now he was a millionaire, and active in Democratic party politics. And when he came to see me that day, I had an inkling of what he wanted to talk about.

"Ben," he said, "if you're planning to run against Ralph Yarborough for the Senate, I'm all for you. But if not, I'd like to get into the race myself."

My chief of staff Robert Spellings was sitting with us in the office, and I hadn't told him yet what I planned to do in 1970. So when I looked right at Bentsen and said, "Lloyd, go for it. You've got my support," Spellings nearly fell out of his chair.

Shortly after that, on Monday, November 24th, I called a meeting in my office with about a dozen of my closest friends and advisers, including Frank Erwin, Ralph Wayne, Julian Read, Larry Temple, Robert Spellings, Howard Rose, Tom Johnson, and George Christian. I'd made my decision, but I wanted to hear the others' thoughts before revealing it.

By this time, media speculation about what I'd do had gotten so over the top that it was threatening to turn voters away. One woman had gotten so sick of me, she told a pollster she wouldn't vote for me because she didn't like my red hair — a fact that reporters happily covered. All agreed that it was time for me to announce a decision.

Each person in the room told me his thoughts on what I ought to do, with most were leaning toward the governor's race. They all were just as supportive as they could be, but in the end, I leaned back in my chair and told them, "I'm going for re-election. And I want to go ahead and announce it tomorrow." In the interim, I decided to call the four men who'd be most affected by my decision: Preston Smith, Ralph Yarborough, Ralph Hall (who'd already declared for lieutenant governor, in the expectation that I'd run for something else), and George Bush.

At 2 p.m. on Tuesday, November 25th, I made my announcement in the Senate chamber. Rumors were flying — one report said I'd prepared two statements, one for governor and one for lieutenant governor, and would decide which to deliver when I got up to the podium. Another said that I'd decided to go for the Senate seat and had been planting rumors myself, trying to throw people off the trail. A third said that I'd get up to the podium and announce that I needed more time to decide. There's no question that all the rumors were getting a little out of hand.

I shot down all the speculation right away with a short statement expressing my decision, within the framework of trying to help the party.

It is my conviction that in that important position [of lieutenant governor] I can make the greatest contribution to the governmental stability and progress of my state, as well as to the unity of the party.

My family and friends and I have discussed many times over these past weeks the future role of Ben Barnes in the political life of Texas, and I have considered the several opportunities for public service for which I might offer my candidacy next year. I am both pleased and grateful for the many expressions of support for any political office I might seek.

I am flattered that the measures of public opinion have indicated that I might be successful in any campaign I might undertake. However, such a decision for service cannot be based merely on personal ambition or merely on an ability to win.

Any responsible public figure must carefully make his own judgment as to how his leadership can best serve the current needs of this state.

I was proud of my decision, and I'll tell you what — to read the newspaper headlines in the next few days, you'd have thought I was personally saving the Democratic party. Papers across the state ran stories like "Texas Wins in Barnes Decision," and "Decision Saves Party from Split," while others lauded what they called my "wise" and "mature" decision. Of course, others printed still more fanciful rumors that either Lyndon Johnson or John Connally would now run for the Senate against Yarborough, so you can't always believe what you read.

I didn't mind all the praise, but the truth is I decided to run again for lieutenant governor in large part, because I needed another term to accomplish a few important things. I wanted to pass a new Texas Constitution, to replace the outdated one that was causing so many problems for state government. I also wanted to push through legislation to lengthen statewide office terms from two years to four, and make the legislature an annual, rather than biennial, event. All these things would be far easier to accomplish as lieutenant governor.

Now that I'd made my decision, the races for governor and senator were wide open. And both would end up with surprising results on primary day.

———

ON JANUARY 6, 1970, TALL, RAIL-THIN, IMPECCABLY DRESSED LLOYD BENTSEN held a press conference to announce he was running for Ralph Yarborough's Senate seat. Gracious and charming, Bentsen was an impressive figure, and as a moderate-conservative in the mold of Johnson and Connally, he quickly became a favored candidate within the business community. Yet, even though he'd served those three terms in Congress, Bentsen still wasn't very well known across Texas. On that day, just four months before the Democratic primary, almost nobody liked Bentsen's chances of beating "The People's Senator."

But Bentsen ran a smart, self-assured campaign, and by the time of the primary on May 2, he was running just about neck and neck with Yarborough. When all the votes were counted, he'd beat Yarborough by about 90,000 votes. A whole lot of people were shocked by those results — including the man who'd been hoping to win Yarborough's seat in November, George Bush.

Bush had made the decision to enter the Senate race against Yarborough, and he'd designed his whole campaign to play up the differences between them. He was perfectly positioned to exploit those differences — Ralph was a die-hard liberal in an increasingly conservative state, and Bush was a fresh new conservative face with a young, dynamic image. Then, all of a sudden, Bush found himself facing an opponent who was more like him than most members of his own party. Both Bush and Bentsen were war heroes, businessmen, and millionaires, and both subscribed to a straight-up moderate conservatism that drew adherents from both sides of the aisle. For Bush, Bentsen's victory over Yarborough changed everything.

The other primary race that surprised everyone was the one that never took place. Governor Preston Smith had no opponent in the primary — the first time that had ever happened for an incumbent governor in Texas. Ralph Hall, who had withdrawn from the lieutenant governor's race when I got in it, had wanted to face Smith, but he was disqualified on a technicality. So even though Smith had been one of the less inspiring governors in recent memory, he ended up waltzing right on through to the general election in November, where he'd face Republican Paul Eggers.

As for me, I found myself facing off against Republican Byron Fullerton, an assistant dean at the University of Texas Law School. Fullerton wasn't terribly well known, and I'm not sure he was running to win so much as he was using it as a platform to poke at me and the Texas Democrats. At that point, I was riding pretty high in Texas politics, and I'd gotten some recent national attention for being named one of the U.S. Jaycees' "Ten Outstanding Young Men" — a group that also included civil rights leader Jesse Jackson, football player Gale Sayers, and Jay Rockefeller, who later became governor and then a U.S. Senator from West Virginia. With a comfortable double-digit lead over Fullerton, I knew that only something scandalous could vault him ahead of me.

The Republicans knew it, too, and they did try to stir things up just a little bit. There continued to be scattered comments and news stories about my finances, but Republicans got another angle to exploit when my wife, Martha, and I agreed to divorce in 1970. Martha and I had been together since high school, and she'd more or less endured my crazy hours and obsessive focus on my political career. She was a doting mother to our two children, Greg and Amy, but by now it was obvious to us both that she'd had enough of the political life, and that we'd grown apart. Divorce wasn't so common back then, so I knew our split would generate some interest. It generated some interesting rumors, too.

I won't deny that I enjoyed being single again after getting married so young, but some Republicans tried to stir the pot, with bumper stickers saying "It's 10:30 p.m. Do you know where your lieutenant governor is?" and other less-subtle provocations. And for some reason it seemed like photographers and reporters were hell-bent on catching me in some sort of "situation." Once, when I went to a benefit in New York, I went out afterward with *Fort Worth Star Telegram* publisher Amon Carter and his wife. The actress Arlene Dahl was there too, and while she and I were dancing, a photographer snapped a picture. Soon enough, that photo was in papers all over Texas, with a caption saying Arlene Dahl and I were out in New York dancing together. It sure sounded scandalous, unless you happened to know that Arlene's husband was standing about 10 feet away.

Some of my "friends" didn't help me too much in that department, either. One weekend in 1970, I took my kids to California to go to Disneyland. The first night of our trip, I met the actress Jill St. John at a dinner hosted by Washington attorney Lloyd Hand and his wife, Ann. Well, Jill St. John and I got into a pretty fierce argument about Vietnam and Lyndon Johnson, and by the end of the evening we just about wanted to kill each other. We said some rude things to each other, and the next day as I walked around Disneyland with Greg and Amy, I felt bad about it. Then, suddenly, I heard my name over the loudspeakers. I was being paged at Disneyland! I got sent to an office where someone handed me a phone — and Jill St. John was on the other end of the line. "I just felt so bad about last night," she said. "I had to apologize. And I want to come out and meet you all there."

I told her to come on, and we spent a very nice day together, the four of us. And that was about it. But much later on, I suddenly got a bunch of calls one weekend. In the gossip section of the magazine insert that comes with the Sunday paper, there was an item where Jill St. John was asked who all the great loves of her life were. She responded with a list of men, including Henry Kissinger, Frank Sinatra... and "Benjamin" Barnes! Now, I had no idea what that was about, but that was a kind of press attention I didn't really need. So I tracked

Jill's phone number down and called to ask her what was going on.

"Oh, Ben!" she said, "Don't be angry with me! My PR man did that — and he got a little carried away!" I'll tell you what, it seemed like just about everybody was getting a little carried away during election years in Texas.

———————

IT WAS PROBABLY INEVITABLE THAT THE HIGHER I ROSE IN STATE POLITICS, the more press attention I'd get — both good and bad. But I got some unexpected attention one evening in August of 1970, at a fundraiser for my reelection campaign.

Lyndon Johnson had agreed to make an appearance at a big event we were holding at the old Palmer Auditorium in Austin. A couple thousand people had come, and everybody was excited about seeing the former President, as he wasn't making a whole lot of public appearances in his retirement. Johnson had prepared some basic remarks, and I pretty much expected a standard-issue campaign speech — but he must have been in a good mood that day, because he suddenly started praising me to the skies.

"He's a redhead, like Thomas Jefferson," Johnson declared, "and, like Thomas Jefferson, Ben Barnes will be President! Show us the way, Ben! Where you lead us, we will follow!" The crowd roared, and Johnson went on, proclaiming that "Ben Barnes will someday be the next President of the United States from Texas!"

I nearly fell over. As far as I'd come in politics, I never expected to hear a former President declaring that I'd make it to his office myself one day. Now, like anyone in politics, President Johnson might have just been talking the talk that day, just saying things to get the crowd fired up. But I'd never heard of him saying anything similar about other politicians he'd made appearances for, and I was flattered and moved by his words.

That same month, a few days after LBJ's birthday, ten thousand people gathered near Stonewall, Texas, for the dedication of a new state park bearing his name. Lady Bird was there, as well as the Johnsons' two daughters, Lynda and Luci, and their husbands. It was a joyful gathering, with the whole crowd singing along to "Happy Birthday" and the former President in high spirits.

I was the main speaker that day, and I stood up at that podium and talked about how, under the Johnson administration, seventy five thousand acres of seashore, four million acres of parks, and almost 10 million acres of wilderness were saved. Johnson was, I told the crowd, "the greatest conservation president since Theodore Roosevelt." People were whooping and hollering with the kind of adoration that great man truly deserved.

When I finished my speech, Johnson stood up next to me at the podium to speak, but first he quietly reached into my jacket pocket. He didn't say a word, just reached right in there and left something heavy. When I sat down, I pulled it out. It was a Rolex watch, engraved with the words "To BFB from LBJ." This day was supposed to be all about honoring him, but instead he'd brought me a gift — one that he knew I'd cherish.

People have said a lot of things about Lyndon Johnson over the years — good things and bad things, and even some cruel things. There's no doubt he was a mercurial, controlling man, and that he left behind his share of hurt feelings and angry people when he left the White House. But from the time he first took notice of me back in the fall of 1963 to his death in 1973, Johnson was just as generous to me as he could be with his support, advice, and loyalty. He truly wanted to help me succeed — and not just me, but the state's Democratic party.

Better than most politicians, Johnson never let the trees get in the way of seeing the forest: his ultimate goal was to improve the lives of ordinary people, in Texas and across the country, and he wasn't afraid to take a lot of lumps trying to make that happen. Despite how history has sometimes treated him, I see him as just about the most unselfish major political figure this country saw in the twentieth century. The United States was lucky to have a man of his integrity and drive in the White House during the difficult years of 1964-68 — and I've been happy to see in the past few years that the pendulum of historical opinion is finally swinging back to that point of view.

With President Johnson's ringing endorsement and a packed schedule of campaign appearances leading up to election day, I was running strong. And the closer we got, the more it looked like the whole party was running strong, too. George Bush never could figure out how to run against Lloyd Bentsen, and his vague campaign slogan — "He Can Do More" — just seemed to leave voters confused. More than what? Nobody knew. The only thing anyone could tell was that he really needed to "do more" to win votes if he wanted to beat Bentsen.

On November 3, 1970, Texas voters went to the polls and soundly repudiated the idea that the South was already falling to the Republicans. Bentsen beat Bush by more than 150,000 votes, despite the fact that Bush was the Texas Republicans' "golden boy" and that they'd spent more money on his campaign than on any other. Gov. Preston Smith beat Republican Paul Eggers by a similar margin, and I won my race in a landslide, receiving more than twice as many votes as my opponent — in fact, my two million votes were the most any Texas candidate had ever received to that point. The GOP's earlier predictions of claiming 35 House seats in 1970 was shown up for the pipe dream it was, when a mere 10 Republicans claimed seats.

It's hard to overstate what a blow this all was to the Texas Republican party. The Associated Press summed it up pretty well with a story by reporter Garth Jones:

> Texas Republicans smarted Wednesday from the good old country licking handed them at the polls. Any way they turned it hurt.
>
> When the dust cleared after Tuesday's balloting it was apparent [that]:
>
> 1. Texas Democrats, headed by former President Lyndon Johnson and former Gov. John Connally, are in better political shape than they have been since Johnson punctured another GOP revival move in 1964. Texas definitely can still be called a one-party state.
>
> 2. Texas Republicans lost their best hopes of ever putting the state on a two-party status with the resounding defeat of Rep. George Bush, R-Tex., and Paul Eggers, candidates for the Senate and governor. It was the second loss for each in their respective fields and made it highly unlikely either will run for a statewide office again....
>
> The election results also likely sent a shiver down the backbone of Sen. John Tower, who has to run for reelection in 1972... With no attractive statewide candidates left and a big pile of campaign bills, the Texas Republican party has a dark road ahead to rebuild in time for Tower's 1972 defense and the 1972 presidential election.

For Texas Democrats, this was the peak. When the sun rose on the morning after election day, it felt like we could see for miles, and the view was just as rosy as it could be. No matter what was going on in other states, no matter that a Republican was in the White House — the Texas Democratic party was as strong as ever at the start of the new decade.

They say it's always darkest before the dawn. Well, sometimes the opposite is true too. Just when it seems like the future couldn't be brighter, the darker times are looming just ahead. Looking back, the three months following election day would mark the turning point for the Texas Democratic party. And it started with a surprising decision by the man who had long seemed the very embodiment of the party: John Connally.

━━━━━━━

ONE AFTERNOON ABOUT A MONTH AFTER THE NOVEMBER ELECTIONS, I WAS with John Connally at his Floresville ranch house when he got a phone call. It turned out to be President Nixon on the line, and he had a proposition for the former governor.

I couldn't hear Nixon's end of the conversation, but I could certainly hear Connally's. And as it became clear what they were discussing, I don't mind saying that I could hardly believe my ears. Nixon wanted to appoint Connally as Secretary of the Treasury, making him the only Democrat on his cabinet. What's more, it sounded like Connally was seriously considering it. In fact, he only seemed to have one real reservation — but it was one that would end up changing the course of 20th-century American politics.

"Mr. President," Connally said, "if I'm going to do that, I think you ought to find something for George Bush to do."

There was a pause as Connally listened to Nixon. Then he said, "Well, he's a Republican, and I'm a Democrat, and he's ahead of me in line."

As Connally later told me, Nixon barked, "Well, what can he do?"

Connally replied, "Well, I don't know, Mr. President, but I've got to live with him here in Texas! If I'm going to take this position, I think you need to find a place for him."

Connally was resolute; he absolutely would not consider taking a cabinet position unless Nixon gave Bush a job. He knew Bush had worked hard on Nixon's campaign in '68 — in Connally's words, he'd "labored in the vineyards" for the party — and he'd been the Texas GOP's next great hope until his loss to Bentsen. Connally just didn't feel it was right to embarrass him by taking a position in the Republican president's cabinet, when his own political future was now so uncertain.

Connally's insistence finally brought Nixon around, and he ultimately made Bush the Ambassador to the United Nations (after first remarking, as Connally later told me, that the U.N. was already so screwed up, Bush couldn't possibly mess it up any more.) Nixon obviously didn't think much of Bush, so if it hadn't been for Connally's browbeating, he most likely wouldn't have offered Bush anything. And because Bush had suffered two devastating losses in statewide races, that probably would have spelled the end of his time as a force in Republican politics.

So it was that John Connally saved George Bush's political career. If it weren't for Connally's pull with Nixon, Bush would have been left twisting in the wind and would never have continued to ascend the party's ladder to the Vice Presidency, then the Presidency. In turn, his son George W. Bush would almost certainly never have been President. It's amazing how even seemingly simple events can ultimately end up changing the course of history.

Connally's decision to take a seat in President Nixon's cabinet stunned a lot of people in Texas. Here was the icon of the Democratic party, the man who'd held Texas Democrats together for so many years, happily agreeing to join forces with the Republican president. And not just any Republican, but Richard M. Nixon. For whatever reason, despite Nixon's lack of ethics in the 1968 election and his already evident paranoia, Connally seemed to like and respect him. But for my part, I still remembered the words of Sam Rayburn a decade earlier. No matter how well disposed my good friend John Connally might have been to Nixon, I still didn't trust him at all. And if I'd known what his administration was already up to, I'd have trusted him even less.

I didn't find out about it until many years later, but apparently the Nixon administration was already plotting how to bring down Texas Democrats, who were the strongest Democratic bloc in the South. In December of 1970, two powerful Texas Republicans — Sen. John Tower and his state campaign finance chairman Julian Zimmerman — had a meeting in Washington with Nixon's attorney general, John Mitchell. As described in court testimony a couple of years later, and recounted in Waggoner Carr's book, *Not Guilty,* the three men sat in the offices of the Committee to Re-elect the President (CREEP), talking about the Connally-Nixon connection and how it might impact Texas politics.

Tower was especially concerned about whether it would give me a boost, as a potential opponent for his senate seat in 1972. As Zimmerman later recounted, Mitchell dismissed that concern outright.

"Don't worry about Ben Barnes," Mitchell told them. "There's an investigation going on that will remove him from the political picture."

If I'd known about the conversation then, I'd have laughed it off as nothing more than political posturing. I hadn't heard about any investigation, and even if there was something going on, there'd be no reason to think it involved me. But all too soon, I'd find out that, in the grand political scheme, none of that mattered. As 1970 drew to a close, Texas Democrats might have been riding high — but they were heading straight for an ambush.

Chapter Eleven

Rumors in the Air

ON THE EVENING OF MONDAY, JANUARY 18TH, 1971, TEXAS DEMOCRATS were in the mood to celebrate. It was the night before inauguration day, and the traditional Victory Dinner was getting underway at Austin Municipal Auditorium. More than three thousand party supporters had paid $30 a head to dine on steak, potatoes, and apple pie and listen to Wayne Newton sing, and the mood in Austin was one of triumph. No matter what was going on across the rest of the South, we'd kicked the Texas Republicans' butts — and tonight was the night to celebrate it.

But there was more than the usual excitement in the air. There was also a rumor going around the room — one that was too hot to ignore. I first heard about it when my chief of staff, Robert Spellings, took my arm and said in a low voice that he'd heard some interesting news. He said he'd heard that the SEC had filed a lawsuit earlier in the day, and that indictments of some major Texas political figures might follow.

Just after that, Frank Erwin came running up too, with a big old smile on his face. "You're not going to believe this!" he exclaimed, just as happy as a child. "Preston Smith and Gus Mutscher are under investigation!" I'd taken in what Spellings had said, but when Frank put the names of the governor and the speaker of the House to it, that got my attention in a whole new way. He went on to say that the investigation had to do with a pair of bills passed in 1969, and allegations that Mutscher, Smith, and others might have taken bribes to get them passed.

Frank Erwin was a loyal personal and political friend, and he also had a little bit of a vindictive streak in him. He knew Governor Smith and I had butted heads over the years, and he wasn't sad to see a man he considered my political foe get in some hot water. But I didn't think there was much to be happy about. "Now, don't start celebrating," I told Erwin. "If either one of those guys gets in trouble while I'm in office, it's gonna rub off on me, too."

"No, it's not," Erwin said, his face puckering. "How can it? You didn't have anything to do with it." On that point, he was right — but he was wrong in thinking that fact would shield me from the mud that was about to be flung all over the Capitol.

When it was time for my speech that night, I stood up at the podium and talked about the future. "In 1970, we made Richard Nixon a better President by sending him a Democratic senator and 20 Democratic representatives from Texas," I told the crowd. "I want us to start right now making plans to make Richard Nixon an even better President in 1972 by making him an ex-president in 1973."

I hadn't told anyone yet, but I was already thinking about the 1972 statewide races too. Having made the choice to run again for lieutenant governor in 1970, I already knew I wanted to run for governor in 1972. Standing at that podium, looking out at all those cheering Democrats, it was easy to believe the future was nothing but bright. But the rumor of the investigation and indictments sat in the back of my mind like a dead weight — I couldn't shake the feeling that things were about to change, and not for the better. Looking back, I believe that the 1971 Victory Dinner was the final moment in Texas Democratic politics where anything and everything seemed possible. What I never would have guessed then is that, more than 30 years later, we still haven't recovered from the fall we were about to take.

THE NEXT MORNING, INAUGURATION DAY, DAWNED CLEAR AND CHILLY. When the church bells chimed noon, there wasn't a cloud in the sky as Governor Smith and I took our places at the South entrance of the Capitol building for the inauguration ceremony. But that perfect blue sky was deceiving, as a cold wind was whipping through Austin, sending chills through the crowd.

The rumors of the night before had been confirmed in the day's newspapers, and soon all of Austin was buzzing with the details. The SEC had filed a civil suit claiming that certain Texas legislators had agreed to push through bills in return for bribes — loans from the Sharpstown State Bank of Houston, which they then used to buy stock in National Bankers Life Insurance Company.

A few weeks later, they sold their stocks for hefty profits, all thanks to the inside dealings of a man named Frank W. Sharp, who owned both Sharpstown State Bank and National Bankers Life. Sharp had apparently arranged the stock deals in exchange for pledges from legislators and other officials to support two banking bills that would benefit his businesses. And sure enough, the House and Senate had quickly passed the two bills in a special session in September of 1969.

Governor Smith and Speaker Gus Mutscher weren't defendants in the lawsuit (though Mutscher and his top aide Rush McGinty would eventually be indicted), but they were mentioned as having received Sharpstown loans to purchase the stock. Neither Smith nor Mutscher denied these facts, but they did deny that the loans and stock profits had influenced their decisions on the banking legislation. And Smith and Mutscher were merely the biggest fish in this particular cesspool — several other prominent Democrats, including former Attorney General Waggoner Carr, Representative Tommy Shannon, and State Democratic Chairman Elmer Baum, were also implicated.

This was a big, far-reaching scandal in the making. Even Texans who didn't have the stomach for reading long articles about stock tips, loans, and banking legislation could understand headlines that screamed "fraud" and "Democrats." What should have been our week of triumph soon turned into agony for Texas Democrats.

I had nothing to do with the Sharpstown loans, the stock purchases, or Frank Sharp himself, who I'd never spoken to or met. I told reporters that when they asked, and they wrote it in their stories. But just a few days after the Sharpstown story broke, another story surfaced — one that was completely unrelated, but which was written in a way that made me look suspect.

Now, I want to make a couple of things clear up front. The fact is, there was wrongdoing by Democrats in Sharpstown. I believe that Gus Mutscher and Tommy Shannon, in an uncharacteristic lapse of judgment, did accept loans and stock tips in exchange for pushing legislation through (even though the legislation probably would have passed anyway). I don't deny that, and never have.

But there were several things that pushed the Sharpstown affair beyond the bounds of a straight-up investigation and into the realm of political witch hunt. Certain forces in the Republican party saw Sharpstown as an opportunity to bring down the most powerful Democratic bloc in the South, and they spared nothing — not time nor money nor effort — in trying to bring Texas Democrats down. The evidence that surfaced later, which I'll describe shortly, makes that absolutely clear.

Even from the beginning, the federal government made some very suspect decisions — for example, the timing of the SEC's lawsuit. Why in the world, when it had been poking around in Texas for several months, gathering information, would the SEC choose to file its suit on January 18th — guaranteeing headlines on January 19th, inauguration day, the proudest day of the year for Texas Democrats? Richard Nixon had been in office for two years, enough time to put his people in place at all the major federal institutions; you'd have to be about as naïve as a child to think the Republicans in charge at the SEC happened to choose that date by chance.

For another thing, the SEC began leaking information intended to further damage Democrats almost immediately. It wasn't enough to file the suit and let the matter play out in the courts, where legal issues belong. The SEC began a campaign of trying Democrats in the court of public opinion — and they started with me. Just a few days after the Sharpstown story broke, reporters began covering the "news" that I'd once received a $60,000 loan from the Dallas Bank and Trust Company, which was also owned by Frank Sharp and named as a defendant bank in the Sharpstown suit. They wrote that I'd bought stock in a data company with the loan, using the stock itself for collateral, and that the loan had become a "problem" loan when the stock price had subsequently dropped.

Now, for one thing, it wasn't illegal to get a loan, and it wasn't illegal to do business with the Dallas Bank and Trust Company. For another, I'd never bought the stock they claimed I did, or used it as collateral. In fact, a friend of mine named Harold Hinn had co-signed for the loan and had personally guaranteed it. Nothing illegal about that either. And besides, by the time the stories came out, the loan had long since been paid off.

The fact was, there was no reason anyone should have cared about that loan at all, which I'd taken out to help pay for my divorce settlement from Martha. But from a Republican standpoint, it surely was useful to be able to put the words "Lieutenant Governor Ben Barnes," "loan," and "Frank Sharp" in the same sentence, instantly tarring me with the same brush as those accused of accepting bribes — which no one was suggesting I'd done.

Having illegally released this irrelevant information just as the Sharpstown story was breaking, sources at the Republican-controlled SEC succeeded in linking my name with the growing scandal, pretty much guaranteeing that in stories about it, my name would appear. Then, to no one's surprise, readers had a hard time keeping the complex details of the scandal straight — and soon enough it just became conventional wisdom that I was somehow involved. Even reporters got confused, as a January 24 correction in the *San Antonio Express-News* showed: "In stories in the Friday Evening News and Saturday Express

News, Lieutenant Governor Ben Barnes was erroneously listed among state officials who have admitted buying National Bankers Life Insurance Co. stock with borrowed money obtained by placing the stock as collateral."

Texas Republicans, left for dead just weeks earlier, were overjoyed at the budding scandal. They offered up all kinds of self-serving soundbites and eagerly wrung their hands for the cameras. With a complicated story like this one, they knew that the investigation would take a while, and that the stench of it would cling to the Democrats for a long time to come, regardless of how everything turned out in the end.

Meanwhile, Preston Smith seemed untroubled by the growing furor. Even though he and his close adviser, Elmer Baum, had made more than $60,000 each on their stock, Smith didn't seem to believe he'd get in any real trouble, either legally or with Texas voters. Perhaps he was so confident because, although Sharp's two bills had passed with Smith's help, Smith had then actually turned around and vetoed the bills. He'd done it at the urging of former Governor Allan Shivers, and I'll tell you what — that saved his butt later. If Smith hadn't vetoed those bills, he almost certainly would have been indicted, like Mutscher and the others.

Preston just went about his business like he didn't have a care in the world, even joking about Sharpstown at a February speech he gave at the Headliners Club in Austin. "I would like to quote from the Book of John — not John Connally," he said, drawing chuckles from the audience, who well knew how much Smith disliked Connally. "'Let he who is without stock throw the first rock,'" he continued, theatrically waving a stone in the air. "I just brought along one rock, because I thought, in this crowd, one rock would suffice." Sitting there in the audience, I thought that was a little bit cavalier on Preston's part, if for no other reason than the stock case was doing so much damage to the party, and he was the face of it.

I wasn't overly worried about how the Sharpstown investigation might affect me, because, unlike Preston Smith, I wasn't implicated in the SEC lawsuit. My advisers felt the same way and urged me just to ignore the rumors and gossip swirling around Austin. There were more important matters at hand, including dealing with the budget shortfall we were facing in the 62nd legislature, and I was anxious to get started tackling the state's problems in the session.

━━━━━━

WHEN THE LEGISLATIVE SESSION OPENED IN JANUARY OF 1971, THE STATE was facing a $16 million budget deficit. Once again, we'd have to figure out a way to make up the shortfall without unduly burdening Texans with too many new taxes. Political observers groaned that the session was destined to be the "worst" and "longest" in years, but I wasn't inclined to sit back and muddle through it. Right away, I broke precedent and declared that the Senate would meet five or six days a week from the beginning of the session, as opposed to the three days a week senators were used to. The state just had too many pressing problems to waste time.

At this point, the Senate's liberals began trying to push through a corporate profits tax. To their minds, the half a billion dollars that would raise every two years was just what we needed to help pull the state out of its hole — but I knew that the tax would ultimately damage us far more than it would help us.

Just as I'd learned in the mid-sixties, when Lyndon Johnson and John Connally were still in office, there was one way to keep the Democratic party strong: we had to maintain ties with the business community and make sure it was always socially acceptable to be a Democrat. Success in politics is a balancing act, and as noble as the liberals' goals might have been in shifting the tax burden to corporations, the ultimate result would have been worse for ordinary Texans. If there was one lesson I wish I could have drilled into Democrats' heads — and could drill into their heads even today — it was that you have to take care of your strong center, and your money base, or else you'll doom yourself to being ineffectual. That's exactly what I was working hard to avoid in 1971 — but unfortunately, more than three decades later, it's exactly what's happening to the Democrats today.

Throughout the spring, I spent a whole lot of political capital fighting the liberals' corporate tax idea. With one term as lieutenant governor under my belt, I was completely at home in the workings of the Senate, and I lobbied the hell out of the 31 senators while putting together a tax package that moderate senators could support. The plan we created would impose slight tax increases on general sales, car rentals, cigarettes, gasoline, and beer, and would solve our money problems without alienating businesses and driving them away from the party. In late April, when it came time for a vote, there was a fierce debate on the floor before we defeated the corporate tax by a vote of 16-15. The result completely deflated the liberals, who thought all along they had the corporate tax sewn up.

Despite working against the liberal wing on the tax issue, though, I continued to push for progressive legislation that would better the lives of Texans. For years, there had been a growing movement to pass the Texas Equal Rights Amendment giving women equal footing with men, and I wholeheartedly supported it. The Texas Senate had passed the measure in 1969, but it had failed in the House. Now, in 1971, it came up again — and we got it passed in both the House and the Senate, one of the first states in the Union to do so. Barbara Jordan was a co-sponsor of the bill, and she'd wanted to speak to the Senate about the measure, but there were enough conservative senators that I figured that might cause more problems than it was worth.

"Senator Jordan," I said to her, "with all due respect, you've got two choices here. Do you want to speak about this bill, or do you want to pass it?" As much as she wanted to make a historic speech on the Senate floor, Barbara was no fool. We immediately put the bill up for a vote, and it passed.

By this time, Barbara Jordan was gaining more and more attention and stature as one of the brightest young senators in Texas. Lyndon Johnson had taken note of her early, inviting her to a group meeting at the White House during her first term and surprising her when he even called on her by name. It was clear that Barbara was interested in a lot more than just being a groundbreaker as a woman and African American, and it was even more clear that Texas — and, in fact, the country — would benefit from having her in a more powerful, visible position.

For those reasons, I took advantage of a constitutionally mandated redistricting effort in 1971 to draw a new district in Houston, one that would benefit Barbara in a run for the U.S. House of Representatives. And I'm proud to say that that new district played a big role in her being able to win that seat — the first African American woman from the South to win a U.S. House seat.

Now, recently there's been a lot of talk about the redistricting efforts of Texas's own Tom DeLay. Prior to the 2004 elections, DeLay used the power of the Republican majority in the Texas legislature to redraw existing districts so that more Republicans could win House seats. It might seem strange that I'd brag on my own redistricting efforts while condemning DeLay's, but here's the difference.

DeLay had no legal right to call for a redistricting when he did. According to federal law, new districts are to be drawn once a decade, after each new census. At that time, new districts — such as the one I drew for Barbara Jordan — are added depending on how much the state's population has grown.

But what DeLay did was totally different. He stepped in and influenced the Texas legislature to call for another redistricting following the first, legally mandated one. This was unprecedented — no one had ever so baldly manipulated the system for partisan gain. Tom DeLay did what he did solely to benefit the Republican party. It's symptomatic of the selfish kind of politicking that's been going on in Texas for the last decade or so.

In addition to drawing Barbara Jordan's new district, there were two pieces of legislation I was particularly proud of in 1971. The first was a consti-tutional amendment giving statewide officeholders a four-year term, rather than the two-year terms we'd always had. I pushed hard for that amendment because I knew it would give the state government more continuity than we'd had to that point. And the amendment called for our statewide elections to take place in the mid-term between presidential elections, which freed us up to focus on Texas's needs rather than on the national races.

The second piece of legislation I worked to get passed was one of the biggest reasons I'd chosen to run for lieutenant governor again in 1970. I'd long believed that Texas needed a new state constitution, and as lieutenant governor I knew I could get an amendment passed calling for a Constitutional Convention in 1973. If everything went as planned, I hoped to be elected gov-ernor in 1972 and oversee the adoption of a new state constitution to replace the current, outdated one adopted in 1876. Our state constitution was simply not adequate to the demands of a 20th-century legislature — a fact we were harshly reminded of in February of 1971, when a new study came out showing that the Texas legislature ranked 38th in the nation according to criteria such as accountability, functionality, and independence. For a state that prides itself on being bigger and better than everybody else, this was a humbling blow, and a lot of it was due to the fact that our constitution really hamstrung what we were able to do.

As the regular session came to an end in May, I felt politically strong. I'd guided the Senate through a rough session and passed some groundbreaking legislation. I'd won a few battles that no one thought I could win. And so far, the mud from Sharpstown wasn't sticking to me. There were hearings going on about Sharpstown, but I figured that, having made it through the first few months without any undue trouble, the worst was over for me.

British Prime Minister Harold Wilson came to Texas for a visit in early May, and he and Lyndon Johnson dropped by my apartment in the Capitol one morning. The next day, Johnson wrote me a short note:

> Dear Ben:
>
> I know we ruined your morning but you did make a great impression on Prime Minister Wilson. We talked about you at length yesterday. He told me after leaving your apartment this morning he wanted to confirm every predic-tion I had made. That is why he said I was only the first President from Texas.
>
> Sincerely, LBJ

At that moment, my political prospects felt as strong as ever. But I was all too aware that it was a dangerous business being the most prominent Democrat in the one Southern state where Democrats where holding strong. As I told the Associated Press a couple of months later, "I would say — and I don't want this to sound vain or wrong — that some Republicans consider me their No. 1 enemy in Texas right now, their No. 1 political enemy. I would say this is a scar, from the standpoint that these people are working on me every day." In the summer of 1971, I was about to find out just how true that was.

———————

AS SPRING GAVE WAY TO SUMMER, THE SEC CONTINUED COLLECTING information for its civil suit. In the meantime, the Department of Justice came on down to Texas and launched its own investigation — and in mid-June, the DOJ made a move that shocked the hell out of everybody, including their counterparts at the SEC.

The U.S. Attorney in Houston, a Nixon appointee named Anthony Farris, offered Frank Sharp full immunity for the rest of the case in exchange for guilty pleas on two felony charges. Those guilty pleas would net Sharp just three years' worth of probation and a $5,000 fine. It was a pretty sweet deal, and with his sudden grant of immunity, Sharp was eager to help out the government that had let him off so easy. Overnight, his motivation turned from protecting himself to implicating anyone and everyone he could in Texas Democratic politics.

There was only one reason the DOJ could possibly have had for granting Sharp full immunity: they wanted his help in going after Texas Democrats. Anthony Farris even said as much when he happily told reporters, "I would rather get all the sharks — and not just the minnows."

But it wasn't Farris, of course, who'd given the go-ahead to Sharp's immunity deal. Those instructions had come from higher up in Nixon's Justice Department. In a June 10 letter to Farris, Deputy Attorney General Richard Kleindienst — the top Justice official behind Attorney General John Mitchell — wrote, "I find that testimony of Frank Sharp is necessary in the public interest. You are authorized to seek a grant of immunity for Sharp." What was a top DOJ official doing rooting around in a Texas case? *The Dallas Morning News,* which reported the existence of Kleindienst's letter, offered its own opinion on June 20:

> ... Farris himself explained the move for immunity for Sharp this way:
> "We felt it would save the government an immeasurable amount of time, money and manpower and get at some important alleged defendants."

But the question can be asked:

Who might qualify as a more important SEC-alleged defendant than Sharp himself, save high Democratic politicians?

At around the same time that Sharp was granted immunity, I announced my intention to run for governor in 1972. If I hadn't already been a prime target for Republicans in Washington, I certainly was now. Gov. Smith was in trouble, I was already leading in the polls to beat him in 1972, and I was now the face of the Johnson-Connally wing of the Democratic party. I was like a nail sticking up, just waiting to be hammered down. And with the SEC and DOJ both continuing their investigations in Texas, and their protected felon Frank Sharp now unleashed, it wouldn't take long for them to find some way to drag my name back into the news.

Sure enough, the next month confidential testimony was leaked to the *Dallas Times Herald,* which dutifully ran a July 21st story titled "Barnes-Heatly Stock Link Told." Once again, my name was in the headlines with the word "stock," which guaranteed trouble for me — even though the "stock link" revealed in the story had nothing whatsoever to do with Sharpstown. The story went on to detail how I'd "introduced State Representative W. S. Heatly to Ling & Co. Inc., the financial firm which handled the National Bankers Life Insurance stock sales to various state officials, according to a document filed Tuesday in the federal clerk's office."

Now, telling someone about a Dallas-based brokerage company was not an infraction of any kind — moral, legal, ethical, or otherwise. The fact was, there was no relevant news in this story at all. But by leaking information that linked my name with an institution named in the Sharpstown scandal, the SEC sources knew they'd cause trouble for me, even if the news was meaningless. When I heard about the headline, I rushed back from a speech I was making in Waco and called an impromptu press conference the next day in the Capitol building.

I'd tried to approach the leaks and innuendo as calmly as I could up to now, but that headline just pushed me right over the edge. I was mad, and I wanted the Capitol press corps to know it. "I'm sick and tired of the attempts being made to drag me into the SEC investigation," I told reporters, my face turning about as red as my hair. "It out-McCarthys Joe McCarthy. I'm disgusted and disappointed that it's taken place. It's got to be politically motivated." I went on to tell the reporters that I'd been informed that that nearly every witness in the SEC investigation was being asked about me. "A federal employee involved in the investigation told three newspaper people in another city, 'We're trying to get Barnes involved any way we can,'" I told the reporters, who duly scribbled it down and reported it in the next day's papers.

I'd like to be able to say that the slew of stories the next day served to neutralize the original story. But, of course, there were many people who saw my objections as self-serving, and who would believe from that point on that I was involved some kind of stock wrongdoing. The truth is, it's almost impossible to get your reputation back fully once you've been smeared — no matter how much you protest, or how right you might be.

From this time on, many Texans began to look at me as just another of those "Austin rascals" who had used their offices for personal gain. Even though I was just 33, I'd been in state politics for 11 years, and so I was part of the "establishment." That alone was enough to damn me in the eyes of many voters, as a July 23rd letter to the editor of the *Dallas Morning News* showed.

> I read a letter to the *News* which stated that the people of Texas have lost faith and confidence in their state government as a result of the findings of the SEC and other recent revelations concerning our state leaders. No statement could be more true. However, I am very puzzled and somewhat amused to note that this same writer looks to Ben Barnes to provide this faith and confidence in our state government.
>
> Barnes may be young and good-looking, but I for one cannot see the wisdom of seeking leadership from a man of the same party, with the same set of strings attached...
>
> As was the reader who wrote the letter to which I have been referring, I too am a college student who will be voting for the first time in 1972. But my first vote will go, if I consider him capable, to the candidate of the Republican party. As one who intends to work and rear a family in Texas, it is the viable and progressive Republican party to which I will turn to provide the leadership for my state government.
>
> Kerry N. Cammack

As the summer rolled on, more and more voters began talking about "throwing the bums out" in 1972. Some cars sported bumpers stickers reading "All New in '72." I could protest all I wanted that I wasn't involved in Sharpstown, but I couldn't rightly claim I wasn't in state government. And for the first time, I began to worry that fallout from the scandal might actually hurt me in the race.

On August 11, 1971, Frank Sharp — protected by his grant of immunity — testified in a deposition that another defendant in the SEC lawsuit, John

Osorio, had implicated me in the bribery case. Osorio was well known in Austin. He'd been an aide to Governor Allan Shivers, a state insurance commissioner, and the head of National Banker's Life Insurance Co., the company whose stock purchases were at the heart of the stock-fraud allegations. Osorio stood accused of being a central player in the Sharpstown scandal, but he said publicly from the very beginning that he believed the case was little more than a political maneuver.

"This whole thing has got deep political overtones," he told the *Dallas Morning News* in January of 1971. "I believe it was politically inspired to embarrass the governor, members of the Legislature, and particularly Waggoner Carr."

In his deposition, Sharp told the following story. He testified that, shortly after the two banking bills passed, John Osorio came to see him in his office at the Sharpstown State Bank. "Well," Osorio supposedly said, "Ben delivered" on passage of the bills. Because he was worried that his office was bugged, Sharp suggested that Osorio join him for a walk outside the office. At that point, Sharp asked, "Are you telling me that we're obligated to Ben Barnes for this?" To which Osorio supposedly replied, "Oh, no, no. I just ... I've already taken care of that... You know, Ben is smarter than most of these other politicians... he takes only cash."

This was the perfect setup to nail me in the Sharpstown case. After all, I could prove that I hadn't ever owned the stock in question or gotten the loans that Smith, Mutscher, and others had admitted to taking. I could even prove that I hadn't done anything extraordinary to get those two bills passed. But there was no way in the world I could disprove the idea that I'd received untraceable, under-the-table cash.

After Sharp offered this testimony, his lawyer Morton Susman walked out of the courthouse with former U.S. assistant attorney Tim Timmins. As Timmins related under oath in a later trial, and also to me personally, he asked Susman, "What's [Sharp] going to come up with next?" To which Susman responded, "Now you know why we got immunity."

SEC officials immediately leaked Sharp's testimony, and it made every newspaper in Texas, with damning headlines like "Barnes Linked to Controversy," "Sharp Links Barnes to 'Deal,'" and "Sharp Ties Bank Deal to Barnes." Even former senator Ralph Yarborough, who was rumored to be considering a run for governor himself, jumped into the fray with glee, declaring that the "boys in Austin" had been caught with their "hands in the cookie jar."

I'd been plenty upset about the "Barnes-Heatly stock link" story the previous month, but this just stunned me. I couldn't believe Sharp would flat lie under oath, and that the SEC would then rush to leak it all over the state. This was just too much — I didn't have a chance in the governor's race if the federal government was going to spread lies about me across Texas for the next 10 months until the primary. So I called my good friend Robert Strauss, who was then the treasurer of the Democratic National Committee. "This is out of control," I told him. "We've got to find a way to stop it! I can't just sit back while they do this."

"Ben," he said, "I'll tell you what. I'm going to set up a meeting with Bill Casey." Strauss figured that the orders to tar me had to be coming from the top — so we'd have to go to the top to get it stopped. He quickly got to work, trying to arrange a secret meeting with SEC Chairman William J. Casey in Washington.

The next day, a courier delivered a transcript of Sharp's testimony to John Osorio, who was then living in New York. Osorio read the deposition and knew immediately that Sharp had made the story up. In the margin of the document, he scribbled, "Cheap trick. Part of the SEC script. Nothing like this ever took place with Ben," and signed his name to it.

If that wasn't convincing enough, Osorio gave a deposition of his own a few days later in Dallas. During his testimony, SEC attorney James Sims asked him point blank whether he'd said the things Frank Sharp attributed to him. "Mr. Sims," Osorio replied under oath, "I don't often get mad. But that's a damned lie."

From that moment on, most political observers understood that I had no involvement whatsoever in the stock scandal. But for thousands of Texans who didn't follow the story so closely, the only thing that stuck in their minds was those big headlines linking the name "Ben Barnes" with Sharpstown.

Chapter Twelve

Nixon's Dirty Tricks in Texas

ON AUGUST 26, TWO WEEKS AFTER THE LATEST DAMAGING LEAKS, I BOARDED a plane after a campaign appearance in Denton, declining to answer reporters when they asked where I was heading. I flew straight up to Washington, D.C., and met with Bob Strauss at his DNC office. That evening, he and I paid a visit to William J. Casey at the SEC headquarters, near Capitol Hill.

A Cold War conservative who would be implicated in the Iran-Contra affair during the Reagan administration, Bill Casey was a hard-core Republican. I don't know about Strauss, but I was ready for a fight when we walked into that room. Strauss opened up by telling Casey we weren't going to put up with any more illegal leaks and smears from the SEC investigation. I knew he intended to do most of the talking, but I had to jump in. "You're trying this case in the press," I said, trying to control my anger. "This is a hell of a way to do things."

Casey seemed surprised, but the other SEC official present, Stanley Sporkin, didn't. Sporkin, who would later gain fame as the presiding judge in the Microsoft antitrust trial, had come with an armload of papers and files. Strauss told Sporkin he'd examined thousands of pages of testimony in the case and had yet to find anything that would implicate me. "And yet this harassment continues," he said.

"Just tell me one thing," I asked Casey and Sporkin. "Am I personally under investigation?"

"No," said Sporkin, a serious-looking man with dark circles under his eyes. Gesturing to the files he'd put on the table, he turned to look at me and went on, "You don't have anything to worry about."

That was probably meant to be reassuring, but the fact was, I was never really worried about the legal case to begin with. I was worried about the illegal leaks that were designed to damage me, regardless of my presumed innocence or guilt. Strauss and I made the point one more time that the leaks and false stories had to stop, and then we left Casey's office. The whole meeting had taken about 10 minutes, but I hoped it would signal the beginning of the end of the federal harassment.

Yet, despite Sporkin's assurances that I wasn't under investigation, the harassment worsened. Soon enough, IRS agents came poking around my office, digging through my files. One night, a couple of agents even showed up unannounced at my parents' house in Comanche County, asking to talk to them about my finances. When my mother told me about it, I tracked down that agent and told him I'd whip his ass if he got near them again. That probably wasn't the most prudent thing I could have done, but I was so mad by that point, I didn't have the strength for niceties.

As I'd find out many years later, the Nixon administration had ordered audits of dozens, if not hundreds, of Democratic officials — most of whom were in the South and Southwest. A year before the Watergate break-in at the DNC office in Washington, Nixon was already honing his skills at bringing down Democrats by any means necessary.

The IRS investigators made a point of checking the records of all the numbers dialed from the Speaker's and lieutenant governor's offices, hoping to find evidence that I'd made personal calls, because if I'd made a personal call from my office phone, the cost of it could have been categorized as "income" for me — and I'd have needed to pay taxes on it. If I hadn't paid taxes on it, then that would mean I'd intentionally avoided paying taxes — and that would be enough of a hook to prosecute me.

Fortunately, my great friend Ralph Wayne (who'd been my campaign manager as well as the chair of the House Administrative Committee) and my accountant, Jim Howard, had long looked out for me on all matters of income and taxes. I mean, I grew up on a peanut farm in Comanche County — what did I know about complicated matters of taxes and accounting? Thank God Ralph and Jim were there to help me out. Every time I'd flown on someone's plane for anything personal, they had me pay taxes on it. And every year, they had me pay taxes on a certain percentage of the phone bill, to cover any personal calls. Ralph and Jim would have made me pay taxes on the air I was breathing if I'd let them.

The fact is, I overpaid my taxes every single year — but that's what saved me in the end. When the government agents finally finished going through all my files and records, they sure enough found something wasn't quite right: the IRS owed me $3,800. But it literally took years for them to reach that conclusion — long after the Sharpstown stench had brought down my career and most of the Texas Democratic establishment.

Now, while all of this was going on, two strange things were happening. For one thing, no matter how many investigators were poking around in my business, no one from the SEC, the DOJ, or the IRS ever asked me a single question about Sharpstown. Not a single one. The stock scandal was supposedly the reason why agents were swarming all over Texas, yet they were spending hours of their time and hundreds of thousands of dollars investigating me — for reasons that apparently had nothing to do with Sharpstown. It was obvious that there was a race on between the various departments to find something that would bring me down politically, or even send me to jail. After all, as the world would learn soon enough, Richard Nixon was not someone who was satisfied simply destroying a man's political career if he could destroy his life too.

On September 4, 1971, Nixon and his attorney general, John Mitchell, were talking in the Oval Office. Nixon's taping system caught their conversation, which was about Sharpstown generally, but also about one of Nixon's assistant attorney generals, Will Wilson.

Wilson was a former Texas Democrat who'd turned Republican after two devastating election losses in the early '60s. He was one of the nearly six dozen Democrats who'd run for Lyndon Johnson's Senate seat in 1960 — the seat that ultimately went to John Tower. And he'd been beaten by newcomer John Connally in the 1962 Democratic primary for governor. Shortly afterward, he'd left the Democratic party in disgust.

Plenty of people believed Wilson was the driving force behind the Sharpstown investigation, in an effort to punish Texas Democrats. They believed he was trying to link as many Democrats to the scandal as possible in an effort to bring down the party that he felt had failed him. But the irony was, Wilson himself had been an associate of Sharp in the 1960s. And he was as deep in Sharp's business as anyone — a fact that apparently caused President Nixon some consternation when he found out.

As the September 4th conversation shows, Mitchell was worried that the Wilson-Sharp connection might throw a wrench into the administration's pursuit of Texas Democrats.

> *Mitchell:* [W]here, I think, you have a prime and vital interest is the politics in Texas. As you know, this Sharp thing has just about destroyed the Democrat Party down there, and will continue to as this builds up. Uh, Wilson —

Nixon: The governor is involved — Wilson, with Sharp —

Mitchell: The governor, the Speaker of the House, the head of the Democratic party, et cetera, et cetera.

So, we have, uh, a hard choice to make as to whether to admit that Wilson, as a lawyer for Sharp, uh, was involved with the Sharp situation — which of course he was, in some of these areas. Not illegally — there's never been anything illegal done.

Uh, or we could toss him to the wolves and, uh, get him out of here and say he's just part of that Texas so-and-so, and then we're losing the stroke that we have in Texas with the leg up on the Democrats.

So, it's a choice that is, uh, rather difficult, and of course I've been quite close to this picture and I thought it was something I ought to run by you and see if you've got some reactions to it.

Nixon: Did you talk to Connally about it?

Mitchell: Ah, Connally and I have talked about this situation from time to time, and, uh, particularly in trying to take care of his boy Ben Barnes, to see that he didn't get —

Nixon: He's in it, too.

Mitchell: Ah, he's, he's in it, yeah.

Nixon: Damn right.

Mitchell: It, uh. He, he is not involved in the fixing of the legislation, like the other Democrats are, but he's, uh, got a lot of things to answer to down there.

Now, this conversation reveals a couple of interesting things. One is that, despite the fact that he'd shocked the hell out of us all by joining forces with Nixon, John Connally was still trying to look out for me in the face of Nixon's pursuit of Democrats. The other is that, despite the fact that Mitchell obviously knew I had nothing to do with Sharpstown, Nixon was determined to try to embarrass me politically regardless. It's just patently obvious that Nixon had a hand in what the Sharpstown investigations, and other investigations, were setting out to accomplish.

Even as his administration was fighting to bring down Texas Democrats, Nixon grew even more infatuated with his own Texas Democratic cabinet member, John Connally. In fact, Nixon liked and respected Connally so much that rumors were soon floating around about a potential Nixon-Connally ticket in 1972. Texas Republicans were reporting gleefully that Connally would campaign for Nixon in '72, and even that he might switch to the Republican party. I responded to all this the only way I knew how. I said publicly that, as much as I respected John Connally, there was absolutely no way I could support a Nixon-

Connally ticket if the rumors turned out to be true. I was a Democrat and committed to the success of the party, and that was the end of that.

But all the rumors, the multiple investigations, and the warring campaigns leading up to the Democratic primary were taking their toll on the party. In October of 1971, less than a year after we'd trounced the Republicans in the '70 elections, state Sen. Oscar Mauzy told the *New York Times,* "Texas Democratic politics is in the most confused, most fluid mess I've seen in 30 years."

My hope was that, over the next six months, I'd be able to overcome the negative press from the investigations and go on to win the primary, and ultimately the governor's office. Sharpstown was, for me, like a low-grade fever that I couldn't shake. I still didn't believe it could do me any real damage, but it just refused go away. I didn't realize it then, but even a low-grade fever can do permanent harm if it lingers long enough.

━━━━━━━━━

AS THE SEC AND DOJ CONTINUED TO INTERROGATE PEOPLE ABOUT ME through the summer of 1971, they soon realized that no one had anything to offer them. They poked and they prodded, but every witness told them they didn't know of any connection I had to Sharpstown. Frustrated, they turned again to John Osorio — who'd already flatly contradicted Frank Sharp's lies about me — and tried to blackmail him into testifying against me.

Osorio had left Texas for New York in an attempt to distance himself from the scandal, but he quickly learned that there was no outrunning the Nixon Justice Department. Not only was he in legal jeopardy from being named in the original SEC suit, but now there were rumors that criminal indictments would be coming down soon for some of the central figures in the case. Osorio still couldn't believe he'd actually get indicted for anything — but when DOJ officials invited him down to Dallas for a meeting in early September, they showed him right away how wrong that assumption was.

Osorio went to the meeting with his lawyer, Emmett Colvin, and proceeded to answer all kinds of questions the government attorneys put to him. Then the conversation turned to me, and they began asking about whether I was involved in the bribery case at all. When Osorio said I wasn't, one lawyer pushed him harder, urging him to provide something — anything — that they could use as evidence against me. Osorio replied that he couldn't do so, because I didn't have anything to do with it. At this, the man got agitated. More than 30 years have passed since that meeting, but John Osorio can still recite the exact words the lawyer said next.

"If you don't give us something on Barnes," the government lawyer warned him, "we're going to indict you from Texarkana to El Paso, and from Amarillo to Arlington."

This was a flat-out threat, but still, Osorio held his ground. He had nothing to offer unless he lied, and he wasn't going to do that. And, sure enough, the DOJ followed through on its threat. In mid-September, shortly after the Dallas meeting, Osorio was indicted on charges of filing false statements to the State Insurance Department. That same day, House Speaker Gus Mutscher, his aide Rush McGinty, and State Rep. Tommy Shannon were indicted as well. Because of the amount of pretrial publicity in Austin, their trial was moved to Abilene, where they quickly became known as the "Abilene Three."

With Sharpstown in the headlines yet again, I made one last effort to call the Nixon administration attack dogs off of the Texas Democrats. Bob Strauss and I had tried and failed with SEC head Bill Casey; now it was time to go even higher up. I flew up to Washington and made an appointment with Nixon's attorney general — the man who, as the White House tapes would later confirm, had talked so cavalierly with Nixon about bringing down Texas Democrats — John Mitchell.

Mitchell was so calculatingly political, he may as well have had antifreeze in his veins. A pipe-smoking, heavy-set man with steely eyes, he was later convicted of conspiracy, perjury, and obstruction of justice in Watergate. He was relentless, and completely amoral, when it came to protecting his President and his party. The comment that best sums up his personal approach to politics came during Watergate, when he warned *Washington Post* reporter Carl Bernstein that Post publisher "Katie Graham's gonna get her tit caught in a big fat wringer" if the newspaper published a story Mitchell didn't like.

I was nervous as a cat when I went to see Mitchell, but I was angry, too, and the anger won out. Right away, I told Mitchell that I didn't intend to put up with the Nixon administration's interference in Texas and my campaign any more. "If you don't get off my back," I said. "I'll go public with what you all have been doing. I'll get out of the governor's race and hold a press conference every day to tell reporters what you all are up to."

Now, this was a little bit of bluster on my part — I wasn't about to get out of the race with just a few months left until the primary. But I wanted Mitchell to understand how angry I was. And I wanted him to feel like there'd be some sort of consequence if he continued to unfairly tar me. I had no leverage against the attorney general of the United States, of course — unless I did do something drastic like drop out of the race, which might have been shocking enough to cause a bit of a ruckus. But Mitchell seemed coolly unconcerned.

I don't remember his exact words, but he said something to the effect that I ought to just calm down, as of course the Nixon administration had nothing to do with what was going on in Texas. He claimed to have no idea who was behind the leaks, the investigations, and the rumors, but I knew better. To my frustration, though, I realized that in the face of his flat denials, there was nothing at all I could do about it.

I returned to Texas and continued campaigning. At every single speech and appearance, I opened up the floor to questions — and every single time, the first question was about Sharpstown. As much as I wanted to, I couldn't simply ignore the scandal, but I still hoped that things would simmer down before the primary — though the publicity surrounding the "Abilene Three" case guaranteed the headlines would continue in the months to come.

That winter, I took a long campaign trip across Texas by train — the "Victory Special." I'd remarried over the summer to Nancy Sayers, the widow of a former state representative and a member of the Texas Employment Commission. Nancy was a gracious, outgoing woman who knew how to campaign. We made appearances all over the state, kissing babies, riding horses, and even eating chicken-fried rattlesnake meat at fundraisers. It was an exhausting schedule, but I loved wading out into crowds of cheering supporters and meeting Texans from all walks of life. With all the mess that was going on in Austin, it was a relief to be out of the capital, meeting ordinary citizens and remembering why I got into politics in the first place.

When the Victory Special trip ended, my poll numbers were high enough that it looked like I'd coast in to victory without even a runoff. If the election had been held then, there's no doubt that I would have been governor of Texas in 1973. But success in politics is very often about timing, and it became obvious that the timing of the May primary wasn't good for me when, on March 15, Mutscher, McGinty, and Shannon were convicted in Abilene.

It's worth noting that even though the "Abilene Three" were convicted, they received just five years' probation — not the kind of sentence meted out for serious crimes. My chief of staff, Robert Spellings, swears that even the prosecutor in the case knew the three weren't guilty of anything, based on conversations they had. And it's a measure of how Mutscher was perceived locally that he later served 22 years as a county judge in Washington County.

But, for ordinary Texans, the convictions were the only proof needed that politicians in Austin were crooked beyond a doubt. The Speaker of the House, his top aide, and a respected state representative had now been found guilty in a court of law. And while the "Abilene Three" would be the ones who were sentenced and punished, the whole of state government was now guilty by association. Once again, cries of "throw the bums out" arose from the electorate — and once again, news stories about the convictions and Sharpstown often included my name.

Primary day was coming up fast, and I needed to be one of the top two vote-getters to ensure a spot in the runoff. A few weeks earlier, I'd been on track to win a majority of the primary votes, but after the convictions in Abilene, my numbers began to drop. Two candidates who I'd been well ahead of — millionaire rancher and businessman Dolph Briscoe, and liberal state representative Frances "Sissy" Farenthold — were pummeling me with references to Sharpstown and calling on voters to make a "fresh start" in Austin.

And there was one other person who was taking a slap at me any chance he got: my erstwhile friend, Bob Bullock. Ever since our falling out a few years earlier, he'd seemed to delight in taking potshots at me, in the press and otherwise. It was all part of the political game, of course, but this election season, he'd turned mean-spirited. He was now secretary of state, and Preston Smith's top adviser in the campaign. And with the governor's poll numbers dangerously low, he started flinging mud with abandon.

Bullock publicly challenged me to testify under oath about Sharpstown — something I'd have been more than happy to do, if any of the dozens of government investigators swarming all over Texas had ever asked me to. He slammed me for going to black churches during the campaign — a common practice — by telling a reporter, "Ben Barnes can sit on the front pew and sing bass and his mama can sing tenor; but I don't believe that the black members of these churches will be fooled by this type of political demagoguery."

I didn't mind his shots at me so much, but when he threatened a friend of mine for a harmless fundraising gimmick, I got mad. At a Dallas rally, my friend Alan Feld had arranged to raffle off a free trip to Hawaii. When Bullock got wind of it, he called Feld in his capacity of Secretary of State and warned him that he could get indicted for doing such a thing. That just about scared Feld to death — how was he to know that a harmless little low-dollar raffle could send him to jail? It was a vindictive move by Bullock, and typical of the way he'd conducted himself since our falling out.

Bullock's provocations were little more than a headache, but in the final two weeks before the primary, I could feel the momentum of my campaign fading away to just about nothing. The convictions in Abilene, the renewed stories about the scandal, and the lingering sense that I'd been involved in wrongdoing finally combined to send my poll numbers down.

On the night of May 6, as hundreds of my supporters gathered at our campaign headquarters for what they thought would be a victory party, I knew that my run in Texas politics was coming to an end. I came in third place that night, behind Briscoe and Farenthold, and just ahead of incumbent Preston Smith. I'd just turned 34 years old, and my career in elective politics was over.

I OPENED UP THIS BOOK BY TELLING A STORY FROM THE VERY BEGINNING of my political career: the day in 1960 when, out of the blue, Sam Rayburn warned me about Richard Nixon. Twelve years later, when I lost in that 1972 primary race, there was already ample evidence that Nixon had orchestrated the destruction of Texas Democrats. There are plenty of lessons we can learn from that — and, more importantly, plenty of things we can learn from the years when Texas Democrats dominated American politics. I'm going to talk about all that in short order, and tell you how we can use that knowledge to pull today's Democrats out of their slump and restore some civility to the political process. But first, there are some fascinating stories that came to light in the years following the Sharpstown scandal, and a few of those bear revealing here.

For one thing, many of the men who'd done Nixon's dirty work in Texas came to regret their actions, and several went out of their way to apologize to me. In the early 1980s, I met with former Attorney General John Mitchell at a Washington, D.C. restaurant called Giorgio's. Mitchell had recently finished serving 19 months in prison for his crimes relating to Watergate, and when we sat down together at the table, he was in a contrite frame of mind. We spent the whole lunch talking about Sharpstown, and he apologized for having helped bring down my political career.

Former Nixon chief of staff Bob Haldeman apologized to me, too. In fact, he went far out of his way to meet with me, flying to little Brownwood, Texas, where I was then living, just to take me to lunch. Haldeman told me he regretted what they'd done, and confirmed that the Nixon administration had intentionally used the Sharpstown case as a way to try and bring me down.

Talking with Haldeman also confirmed something else that I'd long suspected. Back in the summer of 1971, I'd come to realize that it wasn't a coincidence that the SEC lawsuit appeared when it did. I'm not talking about the fact that it was filed right before inauguration day. I'm talking about the fact that those stock transactions, loans, and votes for the two banking bills ever came under investigation by federal authorities to begin with. Preston Smith, Gus Mutscher, and the others did wrong, there's no doubt about it. But the only reason anyone ever found out about it was because federal authorities had come down to

Texas looking for something on me. As I told the *Houston Chronicle* in late August of 1971, "They came down here looking for a way to get me, and Preston and Gus just got caught in their net accidentally."

If Richard Nixon were alive, he'd surely claim he had nothing to do with trying to bring down Texas Democrats. Thanks to the tape of his September 4, 1971, Oval Office conversation with Mitchell, we know that's not true. But what's really amazing is a conversation Nixon had with John Connally on May 9, 1972, just three days after the Democratic primary in Texas. Nixon was so anxious to appear blameless in the whole matter, he actually suggested to Connally that he had no idea who had won the primary! Imagine that — in a year when he was running for reelection, desperate to win Texas's crucial electoral votes, and with a former Texas governor in his cabinet, Nixon tried to claim he had no earthly idea who'd won the Democratic primary for governor three days earlier. Here's the transcript of their conversation:

> *Connally:* I think what you have in this country is, you have a basic unrest of, of fairly enormous proportion. You have a basic frustration. It's true all over. It was certainly true in Texas.
>
> It was aggravated in Texas by the scandals there, to the point where the incumbent governor [Preston Smith] got eight percent of the votes, and my good friend Ben Barnes got about 18 percent. And a woman [Sissy Farenthold] beat the hell out of him, and Dolph Briscoe — he [Barnes] couldn't even get in the runoff. Last Saturday.
>
> *Nixon:* I haven't been following the Texas government. What happened?
>
> *Connally:* Oh! Just murder! Just, they just wiped everybody out — they beat him one — well, [unintelligible] they've got a runoff between Dolph Briscoe and this woman Sissy Farenthold, who's a big McGovern, uh, McGovernite, who's for — oh, hell, Ben Barnes got 18 percent of the vote!
>
> *Nixon:* Who, who in the hell is — Briscoe? Who's he?
>
> *Connally:* Well, Dolph Briscoe is a friend of mine, he's a farmer and rancher, who's a product of this guy [unintelligible] Walker, from Memphis Tennessee, he's a boy that, uh, that this PR firm just took. And he never made a damn speech, wouldn't keep his appointments. And uh, ain't nothing wrong with him, but, uh, he was just nothing.
>
> And uh, hell, just a pure media campaign, and the scandals in Texas — and they just wiped the slate. They beat the attorney general with a very bad fellow, this John Hill, and I, I know him well — hell, I appointed him secretary of state. I say he's bad, he's not —
>
> *Nixon:* Gosh, I — I didn't know all that.

Connally: Oh, they wiped 'em out. Just, just unbelievable. Everybody's stunned, just shocked by it.

I never understood Connally's affection for Richard Nixon, and I'll never know why he took Nixon's unbelievable assertion that day at face value. I didn't know about these tapes until after Connally had died in 1993, so I never got a chance to ask him. Connally was about as savvy a politician as there was, but, for some reason, he just seemed to wear blinders about Nixon. It certainly was odd that, all the time the President's men were orchestrating a Watergate-style operation in Texas to bring down his fellow Democrats, Connally just kept getting closer to Nixon.

That's also what makes Nixon's comments later in that same tape so ironic. When I heard it for the first time, just a couple of years ago, all I could do was shake my head.

> *Nixon:* I can't understand Barnes getting beat —
>
> *Connally:* Oh, it's just, it was a —
>
> *Nixon:* He's a very attractive fellow —
>
> *Connally:* Oh, it's unbelievable! One of the — one of the really bright young men. And was in no way connected with the scandals! Actually. But they thought he was. But they thought he was!
>
> And hell, this woman — this Sissy Farenthold, who's for legalized abortion, who's for legalized marijuana, who's for this, who's for that, a very radical woman! Beat the hell out of him! Got — beat him by 150,000 votes!
>
> *Nixon:* And is in the runoff for governor?
>
> *Connally:* Oh, yes!
>
> *Nixon:* Oh, god.

⸺

IN THE FALL OF 1982, MY FRIEND BARRY SILVERMAN HAD LUNCH WITH Anthony Farris, the former U.S. Attorney in Houston, who had since been elected State Judge for the 151st Civil District of Texas. Farris was the one who'd famously announced he wanted to "get all the sharks" in Sharpstown, and now he had something he wanted to get off his chest. "You're a friend of Ben Barnes, right?" Farris asked Barry. When Barry confirmed that he was, Farris said, "I've got to tell you something." What followed was a surprising series of revelations, straight from the mouth of someone who'd done Nixon's dirty work.

First off, Farris told Barry that, despite his earlier enthusiasm for bringing down the Democratic "sharks," he believed the Justice Department never should have offered Frank Sharp immunity in the case. As Farris put it, "He broke a bank, and then got immunity. Why would he be given immunity? It was politically motivated." Second, Farris said that John Mitchell had told him I was on Nixon's infamous "enemies list." Now, I couldn't tell you for sure whether that's true or not, but given the fact that I found myself a target of an IRS investigation, it certainly wouldn't surprise me. And finally, Farris revealed that the FBI had spent a whopping $5 million investigating me during the Sharpstown era — and they hadn't found a single thing they could use against me. Farris seemed disgusted at the amount of money that had been spent in a purely political witch hunt.

Barry hurried home after that lunch and wrote down everything he could remember of their conversation. He called me as soon as he was done, and walked me through his notes. Anthony Farris died in 1986, so he's not around to confirm the story — but Barry's still got those handwritten notes today.

The Sharpstown investigations achieved what Republicans had hoped for. All three of the state's top elected Democrats — Governor Preston Smith, House Speaker Gus Mutscher, and me — were forced out of politics. Dozens of House members also lost their seats in the voters' rush to "throw the bums out." When the man who would go on to win the governorship, Dolph Briscoe, turned out to be not particularly effective in that office, the momentum Texas Democrats had sustained throughout the sixties and into the 1970 elections was completely destroyed.

And the bad news just kept coming. In January of 1973, Lyndon Johnson died of a heart attack at his beloved LBJ Ranch. He'd been in ill health since the end of his presidency, and while his death wasn't unexpected, it was still an awful blow. Johnson represented an era when Texans, and especially the Democrats, stood tall — and watching that great man being laid to rest under gently swaying oak trees was almost too much to bear. It felt like we were grieving not just for the man, but for the ideals he'd stood for.

Just three months later, John Connally, the last great lion of Texas Democratic politics, announced that he was switching to the Republican party. He hadn't told me he was doing it, but I can't say I was surprised. I knew Connally wanted to run for President, and I knew he'd reached a peak of disgust with the Democratic party at the 1972 national convention that summer, when the liberal wing of the party pushed through the McGovern rules and the party leaders chose to completely ignore the legacy of Lyndon Johnson. Connally did what he felt like he had to do, but Texas Democrats were just as disgusted with him as he was with the party. Lady Bird Johnson's former press secretary, Liz Carpenter, said acidly, "I'm just glad we didn't have to count on [Connally] at the Alamo," while others remarked that this was the "first time in history a rat has swum toward a sinking ship."

Texas had enjoyed a long, proud run of national leadership in the 20th century, from Edward House, to Vice President John Garner, to Sam Rayburn, to Lyndon Johnson. These were men who truly stood tall, who changed the face of American politics through force of will and power of personality. But the era of Texas Democratic dominance was ending. And before long, the man who John Connally had saved from political oblivion, George H. W. Bush, would emerge to begin a new Texas political dynasty — one that would leave a very different legacy than that of the Democrats who preceded it.

Chapter Thirteen

A Bitter Legacy

THIRTY YEARS AFTER SHARPSTOWN DECIMATED TEXAS DEMOCRATS, TEXAS has become the beating heart of the red-state Republican revolution. The legacy of Sam Rayburn, Lyndon Johnson, and John Connally gave way to the 21st-century governance of George W. Bush, Tom DeLay, and Rick Perry — and, sad to say, it's ordinary citizens who are paying the price. Where Texas Democrats in the '60s offered an effective blend of fiscal responsibility and progressive legislation, today's Texas Republicans too often practice the politics of division, fiscal recklessness, and partisan gamesmanship. Let me explain what I mean, and then we'll look at some ways we might straighten it out.

This summer, the U.S. Supreme Court will rule on whether Tom DeLay's controversial 2003 redistricting plan was unconstitutional. I can't predict what the outcome will be, but I can tell you that, in my opinion, DeLay's redistricting scheme was not only unconstitutional, it was a slap in the face to the ideals of good governance. Those districts weren't redrawn to benefit the citizens of Texas — they were redrawn solely to benefit the Republican party. I don't mind if Tom DeLay works his butt off to help his party, but when he messes with the rights of Texas voters to do it, that's just wrong.

Now, some might argue that this is just sour grapes, or that the Democrats would do the same thing if we were in power. It's true that, throughout the decades when Democrats were the majority party in the Legislature, Republicans did challenge our redistricting decisions, sometimes successfully. But it's even more important to point out that when the Democrats held all the power in the '60s — the White House, both houses of Congress, and most of the state legislatures and governorships — Lyndon Johnson didn't step out of line to bring his party more power. In fact, he did the opposite. He made moves in civil rights that he knew would damage the Democratic party. But he made them anyway, because it was the right thing to do.

To me, that sums up the difference between Texas leadership then and now: Lyndon Johnson enriched minorities at the expense of his party, while Tom DeLay enriched his party at the expense of minorities. It's a measure of how backward our political system has become that politicians like DeLay now govern for the sake of their parties rather than for the people they represent.

Tom DeLay isn't the root of this problem, but he's a symptom of it. The real problem is much bigger. It's the culture of corruption and incivility that has grown up over the last couple of decades — a bitter legacy of the tactics pioneered (and honed in Texas) by Richard Nixon.

The Nixon administration's tactics in Sharpstown and Watergate marked the start of a cycle of politics that has only gotten meaner over time. With his "enemies list," smear campaigns, and win-at-all-costs paranoia, Nixon ushered in a new political era. Things didn't change right away — Gerald Ford and Jimmy Carter were both decent, humane campaigners and presidents — but the seeds had been planted. Before long, the American political system was in the hands of people like Lee Atwater, the original bomb-throwing campaigner. Atwater, who got his first national experience working on Nixon's reelection campaign in 1972, once boasted to an interviewer, "While I didn't invent negative politics, I am one of its most ardent practitioners."

I believe the real turning point came in 1988, when George H. W. Bush ran for President against Michael Dukakis. For the first time in American presidential politics, a candidate ran primarily on a platform of tearing down his opponent. This was a sad enough state of affairs, but it was made worse by the fact that this dirty partisan onslaught was coming from a Republican campaign whose candidate owed the resurgence of his political career to a Democrat, John Connally, who'd stuck up for him after his bruising election loss in 1970.

Under Atwater's guidance, the Bush campaign tore into Dukakis, painting him as soft on crime, weak willed, unpatriotic, and worse. The notorious Willie Horton ad, with its stark images of a black convicted felon, tapped intentionally into a deep vein of racism — another classic Nixonian tool. One Republican senator floated false rumors that Dukakis's wife, Kitty, had burned a flag during the Vietnam war. And President Reagan glibly suggested Michael Dukakis was mentally ill, declaring that he wasn't going to "pick on an invalid." The campaign got so dirty, and so far off the track of what matters, that even Nixon himself called it "trivial, superficial, and inane."

I believe the elder George Bush is a decent person, but he surrounded himself with people who did indecent things to try and win the election for him. As the candidate, Bush was ultimately responsible for keeping the tone civil, but finding himself 17 points down just after the Republican Convention, he chose not to do so. With that '88 campaign, the real slide into negative campaigning and character assassination got going.

Today, that kind of negative politicking is everywhere you look. In the 2002 elections, Georgia Republican Saxby Chambliss attacked Max Cleland, a Vietnam war hero who lost both legs and an arm in combat, as having shirked on the defense of his country. In 2004, George W. Bush and Senate Majority Leader Bill Frist broke longstanding tradition by traveling to South Dakota specifically to campaign against the sitting Senate Minority Leader, Tom Daschle. In late 2005, freshman Republican Jean Schmidt of Ohio ripped into Pennsylvania Democrat and war veteran John Murtha on the House floor, implying he was a "cut and run" coward for his views withdrawing our troops from Iraq. And all this incivility isn't just a Republican thing; Democratic Party chairman Howard Dean is equally guilty, with his shameful and divisive generalizations about Republicans.

Over the last six years, the political debate in this country has become as polarized as I've ever seen it. Democrats can't see a single good thing Republicans do, and Republicans have demonized Democrats to an extent I never thought possible. Political discourse from all sides has turned into little more than name-calling.

And it's not just the culture of incivility that's afflicting our political process; there's also a growing culture of corruption that threatens the very integrity of the system. When eight-term congressman and war hero Duke Cunningham can take $2 million in bribes, drive around his district in a Rolls Royce, and not even blink an eye, something's wrong. When lobbyist Jack Abramoff can bilk Native American tribes for millions while referring to them as "morons" and "troglodytes" — while at the same time claiming this country's most high-powered politicians as his friends — something's wrong. And when the vice president of the United States intentionally misleads the American public to garner support for a war in which his circle of friends stands to benefit financially, something is really, truly wrong. Vice President Cheney's assertions that Saddam Hussein's government was involved in the September 11 attacks, his insistence that we would be hailed as "liberators" upon sending troops to Iraq, and his implications that America would fall under attack if John Kerry won the presidential election are all evidence of his willingness to stretch the truth for his own purposes.

Put simply, when the corruption extends to the very top leadership — as it does now, and as it did under Nixon — the problem is officially out of control. How did things get so bad? And, more importantly, how can we pull back from the brink? To answer those questions, we've got to dig a little deeper.

———

NOT LONG AGO I WAS READING PRESIDENTIAL ADVISER DAVID GERGEN'S book, *Eyewitness to Power.* In it, he described the characteristics of a particular presidential administration. This President, Gergen wrote, was openly hostile to the press and deliberately held far fewer press conferences than his predecessors had. His inner circle was secretive and obsessed with ferreting out leaks. The President took his counsel from only a handful of people — while others with dissenting opinions were deliberately frozen out.

Think you know who Gergen is describing? Just wait, there's more. This President had a chip on his shoulder about "establishment" types who, he believed, never had given him the respect he deserved. And, most importantly, he and his top aides believed themselves to be above the law when undertaking certain actions relating to "national interest."

All of this perfectly describes the administration of George W. Bush, of course. But Gergen wasn't writing about Bush; he was writing about Richard Nixon and his cronies. I don't know about you, but I find the number of similarities truly frightening. And I'm not the only one. John Dean, former White House counsel in the Nixon administration, has written repeatedly about what he calls "continuing, disturbing parallels between this Administration and the Nixon Administration."

Way back in November of 2001, Dean wrote this about George W. Bush's administration: "Not since Richard Nixon has there been as concentrated an effort to keep the real work of the President hidden, showing the public only a scripted President." And on December 30, 2005, in response to the furor over Bush's insistence that his government ought be able to wiretap people illegally, Dean wrote:

> Indeed, here, Bush may have outdone Nixon: Nixon's illegal surveillance was limited; Bush's, it is developing, may be extraordinarily broad in scope... No president before Bush has taken as aggressive a posture — the position that his powers as commander-in-chief under Article II of the Constitution, license any action he may take in the name of national security — although Richard Nixon, my former boss, took a similar position.

Now, I want to make a couple of things clear. I do not think that George W. Bush is a bad or dishonest person. Despite the fact that the Bush family wasn't too happy with my decision to appear on *60 Minutes* and talk about the National Guard issue just before the 2004 election, I have always had a fine relationship with the elder George Bush especially, and to a lesser extent with his son. I truly believe both men are personally upstanding, decent people.

But the son, like the father during his '88 campaign, has surrounded himself with people who are doing indecent, unethical things for the sake of power. In George W. Bush's case, Dick Cheney and Karl Rove top that list. Rove has picked up the Atwater banner of negative campaigning and the politics of personal destruction and carries it proudly. Cheney has repeatedly misled the American people. Both seem to believe they're above the law — that the ends justify whatever means they intend to use to gain or solidify power. They're setting an unbelievably dangerous precedent, and so far they've gotten away with it. Yet, at long last, that free ride might be coming to an end — and the reason behind that is every bit as important as the result. Let me tell you what I mean.

When George W. Bush was inaugurated in January of 2001, it marked the first time in nearly 50 years that Republicans held the White House, the Senate, and the House of Representatives at the same time. This was a sudden rush of power to a party that hadn't had so much in a very long time. The result was that it went to their heads a little bit.

The President and party leaders acted like they were answerable to no one — even after Republican Senator Jim Jeffords courageously left the GOP in protest in May of 2001, handing the majority back to the Democrats. Yet even Jeffords' rebuke didn't dampen Republican hubris: after the 2002 midterm elections, when the Republicans won back the majority in the Senate, the cycle started again.

Congress turned a blind eye to its members' ethical violations, and even toyed with the idea of loosening longstanding ethical rules. Party leaders — especially those from Texas — worked to ensure they'd stay on top by any means necessary: potentially illegal redistricting, funneling large national corporate dollars into state races, employing personal smear tactics, and building campaign finance structures designed to skirt the law.

With minority numbers in both the House and Senate, Congressional Democrats had no way to impose the necessary checks and balances on this Republican juggernaut. The Democrats didn't have the numbers to call for investigations, as Republicans resisted the idea even when the behavior in question was egregiously unethical. And the House Republicans even went a step further, effectively disbanding the Ethics Committee, which for the first time in memory doesn't even have any staff. The power pendulum had swung too far, too fast, and Republicans weren't about to let it swing back away from them yet.

Now, here's where it gets interesting. It's easy for Democrats to look at this power imbalance and argue that no party should have a monopoly on all three branches — legislative, executive, and judicial — of government. But on the other hand, I've just spent half of this book telling you how much Texas and the country benefited from Democratic leadership throughout most of the 1960s. During the Kennedy and Johnson presidencies, after all, Democrats held both houses of Congress, as well as most of the state legislatures and governments. So, what's the difference between then and now?

The difference lies in the split between conservative and liberal Democrats that I described in such detail earlier in this book. As much as Ralph Yarborough and his liberal wing of the party drove John Connally and Lyndon Johnson crazy, there were natural checks and balances that grew out of that relationship. As long as we kept the two sides working together, the Democratic party was strong, but never out of control in the way today's Republicans have become.

In the first four years of George W. Bush's presidency, the Republicans showed absolutely no interest in checks and balances — but fortunately, that tide has recently started turning. At long last, Senator John McCain is not the only Republican willing to go up against the President; in 2005, Bush, with his national poll ratings at historically low levels, finally faced a Congress that was unwilling simply to rubber-stamp whatever legislation he wanted. Finally, a handful of Congressional Republicans are making their decisions based on real-world ideas rather than ideology — a trend that both Democrats and Republicans would do well to follow.

━━━━━━━━

THE RISE OF INCIVILITY, RABID PARTISANSHIP, AND CORRUPTION IN GOVernment are all tremendous problems, there's no doubt. But one other trend is far more important and worrying: Today's politicians too often govern with an eye on the next election, rather than on the future, and the people they represent are suffering as a result. This is a national problem, but I'll use the example of Texas to show you what I mean.

In tax revenue raised, Texas ranks 49th among the 50 states. Now, most officeholders in Austin will tell you this is the greatest thing that's ever happened to Texans. Ever since Ronald Reagan rode into Washington proclaiming that taxes were evil, people have treated taxes like a poison that'll kill you, rather than a tool for making sure people's basic needs are met, thereby minimizing even greater social costs and problems down the road. But as they say, freedom isn't free — there's a cost to being the greatest nation in the world, and there are serious consequences when we refuse to pay it.

It would be one thing if Texans paid less in taxes than everybody else and our state was in better shape than the rest. But the opposite is true. Here's a sampling of how Texas ranks within the 50 states in a few important areas:

High school graduation rate:	50th[1]
SAT scores:	48th[2]
Percentage of population with health insurance:	50th[3]
Percentage of insured low-income children:	50th[4]
Amount of welfare and food stamps benefits paid:	47th[5]
Percentage of poor covered by Medicaid:	48th[6]

For a state that brags on itself as much as we do, those are pretty embarrassing numbers. But not all of our rankings are so low, of course. We're at the top of the list in some areas — though you wouldn't want to brag on those, either:

Percentage of uninsured children:	1st[7]
Teenage birth rate:	2nd[8]
Percentage of population that is malnourished:	3rd[9]
Percentage of children living in poverty:	4th[10]
Percentage of 2-year-olds not fully immunized:	6th[11]

And there's more. The high school dropout rate in Texas is 38%, compared to 9.8% nationally[12]. Fully half of all our Hispanic high school students drop out before graduation[13]. Nearly a quarter of all our children have no health insurance[14]. And nearly three-quarters of Texas fourth graders read below proficiency in 2003[15]. It is no exaggeration to say that Texas today is a state in crisis.

The first thing you might notice about all these figures is that the young people are suffering the most. The current government's dogged insistence on cutting taxes and cutting spending, regardless of consequence, is ensuring that a whole generation of Texans is growing up worse educated, worse fed, and worse cared for than any in recent memory.

Earlier in this book, I related what we were able to do for ordinary Texans in the 1960s. That wasn't just talk. Under John Connally's governorship and the Democratic-controlled legislature in the '60s, Texas really did turn a corner in education, technology, and basic human services. We launched one of the first Head Start programs in the nation and enrolled more children than any other state. We raised teachers' salaries, put more money into libraries and scholarship programs, and established a coordinating board to improve our colleges and universities. We guided Texas's transformation from the agricultural/industrial age into the technological age, brought desperately-needed funds into the state through increased tourism and innovative new revenue streams, and gave Texas a head start on entering the 21st century.

Regardless of which party is in power, the evidence is overwhelming that the guiding philosophy of that era — the idea that it's more important to take care of people's basic needs than to offer a couple hundred dollars' tax cut now and again — is far better for the state, and the country, in the long run. That's the difference between governing with an eye on the future and governing to win the next election.

The problems we're facing today are severe. The answers lie not in partisan bickering, but in a return to the long-term strategies and vision that once served the state, and the country, so well. The truth is, both Democrats and Republicans today are guilty of spending more time focusing on short-term gains and political posturing than on real, workable, far-sighted solutions to our problems. It's time to return the focus to improving the lives of our citizens — and the rest will take care of itself.

How do we start? First we should assess the mistakes we made in the years just after Sharpstown, a question I'll look at in the next chapter.

FOOTNOTES FOR CHAPTER THIRTEEN:

(1)   Education Week online: http://www.edweek.org/sreports/qc03/

(2)   The College Board: http://www.collegeboard.com/prod_downloads/about/news_info/
      cbsenior/yr2003/pdf/table3.pdf

(3)   *Austin American Statesman,* July 26, 2004

(4)   2002 State Asset Development Report Card, Corporation for Enterprise Development,
      http://sadrc.cfed.org/measures/savings.php

(5)   State of the Lone Star State, Texans for Public Justice,
      http://www.tpj.org/docs/2000/09/reports/sos/chapter3.pdf

(6)   The Texas Fact Book, The 2004 Texas Legislative Budget Board

(7)   Kids Count Data Book, State Profiles of Child Well-Being, The Annie E. Casey Foundation

(8)   Ibid.

(9)   State of the Lone Star State, Texans for Public Justice,
      http://www.tpj.org/docs/2000/09/reports/sos/chapter3.pdf

(10) America's Health: State Health Rankings — 2004 Edition, United Health Foundation

(11) Ibid.

(12) "Attrition Rates in Texas Public Schools by Race-Ethnicity, 2002-03," Intercultural
      Development Research Association

(13) Ibid.

(14) Kids Count Data Book, State Profiles of Child Well-Being, The Annie E. Casey Foundation

(15) The Nation's Report Card: Report for Texas Reading 2002, U.S. Department of Education

Chapter Fourteen

Where We Go From Here

I'VE TALKED A LOT IN THIS BOOK ABOUT HOW STRONG DEMOCRATS WERE during the era I served in politics, and how successful our legislative efforts were. So, how did it all come down so fast after Sharpstown? The answers reveal the kinds of things Democrats have to do if we hope to recapture the success of that era.

First off, after our impressive showing in the 1970 elections, we needed to elect a true centrist leader in 1972 as governor. Texas Democrats were the most powerful Democratic bloc in the South after the 1970 elections, but by electing Dolph Briscoe governor in the wake of Sharpstown, we set ourselves up to face the growing shift toward the Republican party without a strong leader. Dolph is a good man and a smart businessman, but he wasn't able to take charge the way Texas needed during a critical time in our political history.

It's worth noting that there was one Texas Democrat who did a good job of keeping the Legislature on track during this time. Bill Hobby, who was elected lieutenant governor in 1972 and served in that post for 18 years, succeeded in holding the state government together for a while, and it's largely thanks to him that the education system in Texas continued to make progress through the 1970s. Yet Hobby never ran for governor.

Electing a stronger Democratic governor in 1972 wouldn't have staved off the state's ultimate swing to the Republican party — but we'd at least have had a chance to build on the success of 1976, when Texas went for Jimmy Carter in the presidential election. We also probably would have averted the 1978 election of Texas's first Republican governor since Reconstruction, Bill Clements.

Like John Tower's 1961 election to the Senate, Clements's razor-thin, upset victory over Democrat John Hill (Clements won by about 1 percent, after spending twice as much as Hill on his campaign) gave the Republicans a huge boost in money and momentum. Though Democrat Mark White took back the governor's office in the next election, the Republican run that continues today can be traced directly back to Clements's 1978 victory. If we'd had people in office in the mid-'70s who were better equipped to lead, I believe we might have slowed or lessened the shift to the Republican party, and that our position today might be stronger as a result.

The Democrats who rose to power after Sharpstown also made the mistake of abandoning the "farm team" system for grooming young, up-and-coming officeholders. I'll tell you what, when I was 22 or 23 years old, and men like John Connally and Lyndon Johnson took me into their fold, it meant a hell of a lot to me. Very quickly, I was able to grow in strength and stature as a representative, and I became more determined than ever to work hard for the Democratic ideals they represented. When Barbara Jordan was first elected to the Texas Senate, I tried to do the same thing for her, making sure she had what she needed to succeed and offering to help her however I could. And I spent a lot of hours with Democrats across the state to try and bring other new, promising candidates along. That's the kind of legwork that helps keep the party bonded together.

But even more devastating than losing the farm system was the fact that the Democratic party let the business community slip away. If there was one truth that I'd learned above all others during my time in politics, it was that the party could only be strong with the support of business, and by keeping it socially acceptable to be a Democrat. I know I made this point a couple of times in earlier chapters, and you're probably sick of hearing about it already, but if there's a single message I'd like people to take away from this book, that's it. For that reason, I'm going to talk a little more about it in a minute.

Those are the three biggest mistakes the Democratic party made after Sharpstown, and there's plenty we can learn from them, even today. But there's lots more we can do to help break the losing streak the party has been on. Here are just a few:

Shift the focus away from single-issue politics. One thing Republicans have done well is to pump up their base with a whole host of divisive issues. Abortion, gay marriage, gun control, flag-burning — these are the kinds of hot-button issues that distract from the larger picture of how well or how poorly government takes care of people. We'd all do better — in both parties — to stay focused on the whole picture, governing in a way that provides real, across-the-board improvements.

We need a coalition of leaders who share broad views and broad concerns, and who understand how to apply them to benefit ordinary people every single day. In succumbing to the lure of special-interest politics, we've ended up with polarization of both Republicans and Democrats — of both the ultra-liberals and ultra-conservatives. And that's not helping anybody. We've got to start practicing the politics of construction, rather than the politics of destruction.

On a related note, Democrats — or really, moderates in general — have got to **reclaim our place in the national discussion on religion and morality.** In the 2004 election, "moral values" became the far right's rallying cry. When alarms went off over things like same-sex marriage, the notion of "morality" suddenly became the province of anybody but the Democrats.

But there's a whole lot more to morality than just these scare tactics. Justice is a moral issue. So is fair play. And so is giving a helping hand to a neighbor in need. In the 1960s, ending the shame of segregation was a moral issue — as was helping people out of poverty, and assuring aging citizens adequate medical care, and giving children trapped in hopelessness the chance for an education. These are the kinds of moral questions that really make a difference, and Democrats should be proud of their legacy in confronting them.

During my first term as Speaker, I met with a group of preachers over at the First Methodist Church near the Capitol. These preachers had come to Austin from all over Texas to protest a proposed "liquor by the drink" bill. At that time in Texas, you couldn't buy a mixed drink in a restaurant — an outdated restriction that wasn't doing much of anything but hurting the economy. You could bring your own bottle in to a restaurant, so the restriction wasn't even keeping people from drinking — all it was doing was punishing the business owners for no reason.

But to hear those preachers talk, this liquor-by-the-drink bill was the single most vital issue facing Texas. You'd have thought it was going to corrupt all the youth in Texas, or even bring on Armageddon, the way they talked about it. I listened to them go on for a while, and then said, "I'm so glad you all have brought this up. You're absolutely right, we've got to do something about this bill. I'll tell you what — I'll make sure it gets killed, as long as you help me out on a couple of things.

"Raise your hand if you'll commit your time and your congregation's money to care for single mothers," I said, looking out over the group. "Raise your hand if you'll give money to make sure kids in Texas are insured! Or to make sure our highways are passable, and our education system fully funded!" There were some surprised faces in that group, but they soon got my point. I didn't believe then, and don't now, that the kinds of issues so often seized upon by "moral leaders" have anything to do with real morality at all.

It's time to reclaim the high road by swinging attention back around to the true meaning of "moral values." What good are false morality questions when the most basic rights of people in this country are being eroded every day? The basic values that we all hold dear are in jeopardy: the right to free speech and free assembly (threatened by the Patriot Act), the right to a secure retirement (threatened by efforts to expose Social Security to the vagaries of the stock market), the right to a prosperous future for the country (threatened by the biggest federal deficit that's ever been run up). What good is this relentless focus on narrowly defined "moral issues" when our roads and bridges are crumbling, our children are uninsured, and our schools are falling apart?

When the Catholic church denies elected officials communion because of their political stances, when the U.S. Attorney General pushes his religion on the Justice Department, when our military academies press one particular faith on students — these are the kinds of things our forefathers tried hard to protect us from. We ought to remember that this country was founded by people who got on boats and sailed into the unknown to escape precisely the kind of religious intolerance that many in the religious right are foisting on America today.

I go to church, and I practice the same basic faith as President George W. Bush does, but I'll tell you what — I have a real problem with the narrow religious agenda I've been seeing in this country. If these conservative religious organizations would spend their money trying to take care of teenage pregnancies, and kids who are dropping out of school, and kids who don't have health care, rather than their own pet issues like vouchers and abortion, they'd be doing a whole lot more Christian good in the world than they are right now.

In the same vein, we also need to **bring back the culture of bipartisanship, volunteerism, and service in this country.** John Kennedy famously said in his 1960 inauguration, "Ask not what your country can do for you; ask what you can do for your country" — and people responded. Lady Bird Johnson launched her Beautification Campaign, and thousands of people volunteered to clean up our nation's littered highways. Thousands more joined the Peace Corps and Americorps. There was a real generosity of spirit about those times.

That spirit has been eroded over the last decade or so by an abrupt rise in political extremism. When Lyndon Johnson was Senate Majority Leader, he used to have his Republican counterpart, Minority Leader Everett Dirksen, over for scotch in the evenings. The two men, though political competitors, were good friends — but can you imagine such a scenario today between

George W. Bush and, say, Harry Reid? When Sam Rayburn was Speaker of the House, he had his "Board of Education," bringing lawmakers from both parties over for drinks and real talk about the country and where we were headed. Today, in a time when Americans are at war, and as we face threats on our own soil from a foreign enemy, we should more than ever be working together, rather than at odds with each other. But starting with Newt Gingrich and leading right up to the win-at-all-costs agenda of my fellow Texan Tom DeLay, the political process has been corrupted in the name of power.

We must **find a way for moderation to prevail.** One of the greatest strengths of the Texas Democratic Party in the '60s was that people really felt like we spoke their language, and spoke directly to their needs. When they looked at the Democrats in power, they saw people they understood, and who understood them.

Conventional wisdom in American politics holds that in any given election, 40 percent of voters will vote for the left, 40 percent will vote for the right, and the 20 percent in the middle will decide it — so if you can win at least 11 percent of those voters, your candidate will win. In Texas following the difficult years of 1968-73, the Democratic Party lost its hold on the middle when moderates began shifting in large numbers to the Republican Party. This happened partly because of the fallout from LBJ's civil rights efforts, partly as a backlash against the Democratic moderates who'd been caught up in Sharpstown, and partly as a backlash against the continuing Vietnam War. We need to reclaim that middle ground, and to learn again how to speak to the ordinary folks who make up that vast middle. Too often, I've heard conservative or moderate former Democrats say, "I didn't leave the party; the party left me."

We also need to **cultivate leaders who stand for honest political ideals.** People want to follow true leaders, and when we had charismatic men such as Franklin Roosevelt, John F. Kennedy, and Lyndon Johnson in power, they were able to draw voters in through the force of their convictions and personality. Bill Clinton exhibited that kind of draw for voters, and in Texas, so did my good friend Ann Richards when she ran for governor in 1990. But in the last five years, the Democratic party has struggled to find its faces of the future. Just as Texas Democrats did in the 1970s, we've let our farm system wither, and haven't paid enough attention to grooming the kind of candidates who we know can pull together the multiple strands of the electorate and build coalitions that we need in order to win elections.

As I mentioned above, we desperately need to **cultivate a business community that has a longer-term vision than the next quarterly report.** In Texas during the time I served, we had a whole group of powerful businesspeople who met regularly to talk about the state of the state, and what needed to be done to strengthen it. People like Jimmy Aston, Gus Wortham, and Walter Mischer really did put their money where their mouths were: their businesses were important to them, but they didn't mind borrowing a lot of money to invest in the future of the state. There was a mindset then that's almost completely absent now — a sense of wanting to use power and wealth to help bring everybody up. And you could see the results throughout that whole decade.

Nelson Rockefeller, who was governor of New York during the time I was in Texas politics, told me his secret for how best to solve a serious social or economic problem. "You get the business leadership of the state together in a room," he said, "all the men and the women who are running the big business in the state. Then you lock the door and tell them, 'We've got this kind of problem — we've got to find insurance for our children, or double the number of kids graduating from college, or cut the high school dropout rate.' You lock the door, give those people about two or three hours, and they'll come up with a plan to solve it. Even if they have to tax themselves to make it happen, they'll figure it out."

Rockefeller's suggestion is as true as it is simple. In my experience, people will rise to the level of trust and responsibility you put in them. John Connally and I kept in regular, close contact with the powerful non-politicians in Texas, and we never hesitated to ask their help on issues that could better the state. The current crop of leaders, by contrast, has cultivated an ethic of doing whatever benefits the businesses themselves. This administration has encouraged — and had its own hands in — some of the most avaricious, self-interested corporate behavior in history. George W. Bush and Dick Cheney come from business backgrounds, but that's no reason why they should allow those around them to abandon ethics in the name of making money.

Another way we can start to solve that problem is by **reclaiming public service as an honorable profession.** Starting with the Reagan era and peaking during the 1994 Republican revolution, there's been a real shift in how Americans view those who work in the public vs. the private sector. It used to be that Americans saw their government as a good thing. Wasn't it the government, after all, that protected our Constitutional rights, helped lead us to victory in wars, pulled us out of economic depressions, and looked out for the little guy? Government was the American citizens' protector — and government service was an honorable profession. But since the early 1980s, that's all changed. Instead of seeing the government as on our side, Americans have a real mistrust of just about everything relating to Uncle Sam.

Even those who serve the public seem to suffer this same affliction — I mean, half the Texas legislature right now seems to think it was elected for the express purpose of downsizing government. Serving in the Legislature used to be seen as a high calling, but these days it's considered more prestigious to be in business and make a lot of money. If there's one point I'd like to get across to the many young people who aspire to improve the world around them, it's that there's no more honorable a profession than public service. As I realized all those years ago, when I was 20 years old and went up to the Capitol to blow the whistle on the Health Department scandal, there's something very rewarding about being in a position to make a positive difference in people's lives.

Texas is struggling now, but it will be great again when the men and women in power stand up and take responsibility for making it great. We need to have another form of broad-based taxation in the state, rather than just the sky-high property taxes that are bleeding certain parts of the population dry. We need legislators who won't cling to the false idols of tax cuts and "scrubbing the budget" to make numbers, in the meantime impoverishing the state and creating a need for even more tax dollars down the road. We need to stop sticking it to one group of citizens so that another group can get a couple hundred dollars back in tax cuts — benefiting nobody but the politicians trying to win more votes. We need legislators and statewide officials who have the guts to stand up and say, "This is my time. I'm gonna make a difference in this state. And I'm ready to be judged not by how many votes I get, but by how many people I help."

Which brings me to the most important change we need to make. **It's time for us lead, rather than follow.** For too long now, we've run our campaigns based on reaction rather than action. In the 2000 and 2004 presidential campaigns, Democrats ran against George W. Bush, rather than offering a clear, positive agenda for how we would govern to improve Americans' lives. We've allowed ourselves to be sucked into the politics of name calling and denigration, rather than taking the lead in the race of ideas.

The reality of human nature is that people will act only when they're given leadership. If we can offer that leadership, the electorate will naturally follow. As we saw in the 2004 election, it's not enough for us to simply criticize George W. Bush's half-baked Social Security plan — we've got to offer an alternative of our own! We can't just complain about the fact that our children don't have health care — we've got to offer a workable strategy for how to fix that. And we can't just bad mouth the choices Republicans make — we have to provide a positive, proactive plan for how to do them one better. This is vital not just for winning elections, but for putting in place ideas and policies that will help improve people's lives.

Now, you might be thinking that I'm making all this sound a little too simple. But my approach to governing never was complicated, and I always found that the simple strategies were the ones that worked best. Democrats have just got to re-learn the things we knew back in the sixties and put them into play today. Back then, the Republicans were losing by doing the exact same thing we're doing today — and they kept losing until they figured out how to change tack in order to win. You can see the seeds of that turnaround in this 1971 quote from George H. W. Bush to author Jimmy Banks, as he talked about his 1970 U.S. Senate election loss:

> Our other big mistake, in retrospect, probably was in being a little too negative — talking more about what I was against than what I was for. And I think this, to a degree, has been the disease of Republicans in Texas. We've been opposed to this or opposed to that and, as a result, we haven't identified with the people... I feel more comfortable as an advocate than as a critic. I think people want to know what you believe in, what you're for.

There's nothing I'd like more than to see the Democrats turn around our slide of the past few years — and not just for partisan reasons, but because I believe the nation really needs us right now. The bigger the deficit gets, the more mired we get in Iraq; and the more polarized people become over hot-button issues, the worse off Americans will be, not just now but moving into the future. It's time for us to remember what makes the Democratic party great and how proud the party's legacy truly is.

I'll close with a quote from *Texas Under A Cloud,* a book by longtime Texas journalist Sam Kinch Jr. and historian Ben Procter. In a chapter about my political career, Kinch and Procter quoted me talking about advice I'd gotten from Lyndon Johnson:

> In regard to decision-making, Barnes acknowledged that former President Johnson had given him sound advice. "When you've got a tough decision to make and when both sides are after you tooth and tong," Barnes earnestly exclaimed to the authors, "get off by yourself and decide what you think is best for the people ten or twenty years from now, because it's going to be you that has to live with the decision and not those who are hammering at you."

That's some of the best advice I ever got from President Johnson. And it's the advice I'd give the men and women in public service today. Let's look toward the future, with a perspective much broader than just worrying about the next election. It's time for us to lead again.

Epilogue

WHEN I LOST THAT PRIMARY BACK IN MAY OF 1972, IT WOULD HAVE BEEN easy to feel like my life was over. I'd been in politics since I was 21 years old, and just a few weeks earlier had believed I might soon be governor. Then suddenly, at the age of 34, I found myself on the outside looking in.

I did stay out of politics for a while. After I finished my term as lieutenant governor, I went into business with Herman Bennett, my friend from Brownwood who'd invited me to participate in some of his business developments. Herman offered me a partnership in his company, and he and I went all over Texas developing real estate. As much as I'd enjoyed politics, I loved the excitement of making a deal and building something new.

In 1980, John Connally joined me in the real estate business after an unsuccessful run for the Republican nomination for President. We started a company called Barnes & Connally, and for a while did very well, putting up new developments and investing in properties in towns and cities across the state. Connally and I had worked together well in government, and that same chemistry turned out to apply in the real estate business. In the early to mid-1980s, real estate was booming in Texas, and he and I were two of the happy beneficiaries of that boom.

Then, the bottom dropped out. A combination of things led to a huge economic downswing in Texas — the oil business crashed, the Savings and Loan crisis shuttered lending institutions, and suddenly the state's well of capital had dried up. We'd built our business through cycles of borrowing and building, but now we were left facing a pile of debt — and we had precious few options for how to pay it off.

John Connally and I both were forced to declare bankruptcy in the late 1980s, a wrenching decision that we made only after exhausting all our possibilities here and abroad for a financial lifeline. For Governor Connally and his wife, Nellie, this was a terrible blow at a time in their lives when they were on the brink of enjoying a well-deserved retirement. When they held a public auction of their belongings, putting on the block almost all the items they'd accumulated over their decades in public and private life, it made news all over the world.

For the second time, I'd suffered what some might see as a devastating setback. But even though I lost everything — the only things I managed to save were my dad's red pickup truck and the watch LBJ had given me — I saw an opportunity to start something new. I might not have had any possessions left, but I still had something of value: I could apply my knowledge of the legislative process and of the business world to lobby in Austin and Washington.

The fact is, I'd been doing lobbying of a sort all along. When people would ask me to do a favor or make a call for them, I'd always done it. There was just one difference now. As my secretary, Sheree Kirk, told a caller looking for such a favor just after my bankruptcy, "Well, you know he can't do that for free anymore." So it was that my third career — as a lobbyist — began.

Over the past decade, I've also gotten back into elective politics — though not as a candidate myself. I've worked behind the scenes, raising money for both statewide and national candidates, including John Kerry's campaign for the presidency in 2004. In fact, in some ways I'm just as involved in politics now as when I was in office.

Yet politics doesn't govern my life the way it once did. Losing that primary election in 1972, then enduring the bankruptcy 15 years later, has given me a much broader perspective on life than I ever had as an up-and-coming politician in my twenties. And two other events changed my life as well — the adoptions of our daughters Blaire and Elena. In 1991, my wife, Melanie, and I brought Elena home from Romania after a fierce bureaucratic battle, and then in 1994, we brought Blaire home from Russia.

I have two children, Greg and Amy, from my first marriage, and I love them both. They're grown now, living and working in Texas with families of their own. But there was something about adopting Blaire and Elena — something about bringing these two little girls home and giving them a new and very different life from what they'd have had otherwise — that has really given me a new perspective on my own life.

It has also been really rewarding for me to watch them grow up. When Greg and Amy were younger, I spent a lot of time focused on my political career. This time around, I'm trying to be a better father. I don't think I ever understood before just how rewarding that could be.

═══════════════

AS BLAIRE AND ELENA GET OLDER, I FIND MYSELF THINKING A LOT ABOUT the choices young people are faced with today, and the examples they see around them. And although I wrote this book for many reasons, there's one that really stands out for me.

Fifty years ago, I left a dusty farm in a small West Texas town to make my way in the world. I was lucky enough find a goal and a purpose early on — I wanted to help change people's lives for the better, and I believed that getting involved with government was a way I could do that. I'd never forgotten that day in 1946 when those two men drove up to our house in a pickup truck, telling us the government was going to bring electricity to our farm.

With cynicism about public service higher than it has ever been, I wonder whether today's young men and women will ever find the spark of public service lit in their souls, as it was in mine. I worry that our country's best and brightest see government service as something to avoid, rather than something to aspire to. And that's one of the biggest reasons I wanted to do this book. When all is said and done, if the acts of people like Lyndon Johnson, John Connally, Barbara Jordan, and the other icons of the Texas Democratic era can provide some inspiration for young people, that would be the best thing I could hope for.

Acknowledgements

I'M A LUCKY MAN TO HAVE SO MANY GOOD FRIENDS, FAMILY MEMBERS, AND colleagues, though they probably don't feel so lucky after listening to me go on about doing this book for the last couple of years. It's a long, hard haul trying to get a book finished, and I never could have done it without the generous patience and support of many people.

I've decided to take a chance and list some names here, knowing that I'll probably forget someone — so let me apologize in advance to anyone I've left out by mistake. To everyone who's helped me, whether it's reminding me of a story, adding a detail here and there, or just offering a kind word of support to help me finish, thank you.

My partners and colleagues Jim Sharp, Scott Reed, Wayne Reaud, and Kent Caperton have put up with many hours spent working on the book, and offered valuable suggestions on how to make it better. I owe a great debt of gratitude to all four, as well as to Wyeth Wiedeman in my Austin office.

My dear friend Bernard Rapoport has always been a source of great inspiration to me. He's a man whose heart is always in the right place, and who has never been afraid to step up for what he believes in. I've never known anyone who cares so deeply and does so much, and I draw strength from his example every day.

I've been fortunate enough in my life to have lots of good friends, both personally and politically — and very often, both. There's so much I could say about each one of the following people, but in the interest of saving another forest of trees I'll just list them here (in alphabetical order): Bill Abington, Jim

Berry, George Christian, Stuart Coleman, Everett Collier, Bill Cunningham, mitch Delk, Frank Erwin, Finley Ewing, Tom Fatjo, Wayne Gibbens, Callam Graham, Gary Jacobs, Putter Jarvis, Tom Johnson, Dee Kelly, Al Langford, Lowell Lebermann, Jack Martin, John Mobley, Clint Murchison, Mike Myers, Willie Nelson, Groner Pitts, Julian Read, Howard Rose, Darrell Royal, Reuben Senterfitt, Barry Silverman, Evan Smith, Allan Stanford, Larry Temple, Walter Umphrey, Ralph Wayne, Harry Whitworth, and A. M. "Monk" Willis. Again, my apologies to anyone I've mistakenly left out.

Bob Strauss, a great friend and pillar of the Democratic party, graciously agreed to write the foreword to the book. I appreciate his friendship and counsel more than I can say. I want to thank Jon Huntsman, who sets a wonderful example for us all in both his business and his personal life. And I'd like to thank my business mentor, Herman Bennett, who always had faith in me.

As so many people in politics have discovered, you're only as good as your staff, and I've been lucky enough to have some of the best people around working with me. I want to thank (also in alphabetical order) Margaret Behrens, Glenn Biggs, Peggy Crow, Ann Curlee, Haila Harvey, Diana Heiges, Nicki Beth Jones, Nick Kralj, Randy McClelland, Jason Perlman, Tony Sanchez, Robert Spellings, Patsy Thomasson, Gloria Watkins, and Richard Wayne. I'd also like to thank Susan Martin, a top-rate administrator who manages to keep the office running smoothly in the middle of chaos.

I owe a debt of gratitude to Howard Yoon and Gail Ross for helping me get this book published. I want to thank to Rue Judd of Bright Sky Press for taking on the project. Thanks also are due to Lisa Dickey for helping in the writing process, to Meg Tynan for her diligent work checking facts, and to book designer Julie Savasky. Because parts of this book are based on my recollection of events, we've worked hard to achieve accuracy, checking and double-checking facts wherever possible. If I've missed the mark of historical perfection, it's an error of inadvertence.

Collecting information for a book is a daunting task, and many people had a hand in helping me pull it together. I want to thank the many friends and colleagues who agreed to be interviewed, as well as Tony Black and John Anderson of the Texas State Archives, who were a tremendous help. Joe Youngblood of the LBJ Library also offered invaluable support.

There would have been no story to tell without the many able men and women who served with me in the Texas legislature and state government. Their hard work and dedication to the state serves as a model for us all.

In addition, I want to thank two of Texas's most gracious First Ladies: Lady Bird Johnson and Nellie Connally. Lyndon Johnson and John Connally were more than just mentors and allies to me; they were an inspiration. And neither man would have been what he was without you.

Finally, I want to thank my family for putting up with all my shortcomings over the years. To my mother, Ina Barnes, thank you for giving me the courage to venture off that peanut farm all those years ago. To my brother, Rick, I wish you every good thing life can offer. To my son, Greg, and daughter Amy, I love you both. To my mother-in-law, Dorothy Harper, thank you for all the support you've given Melanie and me over the years. And to my wife, Melanie, and my daughters Blaire and Elena, you mean the world to me.

Bibliography

Banks, Jimmy. *Money, Marbles and Chalk: The Wondrous World of Texas Politics.*
Texas Pub. Co., 1972

Berman, William C. *America's Right Turn: From Nixon to Bush.*
Johns Hopkins University Press, 1994.

Black, Earl and Merle Black. *The Rise of Southern Republicans.*
Belknap Press, 2002.

Bruno, Jerry. *The Advance Man.* Bantam Books, 1972.

Carpenter, Liz. *Ruffles and Flourishes.* Pocket Books, 1971.

Bryce, Robert. *Cronies: Oil, the Bushes, and the Rise of Texas, the Superstate.*
Public Affairs, 2004.

Carr, Waggoner with Jack Keever. *Not Guilty.*
Shoal Creek Publishers, Inc., 1977.

Connally, John. *In History's Shadow: An American Odyssey.* Hyperion, 1993.

Connally, Nellie and Mickey Herskowitz. *From Love Field: Our Final Hours
with President John F. Kennedy.* Rugged Land, 2003.

Crawford, Ann Fears. *John Connally: Portrait in Power.* Jenkins, 1973.

Dionne, E.J. *Stand Up Fight Back: Republican Toughs, Democratic Wimps, and the Politics of Revenge.* Simon & Schuster, 2004.

Dubose, Lou and Jan Reid. *The Hammer: Tom DeLay: God, Money, and the Rise of the Republican Congress.* Public Affairs, 2004.

Gergen, David. *Eyewitness to Power: The Essence of Leadership.* Simon and Schuster, 2000.

Hendrickson, Jr., Kenneth E. et. al. *Profiles in Power: 20th Century Texans in Washington.* University of Texas Press, 2004.

Ivins, Molly. *Who Let the Dogs In?* Random House, 2004.

Ivins, Molly. *Molly Ivins Can't Say That, Can She?,* Random House, 1991.

Judis, John and Ruy Teixeira. *The Emerging Democratic Majority,* Scribner, 2002.

Kinch, Sam and Ben Procter. *Texas Under a Cloud,* Jenkins Pub. Co, 1984.

Lind, Michael. *Made in Texas: George W. Bush and the Southern Takeover of American Politics.* Basic Books, 2002.

Pittman, H.C. *Inside the Third House,* Eakin Press, 1992.

Provence, Harry. *Lyndon B. Johnson.* Paperback Library, Inc.

Reston, Jr., James. *The Lone Star: The Life of John Connally.* HarperCollins, 1989.

Rogers, Mary Beth. *Barbara Jordan, American Hero.* Bantam, 1998.

Schweizer, Peter and Rochelle. *The Bushes: Portrait of a Dynasty.* Doubleday, 2004.

Sorenson, Theodore. *Why I am a Democrat.* Henry Holt & Co., 1996.

Witcover, Jules. *The Year the Dream Died: Revisiting 1968,* Diane Pub Co., 1997

Index